John Hillaby is a writer an[...] [...]ng
things on his own. After a trip among the caribou-hunting
Indians of North Canada he decided to see as much of the
world as he could, alone and on foot. His first African safari
took him over the Mountains of the Moon in the Congo. Then
followed expeditions to Uganda and Tanzania culminating in a
three-month safari to Lake Rudolph on the borders of Kenya
and Ethiopia. *Journey to the Jade Sea* is the story of that long
walk. His next book, *Journey through Britain*, became a
bestseller.

After four years' service in the Second World War, Hillaby
was zoological correspondent for the *Guardian*, and for eleven
years, European science writer for the *New York Times*. John
Hillaby now writes about biological affairs for the *New
Scientist*.

Journey

John Hillaby

through Europe

Paladin

Granada Publishing Limited
Published in 1974 by Paladin
Frogmore, St Albans, Herts AL2 2NF

First published by Constable and Co Ltd 1972
Copyright © John Hillaby 1972
Made and printed in Great Britain by
Richard Clay (The Chaucer Press) Ltd
Bungay, Suffolk
Set in Monotype Ehrhardt

For my wife, Tilly,
the best of all

Contents

Illustrations

The Groundwork

There's an old story about a centipede who was asked which particular set of legs he used to start walking. The question took him by surprise. What had seemed a perfectly normal means of progression became a wholly perplexing problem. He could scarcely move. I'm faced with a similar difficulty when I try to account for – not how I walk, but why. Hopefully the ensuing pages will enlarge on the pleasures of putting one foot down in front of another for another journey of well over a thousand miles.

A young man I met in Lorraine said that all his life he had wanted to travel alone as I did, but somehow he could never make up his mind to begin. What made it so worthwhile? After talking until two in the morning I thought I had got pretty close to the heart of the matter. Independence, I said. Walking means no pre-ordained schedules, no hanging about waiting for transport, for other people to depart. Alone with a pack on your back you can set off at any time, anywhere, and change your plans on the way if you want to. Looking round at his well-appointed apartment, I said of course it depended on what he did for a living. Could he get away for a few weeks? He shook his head, sadly. No, he said. It was difficult. He ran a travel agency.

Now that the walk has become another chapter of personal history I begin to realize how much the independence I enjoyed stemmed from the invaluable help I received. In London, before I set off, I spent many months working out a route, getting information from libraries, museums, embassies, and universities. For this and other reasons I am greatly indebted to Douglas Matthews of that unique institution, the London Library, to Donald Bullough of Nottingham University, and to many other old friends, especially Otto, Renate, and Helli Koenigsberger, Peter Elstob, Jocelyn Kingsley, Mary Usherwood, and John

Worsley. Amid much else, Graham Bishop processed my photographs and designed the maps. The comments and scrawls on them are largely my own. It's impossible to thank all those who made the going memorable, but it's a privilege to mention Annie of Wassenaar, Gerrit the falconer, Gaston in Liège, Moyshe, the sage of Strasbourg, good friends in Belfort, Molaretto, Guillestre and those two young men from Pierrelatte, Alain and Henri, who taught an impudent scrambler how to walk on snow.

On the Beach

Most of the passengers drove ashore. They hooted at each other. They hooted at me. Normally, there is nothing I hate more than being hooted at, especially on what used to be called a public highway. It gives me high-minded notions of being the only traveller in step in a world gone mad on wheels. But at six o'clock that April morning I took those cheerful toots for what they were: the electronic semiquavers of goodbye and good luck. They came from motorists I had sat up with half the night on the ferry from Harwich to the Hook. They were fanning out the length of Europe. The two rally drivers, the pros among the pawns, reckoned if they thrashed it a bit they could reach Monte Carlo in twelve hours.

And me? It took me just over two months to walk from the North Sea to the Mediterranean by way of the Alps. At intervals I felt elated, depressed, self-confident, nervous, heavily over-burdened, and, in big boots among travellers lightly disguised as travellers, at times a bit of a fool. I waved and made for the beach, intent on that elusive thing known as getting away from it all.

For reasons I'll come to in a minute, I struck for Scheveningen, further up the coast, a good place, as I saw it, to turn south. On my favourite map, the page of an atlas, it looked as if western Europe could still be walked through from the mouth of the Rhine to somewhere near Monaco or Nice. Nice – *Nike* – Victory. A track, I knew, had been plotted for the greater part of the way, that is from the Ardennes to the Vosges and from the Alps to the sea. In between the uplands, especially in the Netherlands and north Belgium, in Lorraine and around Belfort in Franche Compté there are belts of heavily industrialized country. It took six months of planning to avoid running the gauntlet of intolerable highways.

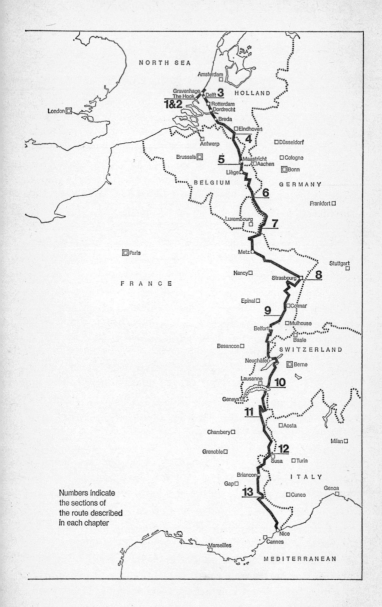

Numbers indicate
the sections of
the route described
in each chapter

Until fairly recently a journey used to be a simple and intelligible matter of going somewhere for a change, for seeing something different on the way. Daniel Boorstin points out that one of the subtle confusions, perhaps one of the great losses of modern life is that we have lost this refuge. As there comes to be less and less difference between the time it takes to reach one place rather than another, space shrinks and all but disappears. The world looks much the same from a modern hotel, a car on a motorway, a seat in a jet plane or from the deck of an ocean liner. We are moving towards Instant Travel. Nowadays, says Boorstin, it costs more and takes greater ingenuity, imagination, and enterprise to work out and endure travel risks than it once took to avoid them. Almost as much effort goes into planning an off-beat route as in surviving it.

In the Low Countries a walker can take to the beach and wander through the canals towards where the upland trails start in the Ardennes. A weed-strewn beach. Sandpipers piped and oyster-catchers pitched through the air like stones. The sea splashed and the hooting died away. All peace now. Keeping to a firm strip near the waves, I strode on.

The sand is pitted with holes like a Swiss cheese. They are dug by holiday-makers to protect themselves from the keen north wind. From one of the holes a youngster emerged, a tousle-haired youth in conspicuously patched jeans. He stood up and stretched. A hippie out on his own for once, I thought. Privately I rather resented intrusion. I waved and walked on. But more figures arose. Five or six girls and boys in one large hole with others beyond. The beach became populated with nice-looking kids, flower children, and beats with bed-rolls, mostly British and American. They had been sleeping rough. Making their way to Amsterdam to some commune, they said. They asked where I was going. Conscious of a destination beyond that far-out city I said through the Netherlands, walking south. At the start I can never bring myself to an outright declaration of intent. It's tempting fate too far. Turning the question round, I asked where they hoped to get after Amsterdam. To India, they said. Probably Kashmir.

Some would almost certainly get there. They wander slowly from city to city in groups of different sizes, sharing the discontents, the searching of youth, and its quick kinship. By contrast, I was alone: in theory as free as a tramp. Yet unlike me with a carefully worked out route to follow, with little time to spare and a need to let a loving and anxious wife know where I had got to, regularly, they seemed far more free than I was. But what is freedom? At that moment I thought in terms of lack of constraints, of being able to act, to choose, to determine one's own fate and all that. True, but ... all lack of constraint is at best relative and perhaps the freedom in which the youngsters seemed to luxuriate was no more than my inability to see their problems because I was so intensely caught up in my own.

For all our differences, including that enormous one of more than a quarter of a century in years, we had a fair amount in common, but little in the way of conversation. Nothing I asked about where they'd been or what they'd seen seemed to interest them. They were questions from some eccentric old square. Maybe it's age or just that I lack something necessary to get through to youngsters. I have tried, often. I tried again that morning.

'Where're you from?'

'Brighton.'

'Like the place?'

'Lousy,' he said.

'What's wrong with it?'

'Oh y'know. Dead square. Boring.'

'What made you choose India?'

'Lots of us are going there.'

'Why?'

'It's logical,' he said.

I turned the remark over as I trudged on towards Scheveningen. Motorists, caravanners, hippies, walkers, all wandering. Looking for somewhere else. Why? It's logical, he said.

'It is a strange madness,' said Petrarch to his out-of-elbows secretary, 'this desire to be for ever sleeping in a strange bed.' Helen Waddell assures us he had been a good secretary. He endeared himself to his master by learning eleven *canzone* in nine days. He copied his patron's verses in a fine clear script. Yet he lacked *stabilitas*. He spoke wildly of going to Constantinople to learn Greek. Years later he came back from Pisa, penniless and starving, a reformed prodigal. But not for long. A wandering scholar, one of the *Ordo Vagorum*, he soon vanished again and is next heard of in Rome. Europe was full of those vagrants. For centuries they were the curse of the Church. Edicts were issued in an effort to keep them at home. 'No clerk may leave the diocese without permission and letter of licence from the bishop; no bishop may receive him without such letter.'

To abuse a debater who claimed it logical to seek the unknown, you called him a *gyrovagus*, an intellectual grasshopper. St Benedict used it of those monks whose life was spent a few days here, a few days there, in the hospitality of different monasteries, ever wandering and never in one stay, 'minding only their own pleasures and their wretched gullets'. Those of whose unhappy conversation, he says, 'it is better to be silent than to speak'.

Logic? According to Milton, a sterile science 'except it conceive from without'. Gerald of Wales tells a long tale of a young man who spent five years at great expense in Paris, and came home able to prove to his father that the six eggs on the table were twelve: whereupon the father ate the six eggs apparent, and left the young man 'those which the hen of his logic had laid'. They sent him back to Paris with a caution.

A far cry from wandering scholars who could live by debating in Latin to the foot-loose hippies of today, but the same urge is there: to get away from the commonplace, to see something different. As for their apparent inability to communicate, to say what they are up to, I wonder the less about it when I think of those kids on the beach that day. For several reasons, I didn't explain what I was doing there. Certainly not why I was trudging towards Scheveningen. But something needs to be said about what the place meant to me as a youngster, since where I come from helps to explain where I stand.

Each year the family moved from Leeds to a rented house in the nearby coastal town of Scarborough. There, from an attic bedroom each morning, I watched the sun rise over a bay of the North Sea. Today I regard that shallow sea as little more than a lagoon, a circulator of warm streams from the Atlantic. It contains reservoirs of oil and gas, the decomposed silt of rivers which are becoming progressively more polluted. The fishing has fallen off. The spawny haddocks, the great shoals of herrings, 'the silver darlings', have all but been cleaned out. But this is sophisticated hindsight. For a child with a Danish name and a romantic sense of history it seemed by far the greatest sheet of water in the world.

The local museum-keeper, a patient, learned man, described how the Vikings had sailed in from Jorundsfjord and Borre, Hollingstedt and Hedeby, a place with a name like my own. Scarborough itself had been sacked by an old pirate called Skadis, the kinsman of Ketill Flat-Nose, Sigtrygg Silkybeard, Thorstein Ox-Leg and Olaf the Fart. Wonderful names. I collected pictures of those longships with terrible beaked prows, and became a Viking on the spot.

Scarborough was a busy port in the early thirties. At first light came the scream of gulls; at dusk the deep, organ-like notes of the incoming drifters. On hot days the harbour reeked of fish guts and tar. During the herring season the Dutch boats flocked in, especially from Scheveningen, the sister port of Scarborough. Unlike our rusty old drifters, the *Black Cat*, the *Rose and Mary*, and the *Herring Queen*, they were trim craft with honed decks and SCH boldly painted in white on bow and stern. I looked on them as ships from the other side of the world. The rival crews drank together; they swore eternal friendship and usually ended up by brawling outside the pubs on the quayside. I fished off the sea wall, feeling that life was somehow passing me by.

One night, with a two-inch cod hook firmly embedded in my thumb, I sat on the harbour steps, not daring to go home with evidence of a forbidden pastime so plainly displayed. 'Push it through the other side,' said an unsympathetic deck-hand. I pushed, slowly, and nearly fainted. Somebody else advised me to go aboard the *Gert Jan*, the Dutch hospital ship. The skipper had it out in no time. He gave me a glass of schnapps, the first alcohol I had ever tasted. With an airy wave of his hand he introduced me to his wife. A galvanizing experience. My metabolism went into an entirely different gear. With her knees under her breasts, that beautiful creature sat upright in a little tin bath of hot water. 'You moost come and see us in Scheveningen,' she said. I thought about her for years.

During that time, a happy time, I rowed out to those dirty old boats with black funnels and brown sails that lay moored in South Bay. There on the slippery decks the fishermen told of herring moons that loom up towards the end of October. They described wonderful white water, the sea blanched by tiny organisms, plankton, the wandering stuff that betokens great hauls of fish. I helped to bait long lines with bits of salted cod and learned how seventy or eighty nets make up what they called a fleet, which is a long curtain of nets, towed astern in such a way that the little drifters rode through the night, head to wind, like herring gulls asleep.

From history books, those same books that seemed so dull under formal instruction, I read how the Danes first caught herring for the Hanseatic merchants until the Dutch took over the North Sea industry. Since the Danes had become my Viking forebears, this rather annoyed me and I read more of Ketill Flat-Nose, and of his daughter Aud, the Deep-Minded, who defected from Odin to Christ. With little thought of what I was supposed to learn, I absorbed everything I could find about the Northmen and then peopled my narrow strip of history with a succession of heroes from the Merovingians to the Sea Beggars who kicked the Spaniards out of the Netherlands. If you add a bit of natural history acquired from fishermen and gamekeepers, for several years I don't think I learned much else that I considered worthwhile.

To get away from the dripping fogs of Leeds, I explored the surrounding dales and moors, walking and collecting plants and insects. History had been replaced by the works of wandering naturalists, especially Lubbock and Waterton, Russel Wallace, Darwin, and Charles Kingsley, whose *Water Babies* is, essentially, the story of a river and a Yorkshire river at that. By unravelling the Latin names of creatures brought home in match-boxes, I picked up a nodding acquaintance with the classics: thus the beautiful peacock butterfly (*Vanessa io*) that settled on the buddleia in the back garden became associated with the priestess of Hera at Argos, the ground beetle (*Feronia*) with the patron saint of all freed men, and the ruby-tail wasp (*Chrysis*) with Terence. I mined dictionaries and encyclopedias. Books were quarries of ideas. The names of things became part of the magic of association which I take to be the fuse of learning. For the young, something close to philosophy begins with wonder and not as it so often does, later on, with doubt.

Later, as a newspaperman, I made up some of the glaring gaps in my education, moving from local weeklies in the West Riding to *The Guardian* and afterwards *The New York Times*. Two enormous steps in an unsettled way of life. They gave prestige and the excitement of working with highly competent professional writers. I travelled to exotic places, to Artic Canada and Africa, but soon discovered that the further I travelled in the hot seat of journalism, the less I began to see in depth. A *gyrovagus*. The trips were too brief for either pleasure or comprehension. News, somebody has pointed out, is literature in a hurry. It's what happens today. It aspires to be history only in so far as it seeks to be accurate. I wanted to slow down the process of absorption. Starting with a long safari in North Kenya, I began to walk through places previously known only through books or brief visits. In a tramp through Britain I had the feeling of a pattern, a mosaic emerging from what had been scattered bits of information and experience. Now I wanted to move on, to try to relate Britain to the rest of Europe. I could not hope to tramp across the whole continent from east to west, but by walking from the Netherlands to the warm lands of the south, I reckoned on passing through the borderlands of countries where the blending processes are most marked. It would have been more practical to set off further up the coast, but I wanted to renew my acquaintance with the sea I had been brought up with.

The waves washed the beach gently, scattering the sand-hoppers, leaving behind jellyfish that glistened transparently, like droppings from a herd of ghost cows. From the grass on the dunes came the endless 'cheep' of pipits migrating west. Swallows clung to the barbed wire, resting, their long journey north nearly over. With no experience of the coast, I thought it would be possible to walk on the dunes, looking down on the sea and whatever lay behind that tantalizing tangle of wire. But the Dutch make sure nobody tramples on their national defence line. It must be easier to get into the palace of the Queen Mother than pierce those protective banks of sand. They are heavily fenced in. The interior is patrolled by police with dogs. Big notices say plainly *Verboden Toegang*. Where there is even a slight dip in the profile, the *zinkstukken* are re-inforced by a palisade woven from willows encouraged to grow behind the wire. If the barrier collapsed, much of the Netherlands would disappear under salt water.

The Dutch don't just resist the sea. They invade it. Engineers keep an eye on the way the tides flow through the changeable channels off the coast. By linking up isolated sandbanks, they are left with a series of lagoons to be fenced in and pumped out. With the help of chemicals, the coarse saltings become rich pastures and the Netherlands gets bigger and bigger each year, but slowly in the way that wood ants increase the size of their nests. Although the outermost dunes are only about twenty or thirty feet in height, this is a respectable elevation in a largely two-dimensional landscape. Limping slightly, I trudged along between their barrier and the sea.

That limp rather worried me. Shortly before I set off, I wrenched my knee. I had read somewhere that Roman soldiers were trained to fight with weapons considerably heavier than those they used in battle. It seemed an idea that could be put to practical use. I knew it wasn't necessary to go into training as a walker. I walk somewhere every day and have done so for years. But there is a world of difference in balance and muscular co-ordination between swinging along without a pack and trudging along carrying thirty or forty pounds. The unencumbered walker is a digitigrade, a toe-user. He leans forward in such a way that he glides along, scarcely seeming to touch the ground. Energy for the initial push off is provided by the ball of the foot and, almost immediately afterwards, by the big toe. Once you get going the power is supplemented by gravity controlled by the rhythmical movement of the legs. The movement is a marvellous one. Step by step, the body teeters on the edge of catastrophe. Yet the ability to stride out in an upright manner sets man distinctly apart from those ape-like shufflers, our earliest ancestors.

By contrast, the gait of a burdened man is inclined to be flat-footed or plantigrade. Until you get accustomed to the change in posture you lumber along like a caveman. But with practice the pack can be carried high and balanced in such a way that after a week or two of weight-lifting you feel unbalanced without it.

During the training period I overloaded. I took long walks daily, carrying about fifty pounds of cast-iron discs sandwiched between the thick volumes of the London telephone directory.

They were strapped down in a rucksack that fitted like a well-made bra. I could shake my shoulders without much side shift in the distribution of the load, but in overlooking the up-and-down movement I rather overdid the Roman idea.

During that period I strode over the South Downs, feeling on top of the world. In a brash gesture of self-confidence I leaped over a small ditch. The outcome was wholly unexpected and extremely painful. I landed like a bird, but the pack slumped down hard, wrenching a wire-taut ligament in the muscles of my knee-cap. There followed anxious days of bandaging and massage and talk of cortisone injections. The pain and the puffy flesh gradually subsided, leaving me with an occasional limp and an uneasy feeling of worse to come.

The rucksack felt light that morning. To economize on weight during the limbering-up period, I'd sent my tent on ahead to Liège. If I wanted to sleep out before I picked it up, I could crawl into a plastic thing called a survival bag, a long transparent envelope. With maps and money and the whole of Europe at my feet, I wondered what on earth I was worrying about. No route-finding problems ahead of the Vosges or the Jura. Any fit man could get to Geneva on his feet. Yet that chronic feeling of apprehension persisted. It took shape in a mental picture of a wall of snow-topped peaks, the Alps, the barrier between the two seas. To screen it off, I scrambled through the barricade of barbed wire to see what the Low Countries looked like from the top of the dunes.

A difficult and disappointing effort. No canals. No windmills. Not even a few tulips. Nothing but glasshouses among acres and acres and acres of corn, carrots, and asparagus. The blanched crop grew under sheets of polythene that rattled dryly in the breeze. And back I went to the sea.

To get the most of that peace that comes from the plash of waves I tried a variation of the numbers game, the last resort of those with nothing profitable to think about. On a brisk walk I stride out at about a hundred and twenty paces to the minute. The waves fell at intervals of about ten seconds. With a little adjustment in pace I could anticipate the gentle hiss of the retreating water by a precise number of strides, and by that simple contrivance I swung along for twelve miles, metronomically geared to the rhythm of the sea.

Dutch light is remarkable. From the beach the impression is of shimmering water seen through exquisitely cut crystal, constantly changing with gusts of moist air, but always a-sparkle even on dull days. The waves are brightest at the water's edge where they rear up and catch the light. Yet Dutch painters of the sea usually put their foregrounds in the shade to emphasize the brightness of the sky. Schools of painting can be roughly dated from the height of the horizons. They became lower in the nineteenth century. The light and the waves dramatized the terror of the sea. Apart from the great estuaries, there are relatively few ports on the Dutch coast. Boats were hauled up on the beach by horses. During storms they were often turned over and wrecked. The fishermen would stand round their smashed-up craft, dazed and stricken as they would be at the death-bed of one who had been the centre of their family.

Scheveningen, that once great centre of the herring industry, the port I had thought so much about as a youth, looked large and unlovely. Where were the men in blue jerseys and sou'-westers of yellow leather; their womenfolk in flowered bodices and coral necklaces, the envy of the girls of Scarborough? I knew where they were. They were in the *hofjes* or almshouses. Or retired to respectable old age in Wassenaar. Or dead in the *Algemene Begraafplaats*, the cemetery in the Little Wood of the Birds. But memory persists. Life must be lived forward but understood backwards. Somewhere in that port I wanted a sustaining glimpse of yesterday, and it was hard to find. The boats, huge diesel-driven affairs, equipped to trawl the waters of the Arctic, lined almost empty docks hemmed in by mean little modern houses. Trams ding-donged through shoals of cyclists, carrying holiday-makers to the modern *plage* beyond the seamen's quarter. Rather saddened by it all, I wandered out through the town, keeping to the coast, towards Katwijk where the blue haze of hyacinths clings to the peaty earth like cigarette smoke.

Far from being as common as orchards in Kent or Normandy, the bulb fields are largely confined to the *geestgrond*, a narrow strip of loam and sand between The Hague and Haarlem, two places scarcely twenty miles apart. The crocus and the narcissus bloom first. Hyacinths spring up in April with here and there a blood-red gash of early and rather vulgar-looking tulips. Here are no short-stemmed Red Emperors or delicately striped Robin Hoods. No China-pinks or Kaufmann hybrids, the descendants of stock for which the tulipomaniacs of the seventeenth century paid thousands of guilders for a single bulb. They are waxy-looking blooms for the sick-room and the cemetery, entirely scentless and too stiff for grace. I prefer them full open, their petals almost falling, revealing their florid inner parts. Around Katwijk, the bulbs are carted about as in other countries they cart potatoes. In that enormous flatscape everyone seemed to be in the flower-growing business.

In horticulture, as in almost everything else they put their hands to, there is a wonderful sense of working togetherness about the Dutch. It's how they came to build thousands of miles of dykes and seawalls and canals and windmills. They are hard-working and thrifty because they created their own wealth. It wasn't to be squandered by self-seeking individualists.

There is a story about how, when he was a young man, Prince Maurice once travelled by a canal barge, an elegant little *trek-schuit*, and helped the skipper to tow the rope. When he was tired the old man told him to butter a piece of rye bread. The prince accepted the invitation and added a slice of cheese. To eat two dairy products at the same time was looked upon as down-right extravagance and bad manners. Notwithstanding the rank of his passenger, the indignant skipper boxed the prince's ears. '*That*'s not how our country grew rich,' he said.

Having an appointment in The Hague the next morning with an old friend, I merely ambled about, looking at nothing in particular. Everyone seemed to have a clear-cut job to do. In the Netherlands you either work or you play, purposively. The Dutch are extremely tolerant towards youngsters, hippies, and the like, who hang about, plaguing authority. It's part of the business of growing up, they say. But if I wasn't on the move, I had an uneasy feeling that someone of my age ranked among the rabble, *het grauw*, those at the very bottom of the social ladder, the trouble-making unemployed. Instead of turning south, I went back to Scheveningen as one might probe a tooth to see if it still ached, and on an impulse, difficult to explain, I slept out on the beach that night.

Under the swinging lights of the boulevard they offer all that's going in several languages. Fireworks fizzle on the front. Large girls half strip coyly in the underground bodegas. Corks pop and *Schottische steacks* cost a small fortune. Dutch food is good, expensive, and badly served. I sat down in an elegant little place, conscious of a bulging rucksack. Nobody looked in the least surprised.

Not so in the seamen's quarter, a place of narrow, dimly-lit streets and dingy houses. At my appearance in the bars there I might have been dressed as a pantomine dame. Seamen ashore are uninhibited about what they find amusing. They laughed uproariously. I could make nothing of the language in the first house. It turned out to be Finnish. A ship from Helsinki had pulled in that afternoon and the whole crew were awash in *genever* and very bitter Amstel beer. The barman recommended another place, where I again ran into appalling linguistic difficulties. The notion that everyone in the Netherlands speaks at least two languages is belied in the docks of Scheveningen.

Through a friendly interpreter I tried to find some of the old fishermen near my own age who had put into Scarborough in the days of steam drifters, but nobody had heard of the place. After pronouncing the word in all the variations I could think of, a not-so-ancient mariner, the captain of a tug improbably got up in the swishest of Italian suits, nodded, '*Haachh-br-chh*', he said. *Ja*, he knew the port. But *soo* long ago. I asked him, did he remember the names of any of the old boats, the *Black Cat*, the *Herring Queen*? Or the pubs on the quayside? He shook his head. But from his reflective smile I had clearly touched some deep-rooted memory. He stumbled for the words.

He recalled a girl. Now what was her name? The one with the beautiful legs. My turn to shake my head. In those days I knew no girls, good or bad, certainly not the bouncy pieces that waited for the boats to come in. Those legs, he said. Everyone knew her. I recalled the girl in the bath. Was she the wife of the skipper of the *Gert Jan*? But he wasn't listening. Of all things, the girl he remembered had worn a top-hat. It came out, eventually, that as a young deck-hand he had seen Marlene Dietrich in *The Blue*

Angel. 'The first film I ever saw,' he said. 'By God, I never forgot it. What a *wooman*!'

Back on the beach I settled down uncomfortably in one of the holes in the sand. From somewhere among the dunes a nightingale sang. A dog barked incessantly. Sand-hoppers rustled about under my plastic envelope, and as the waves washed back and forth it seemed as though they sighed.

The Water Cities

In Dutch The Hague is called den Haag or Gravenhage, a word that simply means the hedge, the hedge or boundary of the old grafs or lords of Flanders. The nobility wanted a bit of privacy and protection in the windy country behind the sea wall. They surrounded their town houses with an imposing arcade of trees known to more humble folk as the hedge. What's left of that little wood or *bosje* lies around the Scheveningenweg, a fine road that drops down from the sea wall to the palace. To keep their royal highway quiet, the city councillors have allowed grass to grow between the tram rails.

Nowadays, the wood is lightly clothed in young oak and beech, for most of the old trees were cut down and burned during the cold days of the German occupation. But what the hedge lacks in solid timber it gains in the music of birds. At six o'clock that morning the thickets of hazel and honeysuckle were rinsed with sound. I could not have been there at a finer hour.

There is no place for laggards or lie-abeds in the bird school. To get the best of what's going you've got to be in class early. Against a mighty clamour of blackbirds and wrens I picked out the contralto of a mistle thrush, the treble of wood and willow warblers, an occasional nightingale and the shrill of a redstart. All babbling and bubbling, trying to outsing each other in a choral claim to an unoccupied corner of that jubilant wilderness.

Whenever I'm out in the country, alone, listening to what's in the air, I remember long and pleasurable days spent in the company of my old friend Eric Warmington, a classical scholar who could identify almost everything he heard, even above the noise of busy London traffic.

This takes some doing. In winter you can see what's singing. The eyes have it. But in thick foliage you need keen ears. At

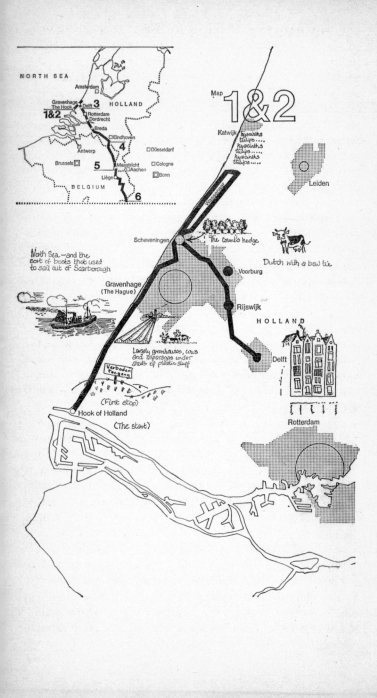

NORTH SEA

Amsterdam

HOLLAND

Gravenhage
The Hook
1&2

Delft **3**

Rotterdam
Dordrecht

Breda

Eindhoven

4

□Düsseldorf

Antwerp

5

Maastricht
Aachen

□Cologne

Brussels▣

Liège▢

□Bonn

BELGIUM

6

Map **1&2**

Katwijk

*hyacinths
tulips....
hyacinths....
hyacinths
tulips....*

Leiden

Scheveningen

The Tomb's hedge

Dutch with a bow tie

*North Sea — and the
sort of boats that used
to sail out of Scarborough*

Gravenhage
(The Hague)

Voorburg

Rijswijk

HOLLAND

*Largely greenhouses, cars
and asparagus under
sheets of plastic stuff*

Delft

Verboden
Toegang

(First stop)

Rotterdam

○ Hook of Holland

(The start)

first the chorus seems as closely woven as the threads of a tapestry, but once the characteristic calls of the commoners have been sorted out, the zones of sound can be split up into their component parts. Like an amateur radio operator, the bird listener is almost constantly combing the air, focusing only on whatever interests him from a mere chip of sound in the foreground – say the call of a hawfinch – to the most distant and faintly heard of the soloists. Eric used to walk in the country with his father, a naturalist who lost his sight at an early age. They walked close together, noting their neighbours and, years later, through the son I acquired a portion of their shared gift.

The birds of the Netherlands are delightfully tame. When I sat down to munch a sandwich, chaffinches pecked at the crumbs; robins took turns at playing at King of the Castle on my upturned pack and, as I sauntered on, tits, nuthatches, and hedge sparrows fluttered out of the trees. This faith in the goodwill of mankind is a tribute to the tolerance of the Dutch who respect their small fellow-countrymen.

During that busy day, shopping and looking at gabled mansions and galleries with my friend, Annie, a schoolmistress from Wassenaar, I recall prodigious paintings and hosts of bicycles and beautiful Indonesian women. With important things to buy like maps and trouser buttons I may have missed much, but I don't think so. With the exception of the Royal Library and some fine town houses by Daniel Marot, the buildings that strike the eye are few and arranged in comfortable clusters as you might find them in a quiet London square. The rest of the town is noisy and rather sprawling.

The Hague is the political capital and the seat of government. If you can ignore the whores that loll behind illuminated shop windows at night – which is difficult – the place is rather self-consciously respectable, even stuffy, but anxious to give a good impression. They tell of Civil Servants who take their midday sandwiches to the office in a violin case, and of course they cycle there.

For the Dutch the bicycle is not so much a useful machine as a balanced way of life. They are ridden with grace. In a corner of the *Koninginnegracht* a girl in a long dress brought her machine to rest by running the front wheel into a rack, scarcely touching the sides. It puts you in mind of a bird alighting on its nest. On bicycles you may see a troupe of nuns or people eating snacks or taking their children and dogs for a ride. In the cities they are a sort of collective entity. Karel Capek likened them to dancing gnats or the swarming of infusoria. He says the art of keeping them upright has taught the Dutch to rely on the force of inertia and the value of self-reliance, for a man on a bicycle gets used to looking after himself and not getting mixed up with someone else's bicycle. I'm in favour of any form of transport that doesn't make a noise or smell, but when a policeman released a wave of cyclists with a flick of his finger I got trapped in the middle of the street like a cowboy surrounded by a herd of friendly steers.

If the Civil Servants and business people seem a bit solemn and over-serious, the balance is partly redressed by increasing numbers of young folk poised, ready for revolt against anything they consider bourgeois and authoritarian. These are the *provotariaat* and their light-hearted successors, the Gnomes, Pixies, and *Dolle Minas* who, from headquarters in Amsterdam, are establishing communes throughout the principal cities of the Netherlands. They have declared a 'jovial war' on conformity. Street posters call for 'pyromaniacal action' against all census forms. Dressed in space-suits and gas-masks they periodically hold up peak-hour traffic just to show what they think of air pollution and noise. In an effort to dent 'the myth of male superiority', their girl-friends, the new liberationists, light-heartedly pinch the bottoms of civic officials in public and wolf-whistle at policemen, whilst a militant group of women aged from twenty-one to sixty threaten to deploy *total* abstinence if they are not given more say in domestic and urban affairs.

But so far the Gnomes haven't managed to make much of an impression on The Hague. A far more important cultural factor there is the arrival in recent years of thousands of coloured repatriates, most of them from the former Dutch East Indies. They now represent a considerable proportion of the already tightly-packed local population. They are a splendid-looking people, the men with soft compassionate faces. And the young women are the very flowers of the Hedge.

Girls with ebony hair and golden skins from Surinam, the Antilles, Java, and Bali skitter through the streets, all prim and beautifully got up. I followed a girl with a pram who looked about eighteen, her baby an exquisite miniature of herself. She was improbably dressed in a bra and shorts which is perhaps as near as she could get to the Balinese *sapoet*, that cloth tied across the top of a sarong, below the breasts. The child tossed out a hair ribbon. It landed in the gutter. Mother took one look at the little bow and skittered on. A flower that falls to the ground during a dance can't be replaced in the hair. Everyone knows that.

The Dutch have made them feel at home. The country's tradition for tolerance came out clearly in Queen Juliana's greeting to the first boat-load of refugees kicked out by President Sukarno. From a land of flowers and warmth and festival they arrived in mid-January, many of them seasick and half-frozen. 'I bid you all a hearty welcome,' she said. 'It must have been very difficult to leave the country of your birth. But you are arriving in your own country, among your own people, and I hope you will feel something of the warmth in the hearts of those who are receiving you.'

The Dutch had a lot of difficulty in making room for what now amounts to nearly three hundred thousand extra people. They had scarcely recovered from the German Occupation. There was an acute housing shortage. But the government assumed full responsibility from the start. They supplied them with housing grants and free clothing; they started familiarization courses, teaching them new skills and how to look for jobs. With uncommon perception they spread the newcomers across the country thinly, like a rich and piquant sauce, knowing that once they found their feet they would tend to gravitate towards certain cities, like The Hague. And almost everywhere the Indonesians have been sympathetically received, certainly without significant hostility. The repatriation machinery has now been closed down, the job done. The Dutch, I think, can teach most of us a lesson in imperial responsibility.

There are many reasons why the programme went off so smoothly. The Dutch are not only tolerant, they are resilient; they know what it means to live under repression. Although they ruled the East Indies for three centuries they got on well with the people there. Their government has accepted the idea of racial integration. There is no colour bar. In the old days the planters often took housekeeper concubines. Some brought them home as wives. They brought them back to cold windy cities, yet places already tinged with elements of Far Eastern culture, in art and design, in food and a concern for life.

In an art gallery you may see a beautiful Balinese girl, perhaps a student, looking at a modern painting. She is unmarried. In her ear-lobes she wears little cylinders of jade or ivory. In Bali or Lambok they would be of rolled-up palm leaves. As she reads about the painting from the catalogue the unoccupied fingers of her left hand are upturned from the wrist. They ripple out a little counterpoint of their own. They are more than mere extensions of her hand; they are a part of her whole body, as expressive in gesture as a smile or a frown. They are the fingers of a girl whose forebears stylized their lives in the dance.

The Indonesians received progressive waves of influences from Buddhist, Hindu, and Chinese sources with a light overlay of Mohammedanism. Their religion is broadly based on a profound belief in the continuity of life. The Balinese, said Margaret Mead, know the day of the week on which they were born but they do not know how old they are. Climax is absent from their rhythms of love and hate. They are insensitive to interruption and, however strong its emphasis upon finality, no death is ever really final. Man is predestined to be born and re-born. As for the souls of the dead, they are babies who must be taught to pray.

Wisdom religions such as theosophy have always flourished in the Netherlands. They recognize human brotherhood as a necessary condition of evolution. These concepts were strengthened by their contacts with the Far East. The repatriates are certainly profiting from what the Dutch learned to appreciate. They have slipped into their new life easily, as into an old garment tried on for a time by someone else.

That morning they were dressing The Hague for the forthcoming birthday of their Queen. Garlands swung between the lamp-posts; great swags of flowers hung from gables. In most of the squares the lofty trees were incongruously laden with plastic imitations of that royal fruit, the orange. Amid the bustle I looked in vain for those anomalies known as national types but saw only a few elderly ladies in mourning. They wore their traditional black- and red-lined capes and head-dresses adorned with little gold horns. A pious gesture, I thought, though Annie, always a realist, said they loved to dress up and might only be in mourning for the distant relative of a neighbour. Elsewhere in Holland, especially among the islands and fishing villages, the local folk put on striped petticoats and winged bonnets which can be photographed for a fee augmented by a subsidy from the tourist bureau. For an unspoiled picture of what Old Holland looked like we went to those treasure houses of oil paint, the *Mauritshuis*, the *Gemeentemuseum* and a curiously painted tent called the *Panorama Mesdag*.

Hendrik Willem Mesdag thought up an impressionistic trick which, as far as I know, has never been pulled off again. He made a glass cylinder big enough to sit in. He stuck this up on the dunes above Scheveningen and sat inside it for weeks, sketching out on the glass everything he saw, full circle. He enlarged his panoramic sketch enormously, painting it on a cylindrical canvas as high as a house. For a shilling or two you can gaze at the Scheveningen of a century ago with boats at anchor and boats on the beach together with local fishermen, their wives and dogs. By turning round you get a view inland as far as the spires of distant Leiden. All is visible to the horizon. To give reality to the foreground he dumped several tons of real Scheveningen sand at the foot of his canvas. A clever device made slightly ridiculous that morning by a real cat that wandered in looking larger than a tiger against the foreshortened perspective.

Mesdag deserves half an hour, but, like the Niagara Falls, the whole thing is a bit overpowering. Apart from its size, you feel you will never see nor, indeed, want to see its like again. More intriguing by far are the works of what Annie called the Little Masters, the painters of interiors and watery landscapes and seascapes which, before they drained the country, must have looked rather alike. They are little only in the size of their canvases. With a few towering exceptions the Dutch tended to paint small pictures for small rooms. When the Spaniards were thrown out there was no market for enormous canvases of the Assumption or the Temptation of St Anthony, nor many places to hang them, for the Calvinists stripped the churches of everything they considered idolatrous. The painters fell back to what the burgomaster and his wife wanted, that is the view they saw every day from their slim windows: of herring boats moored in smelly harbours and ice fairs by Avercamp. They could look at rooks delighting in the light and flowing skies of Ruysdael or Cuyp's chocolate-coloured cows champing away chin deep in wet pastures. The atmosphere is one of intimacy. To look at interiors by Maes, Jan Steen, and ter Borch, is like peering through windows, into private rooms.

The art of the Renaissance was commissioned by popes, by princes, and pious merchant bankers. The marble was cut and the paint put on by artists precariously supported on huge scaffolding. By contrast, Dutch art is, as Capek nicely put it, 'the work of seated painters for sedentary townfolk'. The world in which it sits is restful, talkative, and easy-going. It is cosy, matter-of-fact, and given to tittle-tattle. It notices things nearest to it. It observes at close quarters and with enjoyment. Make an excited man sit down, he says, and he immediately drops his heroics, his grandiose posturing. Nobody can preach sitting down. All he can do is talk.

Annie is a compulsive talker. She is concerned about art, and nature too, but in its place. When I told her about the nightingales I heard among the sand-dunes she agreed they were nice birds, but in her opinion a bit too outspoken. She said a pair were nesting in her garden that year and she had been obliged to throw a shoe at one that sang too early that very morning. She talked about the local health service and the price of butter, about Vlaminck, Toorop, Corneille, and what she intended to do with that clump of azaleas she had planted just inside the gate. This is very much the Dutch way of putting the affairs of the world to rights and one much to my taste. Without standing too heavily on the proposition we agreed that Dutch art is for the most part the work of pictorial reporters. It depicts life as people would like to experience it, either neatly organized and bourgeois, like the tiled floor of an interior, or exuberantly rustic with dogs licking the fallen platters at the marriage feast.

But what of the gloom and lustre of Rembrandt? Or Franz Hals, that painter of hairy-looking he-men? Or of van Gogh, who, from a little square of canvas, looked down on us through wild anguished eyes? That self-portrait in the *Gemeentemuseum* made nonsense of our generalizations.

The eyes are terrifying. In them you can see flashes of shock and horror, the expression of a man who has been dragged from a fearful accident, or of someone who has seen what he dare not describe. Fascinated by that self-portrait I managed to get to Zundert and Neunen where he lived and tried to piece together something about why he died. I don't think I discovered a great deal. Generalizations about genius are usually misleading, but they sometimes give us a glimpse of what we are trying to get hold of.

Van Gogh strove constantly to present a clear and visual image of both sensual and spiritual experience which is largely what all art is about. What is probably more significant is that he wandered from place to place, hoping always for a sense of belonging somewhere, of knowing where he was. Could it be that, subconsciously, he wanted to know *who* he was?

As you may discover from a book by Humberto Nagera, there were two Vincent van Goghs. The painter's father, a fairly well-to-do pastor, called his first child Vincent. The child died in infancy exactly one year before the second Vincent was born. The contention is that that child, a dirty, unruly, life-loving boy, felt he had no personality of his own, that for years he lived under the idealized character of his dead and deeply lamented brother, the person he had never seen. On the tombstone in Zundert cemetery he saw his own name and his own birth date, but they belonged to the Vincent who died before he began to live.

Schoolmasters could make nothing of him. He saw no reality in what they tried to teach him. Asked to define the difference between the nominative and the dative, he said: 'Oh, sir, I really don't *care*.' But he could sketch marvellously well, moving gradually from pastel to oils, trying to capture what he saw, the essence of things. He says God touched his heart, but when he tried to come to terms with his father's vocation, the formalities of theology, the seminarists dismissed him for insubordination. He asked too many questions. Among the potato-eaters, those poverty-stricken miners of the Borinage, he practised faith through works. He became a lay preacher and what today would be called a welfare officer, but the authorities said he was too good, meaning too unconventional.

He banished soap as a sinful luxury; he became dirtier than the people he visited. He gave away his meagre salary. Even his friends thought he was too compassionate. Whenever he found a caterpillar on the ground he picked it up carefully and put it back on a tree. When she was about to have someone else's child he took up, temporarily, with Christine, a prostitute, and described her as attached to him 'like a tame dove'. He lived like a tramp, searching, looking for ways of portraying his concept of reality. He copied Japanese woodcuts, using oriental reed pens for his ink drawings and reproducing the sketches in oils. He tried every technique he knew until at last, under the blazing sun of Provence, the most famous of his canvases – the sunflowers, the cypresses, the cornfields with poppies like blobs of blood – flared under his furious brush-strokes. And ordinary things, too. Writing about the picture of his room at Arles he said: 'It's just simply my bedroom, only here colour is to do everything and giving by its simplification a grander style to things is to be suggestive of *rest*, of sleep in general ... the shadows are suppressed ...' He had begun to see things clearly.

The suicide that ended a life when, artistically, it had just burst into flower is one of the paradoxes of the human journey. In the sacramental meaning of the word he managed at last to acquire the sense of really *being* somewhere, but in the process he destroyed himself. I cling to Gabriel Marcel's belief that perhaps a stable order can be established only if man always remains acutely conscious that his condition is that of a traveller.

Annie went home that afternoon and I set off for Delft, a leisurely waterside walk of a couple of hours. To avoid the traffic on a broad highway with the frisky name of the *Rijswykscweg Sc'weg* I ignored the map and took a resolute compass course right through the back streets of the town, crossing over a number of those muddy little waterways they call *grachten* until I came to a broad inter-city canal in the right direction. There I cruised along among families of stiff-necked Bewick swans who were taking their youngsters out for barge-avoidance lessons among a mighty ring of bells. The music pealed from *speeltorens* or speaking-towers, that nice Dutch word for belfries. The ringers were tuning up for the Queen's birthday.

Delft means the ditch, the place they dug out to freight beer and bales of wool down the Schie to that port now called Rotterdam. There may be water cities more ancient, perhaps more imposing than that little grid-iron of *grachten*, but none more intimate the length of the Low Countries. Tourists pour through the town as through an internationally famous museum, but mostly on foot. The streets are paved with water. The houses seem enormously tall and thin, and they stand on their own reflections, quivering as if seen through tears, but it looks as if there's a lot of domestic sewage in that milky-blue and rather smelly water. In the morning, when they've finished scrubbing down their shop fronts, the traders throw buckets full of diluted detergent into their own bit of the ditch and the foam floats about for hours.

Delft is built of little rose-coloured bricks and stands on sand, and, to judge from the way the houses are jammed together like a packet of sandwiches, there can't be much of it. To save space the staircases are narrow and exceptionally steep. The impression is of a ladder in a hen house. The furniture has to be hauled through the upper windows on ropes attached to a sort of permanent crane discreetly hidden away among the ornamental gables, no two of which are alike. On the ground floor the houses are distinguishable one from another only by their doorways and name plates which might be polished by the wife of a fishmonger, a well-to-do attorney, a barge captain, or a banker. Or you might be looking at the bank itself. A very democratic city. A man's social and professional standing is rarely apparent from the outward appearance of his apartment and, because the lower levels of prosperity are much higher than anywhere else, everyone seems pretty well off.

I should like to know what the old city looked like, but it was burned down in 1536 and whatever remained was devasted in the next century when the arsenal blew up. None of this is apparent from the serene work of Vermeer, at the time of the explosion a promising local boy. His use of light, which gives a kind of magical presence to reality, is loosely called the Dutch style, but it was from the Italians he inherited the hidden geometry of composition.

Much has been made of the serenity, the composure, the wonderful sense of orderliness of Dutch interiors as seen through the eyes of her great painters, but historians and psychologists are beginning to look at the pictures in rather a different way. In the seventeenth century – *de gouden eeuw* – the Dutch had more money that they could use. They were the carriers of Europe, the exploiters of the East Indies. Amsterdam was rapidly becoming the financial centre of the world. Unlike the Spaniards, who squandered the gold they came by so easily, the thrifty Dutch re-invested their dividends. They dug new land out of their coasts, but not fast enough to absorb their profits from trade. The well-to-do bought big houses and stocked them with paintings, furniture and other valuable objects.

Dutch interiors often look deserted – like little museums with ribbons across the chairs – because that's what many of them were. Apart from the very rich with a lot of social obligations, the Dutch were content to live in a small part of their homes. The untenanted rooms were treasure stores: they were Victorian drawing-rooms on the grand scale. G. J. Renier, one of their official historians, says even the kitchen with its glittering brass utensils was far too fine a place for daily use: food was cooked there once a week; on the other days it was heated up on the small oven in the recess behind the kitchen where the family dwelt throughout the winter. When better weather returned the family went to live outside in the courtyard or even on the pavement from which all dirt and untidiness had been banished. The word *schoon* for 'beautiful' began to acquire the meaning of 'clean', something which had to be polished and dusted. The connection between possessiveness and extreme tidiness is well known to psychologists. The current word for conveying the notion of 'beautiful' is *mooi* which means pretty.

By working outwards from the busy market place between the *Stadhuis* and the musical *Nieuwekerk* you can get hold of the spirit of a little place like Delft in two or three hours. Other cities may take longer. Nobody can take in all the tourist boards have to offer, even in a sampling survey. To make the most of your time you need a map, guide book and compass, a fair sense of direction and enormous curiosity tempered only by what you reckon irrelevant to the particular place. This calls for a lot of leisurely homework or some rapid reading in the most attractive open-air café you can find.

Before you get trapped in what may turn out to be a dull museum, it's best to compare what the expensive antique shops have to offer with the stuff they sell in the bric-à-brac parlours. Likewise, a Roman Catholic church – in Delft it's St Hippolyte – can often show what treasure the Calvinists threw out. The cultural spiral properly carried out should proceed from the general to a more leisurely inspection of the particular. I settled for a few shops, three churches, two museums, a walk through the back streets and a chat with a man I took to be the burgomaster's social secretary.

At intervals the carillon of the great *Nieuwekerk* plays popular tunes from *Traumerei* to selections from *Oklahoma*. Verhulst's famous statue of van Tromp, that admiral who trounced the English fleets, lies stretched out in a niche of the equally huge but silent *Oudekerk*. In that cold green light he looks as if he has been dredged up from the sea floor. I find churches without altars extremely depressing and went off in search of the town's famous porcelain.

The old ware is so delicate, so finely painted that I'm surprised that over-glossy modern reproductions are still so popular. The technique is based on soft paste, glazed and fired with lead, silica and tin. This is *majolica* or *faïence* derived, I'm told, from Faienza in Italy where the Dutch seemed to have learned the whole business. With little brushes made out of the whiskers of a mouse they put the sign of the Peacock or the Star on an ever-increasing range of wares from tiles to the framework of bird cages. Delft got into the trade ahead of their rivals in Haarlem because the local brewing business failed, leaving factories empty and skilled men unemployed.

Other countries imitated what the Dutch did supremely well, even though within a century Delft began to go in for ceramic oddities such as porcelain models of court shoes, windmills and wide-eyed Friesian cows. But for a time they sold only stuff that could be used. Mugs and plates were inscribed with the words and music of drinking songs so that when the eating was over, the company could burst into song by holding up their pots. Tiles were used for instruction in schools much as we use posters in the infants' department today. Series of blue and white squares depicted the expulsion of the Spaniards or the history of the herring fleet, and from inlays over his head in barracks a young recruit could learn how to clean, load, prime and fire his blunder-buss.

As I mooched about in the dusk, looking for a room, the swans called to each other in a bugle-like voice and the carillon of the *Nieuwekerk* slowly tolled *Home on the Range*. At the back of the *Prinsenhof* I found a little place where Madame looked at my bulging pack with some apprehension, for, in mounting the ladder-like staircase, I grossly threatened several bits of pottery difficult to see in the half-light.

What we both feared took place with a terrifying musical accompaniment just outside the bedroom door where, despite some delicate manoeuvring, I nudged the edge of a baroque grandfather clock, a beautiful object with a lot of gadgetry built into the dial. Immediately it began to chime, wildly, like a tram bell. Something behind a picture of Old Utrecht played a folk-tune, apparently backwards, and each time the minute hand raced past the figure XII on the dial it gave impetus to a number of miniature windmills, spinning wheels and two-dimensional storks that flapped their wings, violently.

I watched aghast yet fascinated that so much could happen so quickly, but Madame seemed stoically unconcerned. She looked on, saying nothing until the clock had expended what seemed the pent-up energy of centuries. 'It has not spoken for some time,' she said, adding that she would come back for my pass-port later.

Across Brabant

How I came to get a brick thrown at me in a peaceful place like Holland was due to my own stupidity, but I couldn't have foreseen all that happened that day, certainly not an encounter with an elk at the foot of a huge clover-leaf road crossing. But I am anticipating events that began peacefully enough on the canal between Delft and Rotterdam.

If you walk pretty nimbly it takes about three hours. I emphasize the speed, not because I was in any particular hurry. But under the *Waterstaat* regulations the barges are not allowed to chug along at more than about five miles an hour, which means that if one comes up behind you can keep up with it for a few minutes by jogging along a notch or two above normal.

'Joomp on!' shouted the master of the *Pieter de Roose*.

Now there was temptation for you. A smart boat. A short haul to the Rhine. Or was it the Maas? I could have found out if I had jumped aboard. And I might have learned something about barge life. But I didn't joomp and if you think that stupid you are dead right. As the *Pieter de Roose* slowly hauled ahead, I gave myself a good talking to.

'Gootbye,' shouted the master. 'Gootbye. To carry all zat vate you moost be fairy stronk.'

Sure, I thought, and weak in the head, mister. I was still in the middle of silent argument when up hove the something or other from Bremen. The captain hailed me in German and what I took to be Swedish.

'*Ainglander*,' I said, crossly.

'Engländer?' he repeated. He nodded and smiled and I knew just what that smile meant. I had worked out a few Germanic pleasantries for the next boat when, quite unexpectedly, the canal swung away to the west, away from Rotterdam.

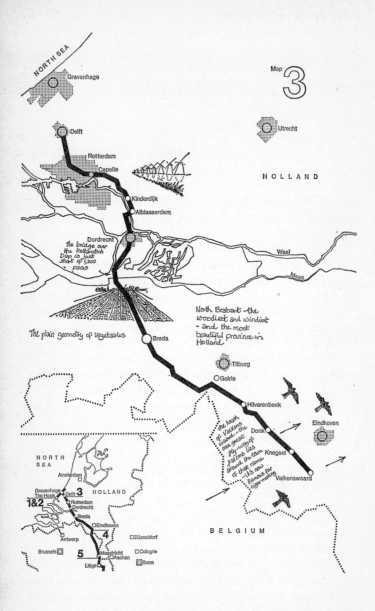

NORTH SEA

Map 3

Gravenhage

Delft

Rotterdam
Capelle

HOLLAND

Utrecht

Kinderdijk
Alblasserdam

Dordrecht
*the bridge over
the Hollandsch
Diep is just
short of 1,500
paas*

Waal

Maas

The plain geometry of Vegetables

Breda

*North Brabant – the
woodiest and windiest
– and the most
beautiful province in
Holland*

Tilburg

Goirle

Hilvarenbeek

Donk

Eindhoven

*the heath
of Valkens
waard – the
once great
fly-way of
falcons lies
around the town
of that name
it's now
famous for
cigar making*

Knegsel

Valkenswaard

BELGIUM

NORTH
SEA

Amsterdam

Gravenhage
The Hook

Delft 3

1&2
Rotterdam
Dordrecht

HOLLAND

Breda

Eindhoven

Antwerp

4

Düsseldorf

Brussels

5

Maastricht
Aachen

Cologne

Liège

Bonn

With a mist floating about in rather an eerie fashion, I climbed up a ramp and found myself at one of the entrance lanes to the biggest clover-leaf crossing in Brabant.

As an almost full-time pedestrian I have never studied the anatomy of these intestinal affairs. Here were at least six roads interwoven, one above the other, on an arrangement of ferro-concrete stilts. With traffic whirling past at an appalling speed, I went up to the topmost whirlabout with much angry hooting from all concerned. Up there the traffic fanned out in lanes to Dordrecht and to Utrecht, to Gouda and the Benelux Tunnel, but not, as far as I could see, to Rotterdam.

And down came the mist, warm and white and more blinding than the dark. I became thoroughly scared, for with their yellow fog lamps blazing, the traffic scarcely slackened speed. And from the harbour, far below, all the ships in the world began to moan like a herd of cows.

Inching round the loops, nervously, I eventually found a thrice-blessed sign that said *Centrum* and down I went, down to the *Vroesenlaan* where the sound of ships' hooters seemed curiously intermingled with the roaring of lions and a deep-throated bellow difficult to identify in the mist and the confusion. But it sounded quite near.

It came from a fine specimen of a Canadian elk with its head through the railings of the Rotterdam zoo. It bellowed unhappily as if challenged by those elks down on the waterfront. I felt rather sorry for the animal, a fellow-pedestrian in distress, and I sat on the pavement quite near it until the mist lifted and I marched on.

This habit of striding briskly through populous places is sometimes an embarrassment. I forget that I'm walking like a guardsman and the spectacle clearly amuses those with memories of drill sergeants and the barrack square. On many occasions in Britain and elsewhere people have stopped digging holes in the road and bawled out: 'Left, right, left, right,' or, occasionally, 'Shun!' or 'H'order – H'arms!' It happened again in Rotterdam.

From the platform of a partly-constructed building, a labourer shouted *links*, *rechts*, *links*, *rechts* and imagining, perhaps, from my dark green pants and jacket that I had once been in the German Army, he added: 'Heil Hitler!'

This annoyed me. Quite stupidly I half turned round and raised my right arm in a Nazi salute, whereupon half a brick crashed down on the pavement and I marched on more rapidly than before.

It doesn't do to make jokes about the Nazis in Rotterdam. No visible scars remain of that bombing raid when thirty thousand civilians were stricken down in little more than half an hour. The city has been almost entirely rebuilt, but few over the age of forty forget why.

They say the order to pulverize the place came direct from Goering. You would have thought the city would have been more use to the Germans if they had left it intact. But the news came through that British troops were landing on the Dutch coast to the south of the Maas river. This, they thought, constituted a danger to their own spearheads coming up from Dordrecht and they sent the Dutch an ultimatum to surrender at once or take the consequences. Scarcely had the terms been considered when the first planes droned over.

They were Dornier Flying Pencils, those same planes that took part in the terror bombing of Guernica. Within minutes the centre of Rotterdam was in flames. People trying to get out of the city added to the confusion. Streets were jammed with traffic before the first bomb fell. And the civilians were bombed and bombed until scarcely a building remained upright.

Five hours after the attack the Germans marched in. The city burned for days and the world gained a new and terrible expression – to be Rotterdammed.

Today you walk through street after street of new apartment blocks. No matter whether the rooms are on the ground floor or thirty storeys up in the air, they all have three very noticeable characteristics. The first is cleanliness of an uncommon order. They might have been spring-cleaned and re-painted the day before. The second is that behind the windows are not just a few bowls of flowers, but a potted garden. The plants are wildly exuberant. Perhaps it's that light.

The third characteristic is the Dutchman's curious love for little burgundy-coloured rugs, something like a Bokhara, which owe their design in part to Javanese batik. You find them on wooden tables and used as coverings. They hang over the backs of seats, but they are never put on the floor. Nobody has been able to explain to me why they are quite so popular and until you point them out the Dutch don't seem to realize how unique they are.

At sundown, the best viewing time, I stood on the topmost turret of the Euromast and looked down on the islands of Rhenish silt spread out like a map. On a good day you can see for over twenty miles. Some islands are clearly visible, others are mere smudges of smoke in a vast, two-dimensional landscape. There is Voorne and Over Flakkee and Putten and Hoeksche Waard and Schouwen and Walcheren, where, in the middle of the sixteenth century, Charles V had that long talk with his son Philip and his brother Ferdinand. There in the castle of Oost-Souburg they decided to split Europe up into two parts. Philip could take the Low Countries, Naples and the Indies, and Ferdinand the Holy Roman Empire. The greatest division of power for over a thousand years.

Holland, like Egypt, is an enormous delta. The islands are composed of silt. But Holland is not only flat; it is also hollow. Much of that silt lies under water, awaiting yet another reclamation project. The silt has been slowly washed down from the highlands of Europe by three very large, very sluggish and now very poisonous rivers. Those poisons are oozing out into the North Sea. Some are virtually indestructible. Holland is the vent of some of man's most insidious filth, the pesticides, biphenyls, and oil waste, the over-saturation of phosphates and nitrates, all that stuff that stockholders assure us is indispensable for national growth.

But that isn't the picture of the delta as a smooth young man with a brief-case described it to three East Africans. They were getting the treatment from a salesman of one of the biggest petro-chemical countries in the world. With the air of a modern Moses he pointed down to the Promised Land, the pastures of Capelle, the orchards of Spui, an enormous panorama of Ceres abounding. All due, he implied, to poisons that merely acted on the central nervous systems of hosts of small animals. Their products, he said, had transformed the world.

And by God he was right! I thought of penguins around the South Pole contaminated by pesticides from Europe and America sluiced down the whole length of the Atlantic. I thought of rivers so foul they have caught fire at the surface and burned for days. I thought of the millions spent on advertising and propaganda to conceal what's really going on and wondered about tackling the man in front of his potential customers. But as I thought about what to say without sounding downright aggressive they turned away and some children began to sing that rousing song, the *Zilvervloot*, the song about how the great silver fleet of the Spaniards was captured by old Piet Hein and his men.

The schoolmistress in charge of the party told me she was fed up with talking about the Eighty Years War. It was about time they thought of something else. But what could you do? They all wanted to know about it. Now listen! she said, and pointed out Brielle on Voorne where in 1572, on what the Dutch call the Night of the Red Stars, the forces of the Prince of Orange struck the first blow in that long fight for independence. A great story.

The stars were the poop lanterns of two and twenty ships including the *de Hoorn*, the *d'Egmont*, the *Compromise* and the *Swan*, the *Annie-Mie* and the *Willem de Zwyger*. They were the ships manned by the Sea Beggars. After the fall of Brielle, the ships skulked among the Wet Lands like foxes waiting for the passing by of Spanish poultry. They sailed with their three pennants rippling ahead, white for freedom, blue for great heart and orange for the prince. After much blood had been spilt, and much infamy done on both sides, Philip died and the Spaniards marched home under Alba. The Sea Beggars, those desperadoes without a decent shirt on their backs, became the rich men of Europe.

To see something of that fine avenue of windmills, the *Kinder-dijk*, I set off for Dordrecht by way of the Nieuw Lekkerland, but found that for the pedestrian the problem of how to get out of Rotterdam is – if anything – worse than how to get in. It's all very nice and orderly at the centre. They set off for work at half past seven. The streets are full of bicycles and pedestrians. At crossing-places the crowds wait for a mere nod from a young and self-confident *politie*. They flock down towards the William Bridge on the water-front and I flocked with them, thinking how nice to live in a city that deeply respects pedestrians. And so it does, but not beyond the city limits. There all the bicycles and walkers disappear and I strode out towards Capelle amid the thunder of traffic. The road is wholly devoid of sidewalks and, worse, beyond Krimpen it climbs up on to an embankment at least a hundred feet above the polder where you are horribly exposed. Scared by the noise and the thumps of air from large trucks, I clambered down to the green floor of Holland. A bit soggy and decidedly slow going since I had to work through a network of ditches and canals in the making. But gloriously peaceful.

Black and white cows chomped away in grass bright with dandelions, king cups and cardamines, those lilac-coloured crucifers which country folk call lady's smocks or cuckoo flowers. Old Gerard, the herbalist, describes how they come out 'for the most part in April and May, when the cuckoo begins to sing her pleasant note without stammering'. But this is less than half the story. The popular French name is *fleur de tonnerre* and in German *Donnerblume*, the belief being that in profusion they betoken storms. Some folk in the Vosges say that if you so much as touch the flowers your house will be struck by lightning. But not a cloud marred the sky that morning, and I strode on, gathering momentum and watching mallards.

In the spring, the Dutch polders are densely populated by what is probably the best-known wild duck in the world. I put them up in flights of forty or fifty. They whistled overhead and sought their mates in little pools among the reeds. Only the drab females make that direfully flat *quaaaaaack quack-quack-quack*. The glossy-headed males utter a high-pitched *queck* and not too often, as if unanxious to disclose what they are about. They don't want rivals around.

The females have other ideas. The more boy-friends, the better. They can out-fly their suitors. In all senses of the word they are the pace-makers. When they are ready for serious courtship they become coquettish, swimming from one excited bird to another until they are hemmed in. Then suddenly they leap into flight and lead the gang on as wild a chase as ever you saw.

As they twist and turn, the males try to grasp their mates in mid-flight. I saw one pull some tail feathers out, but after a long chase he was beaten to it by a wily bird that just kept going.

He took her under a little wooden bridge, but only briefly. They were soon off again, with the female still in front, this time in search for a place to settle down. She decides where they could probably raise a family of mimosa- and chocolate-coloured chicks. It might be quite a long way from water. Sometimes up in a tree. She sits on the eggs and keeps the grass-lined nursery tidy. His job is to keep the neighbours at a respectable distance and for this he can have her now and again, but only when she's nothing better to do. Among the mallards of the Lekkerland there's a lot to be learned about connubial life in general.

For six miles on either side of that waterway they call the *boezem* of the Overwaard you may see more windmills than in any other part of the Low Countries. It puts you in mind of an illustration from *Don Quixote*. This is the famous *Kinderdijk*, the Child's Dyke, a memorial to a disastrous flood in the fifteenth century. There are many legends about this dyke and I shall relate the one I heard from the postmaster at Alblasserdam, but first something about the windmills themselves.

There are just over a thousand left in Holland of which only about a third are still in use. They are of two kinds. There are those used to keep the land dry. Essentially they are wind-driven pumps. They are so arranged that the slow-turning sails drive scoops or a screw-like contrivance that lifts water out of a ditch or a mere to where, with a helping hand from another series of mills higher up, it flows into a river and down to the sea, leaving more polders ready for cultivation. The other kinds of mills are used for industrial purposes such as grinding wheat or extracting oil from edible nuts, but there are not many of these left and from the interior of some you may hear an electric generator.

In the old days the Dutch used to speak of the language of the mills which is a pretty way of saying that when the sails were set at rest in certain positions, they could be used for signalling purposes. For example, when one pair of sails remained vertical and the other horizontal, the miller was saying he was ready for work. All he wanted was something to do. But when the sails looked like an enormous X, his neighbours knew he was in trouble. It might have been no more than lack of wind or over-much weed in his particular length of the dyke. Whatever the cause, from afar the mill looked like a man with his arms raised in despair. Between those two basic positions were several variations used to convey news of a birth, a death, a marriage, a public holiday or the sight of an invader or an income tax collector.

The great flood on St Elizabeth's Day in 1421 arose from what geographers nowadays call a surge, that is an abnormal rise in the level of the sea brought about by high winds, storm waves and exceptionally high spring tides acting together. A similar one occurred in 1953. The North Sea is shallow. When Dogger Bank is thrashed by winds from the north, immense quantities of water pile up between the mouths of the Thames and the Rhine. Only a limited amount manages to escape through the Straits of Dover. The rest swirls round towards the Netherlands, pouring over the thin rim of that basin.

The flood of 1421 was truly catastrophic. The swollen rivers ran into an advancing wall of water from the North Sea. They rose twenty feet. The sea walls collapsed. The contours of the land were completely changed. Overnight, the Biesbosche, that land of lakes to the east of Dordrecht became an inland sea. At least sixty villages were wiped out. Thousands of people were swept away and for weeks afterwards their bodies fattened crabs at the mouth of the Maas.

These are facts set down at the time. But the postman's story of how the *Kinderdijk* got its name is so fragile that even to enquire into it deeply is perilous, yet it deserves telling.

Not far from Alblasserdam there lived a woman they called the Good Wife, though she was married to an impious *Water-Signeurke* of whom no good at all was said. He spent most of his time hunting and drinking; he neglected the dykes, and he taxed the people so heavily that had it not been for her charity secretly bestowed, many might have starved.

They swore that one day they would see him die, miserably, in his own house, and die he did, but they were not to know that on St Elizabeth's Day most of them would die with him.

That night there had been a great feast in the great house. The Good Wife had given birth to a daughter, their first child in twenty years of marriage. From a caul on the little girl's shoulder, she foretold it would be loved by everyone.

When the house collapsed, the wooden cradle bearing the child was swept out of an upper window. It would have been swamped in the deluge, but a tabby cat leaped into that little boat and, with that animal's instinct for preservation, it moved from side to side so that the little craft kept upright. It came to rest on the little patch of dry land near the present city of Dordrecht where villagers adopted the waif. They called her Baetken or Beatrix, meaning the happy one. On becoming of age, she married Jakob Roerom, a name still known thereabouts. It would be fine to think they went back to Alblasserdam and lived happily ever afterwards, dispensing charity to the flood-bereaved, but from all accounts it was long before anyone returned to the mud that covered the Lekkerland.

In the mild breeze on the *Kinderdijk* that day the sails of the mills turned full circle in just over four seconds. With larks bubbling overhead, I sat among the lady's smocks and watched them. In a moderate wind they spin round merrily, reefed down, that is to say with their slats partly folded, but when gales blow they sail on empty poles or, as the millers say, with their legs bare. The cumbersome sails can be checked from inside by a cap on the main axle, a primitive sort of drum-brake, but from charred marks on the blocks it could be seen that over-zealous braking might easily set fire to the whole contraption.

I can think of no simple way of describing what happens to the Rhine thereabouts except that one of the main arms is called the Waal and another the Lek. Near Dordrecht these foul-looking waterways are joined by tributaries of the Maas or Meuse and together they amble off to pour their sewage into the sea through a maze of complicated channels.

Dordrecht is a large island with a very old town tucked away in the corner opposite the factory chimneys of Zwijndrecht. Seen from the river – and what river it was I couldn't make out – it has an air of dilapidated splendour. Here, as in Delft, the streets are paved with water. There were narrow streets, a great Gothic cathedral and the smell of onion soup and boiled bacon, for it was the eve of the Queen's birthday. From upper storeys came short spurts of sound – the squeal of a pipe, a trill on a flute and deep and vulgar notes from wood and brass. The impression was of an orchestra tuning up before the conductor raises his baton.

I had scarcely got down to an immodest breakfast of ham, cheese, gherkins, salami, three kinds of bread and coffee the next morning when the whole town blew up. The noise was tremendous. Out they came, the bands and the choirs. They marched through the streets with hand-clapping children and proud parents in the slip stream of the *oompah-oompah-oompah, bang-bang-BANG!* They marched up to the Great Church. They sang of Koppelstock, the ferryman who acted as a national negotiator at Brielle. They sang of the Silver Fleet and of *Gelukkig is het Land.*

> O happy is that country
> Protected by the Lord
> When 'gainst the fearful murderers,
> He conquers one and all. . . .

The bands intermingled. There were times when you might have thought they were playing against each other. I had scarcely sorted out the Dordrecht Fire Brigade from the Flemish Bull Club when along came three jolly fellows pushing a barrel organ of a kind peculiar to the Netherlands, an affair of mechanical drums and pipes. It rattled out clog dances, waltzes and what appeared to be Spanish tangos, which is perhaps not altogether surprising if, as some people think, *flamenco* means Flemish. And above carillons everywhere boomed the bell of the Great Church.

Bemused by it all, I wandered down to the Catharijnepoort where a shrivelled old man brought out the treasures of his antique shop. He showed me coins and bits of porcelain; he brought out ancient pistols with 'God is for the Right' engraved on the stock and some little rods of boxwood I could make nothing of. The old man slipped them over his finger and half clenched his fist. They were *baguettes.* Instruments of torture. Inserted between the fingers or toes, they could be tightened so precisely that the ligaments were distended and the bones stripped of their flesh and slowly smashed in the sure knowledge that the victim would fall down screaming, ready to confess doubts about God's grace, Original Sin, or where he'd hidden a hundred florins.

From somewhere outside came the sound of brass bands and children's voices.

> We must be thankful to the Lord,
> To God who lives for ever,
> That He who for His honour's sake,
> This victory has given. . . .

He said *baguettes* were often used in the Eighty Years War, and he wasn't sure they were used more by one side than the other.

To the south of Dordrecht the road spins round once or twice, gathering momentum for its great leap over the *Hollandsch Diep*. The bridge, as I can personally attest, is nearly thirteen hundred paces in length and I have nothing whatever to say of the sullen water it spans except that, considering the pollution, it looked its best under an immense sky dotted with little puffs of cloud, like cannon smoke.

For mile upon mile you walk through landscape almost wholly devoted to sugar beet and potatoes, very productive, but scenically unrewarding. Towards nightfall, little bits of woodland begin to appear in the barony of Breda. The churches become more Roman in expression. This is North Brabant, one of the most beautiful provinces in the Netherlands.

For two days I walked straight into the morning sun, towards Hilvanrenbeek and Donk, following little mushroom-like signposts through the birches of Chaam and Gorp, heading for the Valkenswaard, those heaths famed for centuries for the hawks they caught there. It began to blow, hard. Hard as a shove in the back, and I relished every moment of that wild, warm earth-mothering air from the South Atlantic. It made the birches sing. It blew clean. It blew away all doubts about adventure scarcely begun. I thought of what I had in store, of the hills ahead, the Ardennes, the Vosges, the Jura, and the Alps and I walked the faster.

Brabant lies across the north-western flyway of migratory birds, a veritable river of birds ranging from little songsters to what are left of the great raptors that prey on the aerial traffic. Though I swept the sky with glasses, in two days I saw but a few buzzards mewing sadly and a solitary harrier flapping over a sea of reeds. On high no goshawks nor gyrfalcons. Certainly no eagles. If they are there to be seen in these hawk-barren days they had flown on, the passage almost over. But kestrels hung poised in pockets of still air and few sights are finer than a kestrel striding.

> High there, how he rung upon the rein of a wimpling wing
> In his ecstasy! Then off, off forth on swing
> . . . the hurl and gliding

> Rebuffed the big wind. My heart in hiding
> Stirred for a bird – the achieve of, the mastery of the thing!

I walked to the Valkenswaard to meet the master falconer. Gerrit lives near what is now a modern town largely devoted to making cigars. But in the old days the villagers sold the finest hawks and falcons in Europe. To the annual fair at Valkenswaard came the emissaries of lords, cardinals and kings, knowing they could buy any bird they wanted.

> An Eagle for an Emperor, a Gyrfalcon for a King;
> a Peregrine for a Prince, a Saker for a Knight, a
> Merlin for a Lady; a Goshawk for a Yeoman, a Sparrow-hawk
> for a Priest, a Musket for a Holy Water Clerk
> and a Kestrel for a Knave.

The Valkenswaarders specialized in passage hawks, that is adult birds trapped locally. They are faster and more powerful than youngsters taken from nests and trained. But none are sold there today. Birds of prey have become perilously scarce. They are among the principal victims of pesticides. Peregrines are now worth about £100 each, which means that nest-robbing is a highly profitable exercise.

Until I met Gerrit I thought a good case could be made out for banning falconry altogether, but now I'm not so sure. The secretary of the Dutch *Valkeniersverbond* is both a conservationist and a skilful falconer. He loves falcons and unlike those showmen who appear on television programmes in fancy dress, he is very concerned about publicity given to the sport since most of his time is now devoted to setting captive birds free. This is called hacking back. On the edge of that heath where uncountable numbers of birds were caught and sold I spent a day in the company of a man who is a very prince among hackers back. He runs something between a convalescent home and a training school for strays.

From a cage in the garden, a bird with a barrel tail like a large sparrow-hawk began to shriek wildly. It sounded tormented. An anguished cry that upset her neighbour in the next cage, a kestrel who responded with a reproachful *kee-kee-kee*. Several other birds looked round, nervously.

'Don't take any notice of the old goshawk,' said Gerrit. 'She's a bit greedy, a screamer. If only she'd fly away I'd let her go, but

I know she'll hang around and get into trouble again. I'll be able to do something with her in time. But it takes a lot of time.'

Falconers distinguish clearly between emotions as we understand them, and what they know a bird is saying. The language of falconry is carefully stylized. Wings are sails, breast feathers mail, talons are called pounces and the bird doesn't dive on its prey, it stoops.

Screamers are birds unable to restrain themselves at the sight of food. Socially speaking, they are a bit of a nuisance, but no more than that. Gerrit put on a leather glove and handed her a bit of meat, speaking to her quietly as he did so. It was wrong to scream the way she did, he said. And the goshawk made a contented noise that sounded like *gig-gig-gig* at which he slowly stroked her breast with his bare fingers.

Gerrit gets his birds from the police and from people who turn up with an injured owl or a sparrow-hawk they don't know what to do with. Some come from ships at sea. He told me of the exhausted Lanner falcon that alighted on a tanker off Port Sudan and refused to leave the corned beef that the cook laid out for her every day. These are his problem birds. Wild creatures which have become thoroughly accustomed to the presence of man.

Starved birds can be fed and wing feathers patched up. In time they will grow again. But during that time, if it's fortunate, the bird has been the guest of a thoughtful host, and some guests won't go away. They have to be thrown out. And only a falconer knows how they can be trained – or de-trained – to fend for themselves. Gerrit found that when buzzards had been in captivity for a few months they became as tame as puppies. They followed him about. They get the impression that all human beings are nice people who'll feed them and offer them shelter. They forget, if ever they knew, that men use guns and dogs and boys throw stones. Gerrit releases his buzzards in remote parts of the country where he pegs out dead rabbits and muskrats until they get into the habit of looking for carrion on their own. A big part of the problem is how to get the birds back on their natural diet.

There was the case of the honey buzzard which had been picked up on the Valkenswaard with its breast feathers completely frozen. It had been caught by a frost on its flight south. Now honey buzzards are not really birds of prey at all. They sit motionless, for hours, just watching the flight of wasps and bees from a great distance. In captivity they can be fed on honey-combs buried in the ground. But there were no honeycombs available for the bird found in November. Gerrit fed her on pancakes and syrup and apple sauce and cooked pears until he hacked her back the following year with her taste for the grubs of wasps and bees regained.

One day they brought him a hobby, a beautiful little falcon that looks like a miniature peregrine. It had been fed on meal-worms which are not unlike the insects they chase at dusk. But hobbies need bone and when they brought it in, the creature suffered so badly from a calcium deficiency that it could scarcely stand. A year elapsed before it could be persuaded to fly away.

Gerrit considers that sparrow-hawks are among our most delicate birds of prey. They glide over hedges, pouncing on young birds and animals. He gets them from boys who take them as nestlings but don't know how to handle them when they grow up. And by that time they are poor hunters. Before it could be released, one bird needed to be flown over a hundred times before it caught a few sparrows.

The Lanner falcon from the ship had to be taught plainly to fly off when there were human beings about. Gerrit tried her out with an artificial lure and found she responded beautifully, but she didn't seem in the least interested in flying at birds. But knowing she was an old bird herself with some experience of hunting, he set her free.

Within a few weeks they rang him up to say she had been caught by some boys in North Holland, crouching over a wader she had struck down. After some difficulty he managed to make her shy by taking away her meat as soon as she started to eat it. The Lanner was released once more and never seen again.

At high sun Gerrit and I walked over the shreds of that great heath where, for days on end, the falcon-catchers used to crouch in holes in the ground, like spiders at the centre of a web of wires to control the nets and decoys. The holes were covered with a framework of heather and osiers. The catchers were adept at concealment. They were intent on those most keen-eyed of predators: the short-winged hawks that kill with their beaks. And the long-winged falcons such as the peregrine, that pounce with talons down. The holes remain forlorn and overgrown. But we saw no falcons except a swift-like hobby intent on dragon flies.

The catchers went out long before dawn and since they were obliged to spot the falcons when they were a mere dot in the sky they matched bird against bird by using a captive grey shrike as a look-out. The Latin name for this bird is *excubitor*, the sentinel. For some reason they become wildly excited at the sight of even a distant bird of prey. Guided by the shrike's reaction, the falconers released a tethered pigeon. Some used a whirling bunch of feathers or a trained hawk to lure the prey down towards some bait on the ground where, hopefully, it could be quickly netted. The operation can be described fairly simply, but in practice it often took many hours, sometimes more than a day, to capture a bird that soared round, intrigued but suspicious of what had been laid out for it.

During the golden days of falconry, there might be twenty or thirty skilled men at work on the Valkenswaard. Some families specialized in the business. There were the Bots, the Dams, the Dankers and Peel, the van Heuvels and the last of the great catchers, the Mollens family, particularly old Adrian, falconer to two kings, and his son Karel who died about forty years ago. A street in the town is called Mollenstraat; a picture of him at work hangs in the town hall. And they all know Gerrit in Valkenswaard. He is the keeper of what he calls the things that must never be forgotten.

North Frankland

My reaction to a frontier post is that of a shrike to a hawk. At the mere sight of a striped pole I start to chatter nervously, rehearsing all sorts of little speeches that never quite come off. Trying to suppress deep and quite inexplicable feelings of guilt, I tell myself that my French or maybe my thought processes are a bit too erratic for those obliged to live by a book of regulations.

I had something polite to say to the man at Schaft-Achel since Belgian *gardes* are apt to be testy, if not downright surly.

He stood there, looking at me impassively. Before he could say a word, out stepped a pink-faced young Dutchman at which I relaxed considerably, for they are courteous people who lapse easily into two or three languages.

'*Goede morgen*,' I said.

To my dismay he responded in voluble German, asking me, I thought, if I had anything to declare.

I shook my head vigorously. No! Not a dam' thing. *Absolument rien. Gar nichts.*

At this he became extremely abusive in English and German. If I understood him right, I had no right to be walking about the country like that. It was against the law.

The Belgian standing nearby grinned and in English said: 'He only wants to see your passport.'

I handed it over without a word. The Dutchman looked testy. The Belgian winked and thumbed me on. 'Have a good time,' he said.

Belgian Limburg is a mixed-up sort of place. The cherry blossom that foams on the slopes of the Campine leaves you wholly unprepared for the dreadful sprawl of collieries and smoke around Mechelen on the Meuse. People speak Flemish

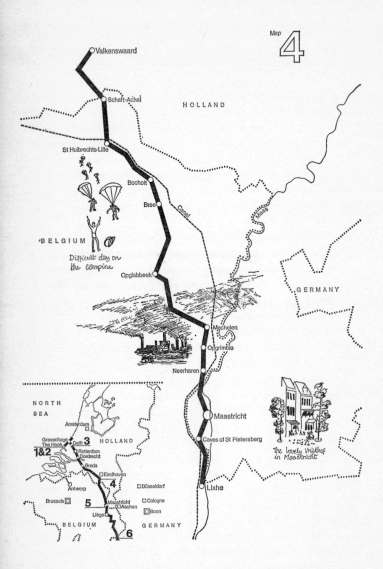

Map 4

Valkenswaard

Schaft-Achel

HOLLAND

St Huibrechts-Lille

Bocholt

Bree

Canal

Maas

Difficult day on
the Campine

BELGIUM

Opglabbeek

GERMANY

Mechelen

Opgrimbie

Neerharen

Maastricht

NORTH
SEA

Caves of St Pietersberg

Amsterdam

Gravenhage
The Hook
Delft **3**
1&2
Rotterdam
Dordrecht
Breda
Eindhoven
Antwerp
4
Düsseldorf
Brussels
5
Maastricht
Aachen
Cologne
Liège
Bonn
BELGIUM
GERMANY
6

Lixhe

The lovely Vrijthof
in Maastricht

and swear in German and French. Belgium thereabouts is not so much an entity as a state of mind. With some experience of the Congo in the old days, I flatter myself I know a bit about the Belgians. They are a nation of hard-working hand-shakers; they go in for a great deal of high finance and sport and tax evasion. They are litigious and house-proud and secretive about what goes on inside those trim family apartments, rarely asking you home unless they have known you for years. They are warmly disposed towards the British and I can never quite understand why, for although we fought for their independence in 1914, the object was not so much paternalism as maintaining the balance of power. They are great eaters and drinkers.

If you were dropped into Belgium blindfolded you would know where you are at eleven o'clock in the morning when the aroma of coffee is replaced by the pungent, all-pervading smell of *frites*, those potatoes cut lengthwise and fried deep in fat or oil. If you opened your eyes in a provincial market place you would see rows of stalls that sell caged birds and fresh doughnuts and nougat. And priests everywhere. They swarm in Belgium, breaking away only to found new colonies abroad. If I hadn't met one of them in north Canada years ago, I might have avoided the industrial belt and struck across country, to Liège, to meet another old friend from the Congo. But the memory of those spectacular days on the fringe of the Arctic haunted me. I had a mind to enlarge them, the more since Father Leo's last words had been: 'When I go back to Belgium, come and see me in Neerharen where I learned to pray.' That was at Stony Rapids, an Indian settlement at the Athabaska river. I had gone up there as a correspondent for the BBC, making recordings in the uranium mines.

Although I didn't know it at the time, that chance trip, a combination of mishaps and good luck, became a turning point in my life. Instead of being tied to routine newspaper assignments in Britain, I became a wanderer. I glimpsed a world infinitely more exciting than anything experienced before. I saw the cold top of the world and flew over herds of migrating caribou. By sleeping in the bush I met trappers and game wardens, and when money began to run out I learned how to travel cheaply on foot.

Someone at the Hudson Bay store told me he'd heard that at an encampment up-river the Red Men were 'lighting a fire'. They were Chipewyans, one of the last tribes to dance before they set off to slaughter caribou. If I could get through the bush he knew a trapper with a canoe who would ferry me upstream for the price of a bottle.

'Father Leo isn't all that keen on the old Indian stuff,' he said. 'But he's having trouble with the Chips this year. They're real hungry. There's nothing in trapping. White fox has slumped to ten bucks. I recall it nearer fifty.'

For hours I walked through the Jack pine scrub alone, beating off more mosquitoes than I met in the Congo in months. The trapper took one look at my bulky BBC tape-recorder and said it was the finest Geigy he'd ever seen. 'Don't wobble if you want to keep your ass dry,' he said, and pushed off, paddling deep.

Up there, in those high latitudes, there is no night and day as we know it. In May the sun dips below the horizon shortly before midnight, and rises again at half past one. During that brief afterglow the sky is the colour of blood and the foaming river takes on the colour of the sky.

As we paddled through that Wagnerian light towards the village, we heard the wail of the husky dogs and the sound of children's laughter. They were playing baseball with a pine cone tied up in a bit of caribou skin. What they shouted to each other was in Chipewyan and incomprehensible, but the laughter was that of children anywhere.

At midnight the mission bell began to clang and at each stroke it wiped out more and more of that laughter until there was no sound except the wailing of the dogs. The congregation dutifully filed into mass, for Father Leo had struck a bargain with his flock. If they insisted on dancing that night, he said, they had to go to church before they lit the fire.

It blazed like a haystack. Like most poverty-stricken people the Chipewyans are wildly improvident. They burned everything they could lay their hands on. After a few swigs of some ferocious stuff called moose milk, made, as I recall, from methylated spirit and raisins, they bashed their *tam-tams* and hopped round the flames, growling like dogs.

Eventually they grew tired of capering about and settled down to listen to an old man who began to sing in a quavering voice, rather like a counter-tenor. Against the monotonous rhythm of the drums, he sang a few low notes and then quite unexpectedly threw his voice up into a falsetto wail. They told me through an interpreter that he was 'asking help from the sky'. They called it a Bridge Song, a pathway between earth and heaven. I listened fascinated, and recorded what he sang.

Back in the mission station, Father Leo gave me a hunk of pemmican, some bread and a glass of Communion wine. He listened impatiently to the noise outside and looked at his watch. He said I must understand that they were not heathens. But they insisted on dancing. He couldn't understand why they weren't satisfied with the hymns he had translated for them. He hoped at least a few would turn up for the eight o'clock. But not a soul came. The whole village got uproariously drunk. They were still throwing wood on the fire when I left the next day.

Father Leo almost wept. It was *soo* bad, he said, that I should have *soo* wrong an impression of his people. He allowed them to dance twice a year and he intended to find out where that liquor came from.

I looked into Stony Rapids on the trip south and discovered what it meant to be a Treaty Indian. As a tribe, they were all but done for. They lived in squalor; most of them were hopelessly in debt to the Store. Their womenfolk were syphilitic and infertile, and the caribou on which they had lived for centuries were becoming increasingly scarce. I often wondered if they got any help from the sky, for, God knows, they needed it.

Father Leo's little town of Neerharen lies on the Meuse, a few miles north of Maastricht. With any luck I reckoned I should be there the following day.

One of the serviceable tricks I learned from my walk through Britain is that canal banks are a fair substitute for country lanes, and in industrialized country they are the only life-lines available to a whole-time pedestrian. At St Huibrichts-Lille I struck out along the tree-lined *Maaskanaal* that links the Scheldt to the Meuse. The towpath is flanked by willows and briars and in that bird haven sang more nightingales than you could hope for in

Arcady. The singers were spaced out at intervals of about three hundred paces, which is just about as far as you can hear the individual songs above the murmer of a breeze.

It began to rain, that soft spring stuff that hurts nobody. It certainly had no effect on that sustained *chook-chook-chook*, that *tee-oo*, *tee-oo* of those passionate singers. Country folk believe they sing best with their buff-coloured breasts pressed hard against a thorn 'to keep their sharp woes waking'. The Greek legend is that Tereus, the young king of Thrace, cut off the tongue of his wife Procne for fear she might disclose he had violated her sister, Philomela. They did dreadful things in ancient Hellas. The gods turned Procne into a twittering swallow, a bird with almost no voice at all, and to this day Philomela, the nightingale, still sings of that cruel ravishment.

> Fie, fie, fie! And then she'd say
> Tereu! Tereu! by and by.

Memories of that canal are coloured vividly by the glimpse of a young girl on the opposite bank lying on her back, naked, her arms and legs gracefully outstretched to the rain. How can I describe dispassionately a brief sight of what I still think about? A little incident without a beginning and without an end. I don't know why she was there. She might have been for a swim. She might have been waiting for her lover. She might have been entirely alone and glad to see me. I shall never find out, for I walked on, unseen behind a discreet screen of reed mace and willows. But like Turgenev's friend she is an indelible fragment of memory.

As Edmond de Goncourt tells that endearing little story, they had been to one of Flaubert's parties. The company was discussing incidents they would always remember. Looking back on his life, Turgenev said: 'When I was a young man I had a mistress, a miller's daughter who lived near St Petersburg whom I used to see when I went hunting. She was a delightful girl, very pale with a cast in one eye, something which is fairly common in our country. She would never accept anything from me. One day, however, she said: "You must bring me a present." "What do you want?" I asked. "Bring me some soap." I brought her a tablet of soap. She took it, disappeared and came back covered with blushes. Holding out her scented hands she said: "Now kiss as you kiss the hands of the ladies in the drawing rooms of St Petersburg." ' Turgenev says he threw himself at her feet.

They are proud that the king has stayed in the little town of Bree. They say he may come back next year and I am sorry he will find no shade in the square opposite St Michael's Church at noon, for they were cutting down the last of eight splendid lime trees the day I walked in. Six had already fallen. They were lying flat in a row, like hostages shot down, but though I asked several people including a notary and a clerk from the *mairie* why they were being felled, nobody seemed to know. The notary said it was none of his business and implied it was none of mine. The shopkeepers were puzzled. They rather liked the trees they said, and one man, who I believe sold honey, said, 'Is it not a fact? No trees, no bees. They are destroying the whole place.' A crossing sweeper thought it would now be easier to keep the place tidy and leave more room for cars. The clerk, a fussy little *fonctionnaire*, told me they were being chopped down 'by the wish of all the people', and I had to leave it at that.

Away to the east a loop of the Meuse caught a shaft of sunlight and slowly faded from view as rain swept across North Frankland. A much troubled region. *Vexata et afflicta*. The ancient Celts who lived there – the Gauls as the Romans called them, were conquered, subjugated and partly colonized by the Legions, though, with few exceptions such as the Treveri, their conquerors thought little of the inhabitants. They were brave, they admitted, but boastful in speech and known for their inconstancy. With Rome pillaged, sacked and robbed of her imperial dignity, the outer barbarians swept in. New blood, new ideas, new customs poured into Europe. Great waves of Germanic infiltration broke westward from the Danube and flooded southwards across the Alps. The Huns were routed, but the Germanic expansion continued, growing. By the end of the sixth century, the Salian Franks were established in north-east Gaul and the Riparian Franks on the banks of the Rhine, the Meuse and the Moselle. Faint patterns of unity began to emerge.

The first Frankish chief we know of, a Salian called Merovech, founded the dynasty of long-haired Merovingians, a succession so violent that I shrink from saying much about it here. The life-long quarrel of the two queens, Brunhilda in Austrasia and the beautiful cat-like woman, Fredegunda of Neustria, is as fearful as anything in history, yet in their conflict they helped to bring Charlemagne, that Frank of the Franks, to imperial stature, and it was through the Middle Kingdom of his grandson, Lothair, that, by chance, I had plotted my course to the Mediterranean. I wanted to see what was left of that great palace at Aachen, but I never managed to get there. The heavily industrialized river looked forbidding. Instead I wandered through the Ardennes where the king's estates lay thickest, and in the country between the Meuse, the Moselle, and the Rhine.

After the death of Charlemagne the longships of the Northmen were seen for the first time on the Meuse. At Maastricht and Liège, Tongres and Malmédy, the monks fled at the sight of those terrible prows. The king knew they would attack him. From Alcuin's own lips he had heard of their onslaught on Northumbria, Scotland, and Ireland. Ambassadors related how they had reached Constantinople. Gotfried of Denmark, 'puffed up with false hopes' (*vana spe inflatus*), swore he would invade Frankland and make off with the treasure at Aachen.

Through the window of one of his palaces, Charlemagne saw the ships in the distance. Notker of St Gall says he broke off his eating and wept. Nobody dared speak to him. At length Charlemagne turned to his household and said he had no personal dread of the pirates, but he grieved to think of the evil they might do to those who came after him.

Evil they may have been. Resourceful they certainly were. To strike where they were least expected they sometimes hauled their ships overland from one river to another. The initial raids were always carried out by 'picked men unacquainted with fear'. They set up principalities on the shores of the Caspian and the Black Sea. Canute ruled over not only England but also Norway and Denmark, but his short-lived empire fell to pieces at his death. It fell through that political weakness of the barbarians: conflict among their ruler's sons. Had he not been attacked by the Northmen who settled down as Normans, a great sea-faring power stretching from America to Russia might have emerged from the house of Canute.

Scheveningen

Delft

Kinderdijk

Meuse canal

Spring in Hautregard

High Fagne

The young Our

Oompah in Echternach

Beaufort in Little Switzerland

Everyone dances

Vosges at dawn

Sisters of Alsace

To reach what looked like good timber, I walked south, towards Opglabbeek and Genk and places with even stranger names. This is the Campine, hummocky country of pine woods and sandy soil, ready-made for army manoeuvres. To a Belgian conscript the word Beverloo is much what Aldershot means to a British recruit, and the two places look alike. From afar came the stutter of automatic weapons. Whistles blew and the cough-like *croomps* that followed sounded unpleasantly like mortar fire remembered from long ago. On the roads were convoys of cheerfully derisive men in trucks that towed long thin guns with a bulge at the muzzle. I didn't like what was going on and walked on fast, the more since it began to pour down.

Oh that rain, that ever-besetting blight on those who walk under mixtures of warm and cold air in high latitudes. How pleasant to have been there on a sunny day! Like that anonymous poet who is known only for the lines he wrote in exile, I thought of shelter more attractive than a thin canopy of pine needles.

> Western wind, when wilt thou blow
> That the small rain down can rain?
> Christ, if my love were in my arms,
> And I in my bed again.

Far to the west, some transport planes disgorged scores of parachutists that floated to earth like little white mushrooms. More firing, but louder this time. It looked as if I had strayed into the front line. A soldier on a motor-cycle bumped along the track ahead, but as soon as he saw me he turned round and bumped back. I struck off into a forest ride, a ribbon of grass between tall stands of spruce, yet even there it seems I was observed for a helicopter clattered overhead. For half a minute it paused, scarcely ten feet above the crown of trees, and then it clattered off, sideways. I marched on, faster now.

The conifers gave way to straggly oak and birch that made a high-pitched breathing noise in the rain. This is a peculiarity of deciduous forests. During a downpour, coniferous woods are strangely silent. The needles are wonderful insulators of sound, but among broad leaves you are aware of the squalls, for the rise and fall of the gusts sound like a long-drawn-out sigh.

At some point in that wet wood I got ambushed. There is no other word for it. Five young men in red berets and mottled battledress sprang out from behind a clump of bushes. Until a sergeant with a tommy-gun shouted 'Halt!' I had no idea they were there. Had I known I had strayed into an important Nato exercise I might have been less insistent about the rights of a civilian but, as I have said, it was raining. I wasn't prepared to peel off protective oilskins to get at my passport. They had become as important to me as fur to a bear. I said politely, but, as I discovered later, quite wrongly, that only a gendarme or a civil guard had the right to ask for my papers.

At this they ordered me to follow them, and they pointed down the track. Not so, I said. They could follow me in the opposite direction where, no doubt, we should arrive in time at a *gendarmerie*. To my surprise and relief they agreed, although with some understandable reluctance, since, invisible in the bushes, they had dumped a small arsenal that included a portable rocket-gun, various small but not light arms and two folding motor-cycles which for some reason had to be carried.

That portion of my walk through Limburg with a military escort can be related as briefly as it lasted, which wasn't long. Heading the column, I stepped out more briskly than I had walked for days. The rain felt less sullen than before, and I even contrived to whistle that marching song called *Georgia* which is the mark of those who have served among field gunners.

The first to break ranks were the two who carried the rocket gun which looked about as heavy as a plough. After half a mile of heavy breathing the small-arms men followed suit with a loud and uncomplimentary remark. This left only my interrogator, the sergeant with the tommy-gun, who also carried a box of ammunition.

He began to lag behind, at which I, too, shortened pace so that we kept more or less abreast of each other. I asked him where he came from and how long he had been in the army.

He stopped and instead of replying he began to swear, almost dispassionately. The words poured out in a monotonic stream. As he turned round and walked off, I recall only his last words, for they were the only ones that seemed directed at me and they can be translated easily.

'. . . *and* your sister,' he said.

Towards evening I took stock of misfortune in a bar where they were civil enough, although much too preoccupied with the condition of an almost hysterical fighting cock in a wickerwork basket to pay much attention to a wet English walker. But I sat there, gratefully, and got the stiff drink I needed.

I had reached Mechelen and Opgrimbie, which together compose as grim a landscape as ever you saw. In that half-light you could see nothing except smoke and industrial spoil heaps, the chimneys and brickfields and coal mines with their wheels spinning round like upturned bicycles. This is the industrial heart of the Meuse and I felt low. I had experienced a great ebb of vitality. Hilaire Belloc says one of the saddest things about us is that the bright spirit that lights us from within, like a lantern, can suffer dimness. It wasn't the sort of place for enquiries about a priest. As for Neerharen, the landlord walked to the door and pointed out a smudge scarcely distinguishable from the other smudges in that satanic valley. 'It is there,' he said. 'Perhaps seven kilometres. Give our regards to the girls.'

It turned out to be scarcely worth the name of village. The sad assortment of modern bars and bungalows on both sides of a great highway were strung together by festoons of cables and telephone wires. Nobody had heard of Father Leo there, for nobody seemed to be a native. And there was clearly more to the discreetly lit bars with large cars parked outside than the sale of liquor. I tried two. The doors were locked. The curtains parted. Somebody looked out and after no more than a glance, the curtains promptly fell. From within came the jangle of a juke-box. No other sound except the trucks bound for Maaseik and Maastricht. Thoroughly depressed by it all I walked on and on until I found a bar with an open door.

Inside, about a dozen poorly dressed folk were drinking beer. I greeted them with that carefully intoned *May*-sieurs. A nod to the landlord and I settled down to a drink asked for quietly and sipped alone, at the end of the bar. My host was solicitous. Yes, he said. There was a hotel just down the road. He offered to phone. Was I Swedish? British, I said.

At this a well-dressed but slightly intoxicated youth shouted: 'Tell the truth. You're a damned German.' Instant silence. A confrontation. Liquor works in a curious way. I can't explain the hostility so often aroused by those unprepared immediately to explain who they are in company less sober than themselves, but I know it for a fact and have experienced it before.

The youth – who was of no great stature – walked over. He repeated the charge that I was without doubt a *sale Boche* and for the second time in that ill-starred day he challenged me to produce my *carte*.

Much cross talk ensued. I forget how it went, for he became incomprehensibly aggressive and I felt testy and tired. Stretching my French to its outermost frontiers – for I had to employ the conditional – I said with ponderous irony that were he a man rich enough to put down a hundred-franc note on the bar, the affair could be settled immediately.

He looked surprised. We used the bar top for the game. He led with a green bill. I countered with a note of equal value. The stakes were laid out. As the company watched, fascinated, he produced a little white card signed by the Burgomaster of Mechelen. I won point and game by slapping down a signed photograph attached to the passport issued by Her Britannic Majesty's Principal Secretary of State for Foreign Affairs.

A hundred francs represents nine beers. By adding another small bill I gained a dozen temporary friends with that easy phrase, 'Drinks all round'.

During a reciprocal from the landlord, my youthful aggressor retired to an isolated chair where he sat with his forehead cupped in his hands in the manner of the *jeune premier* in an early French film. He looked very sad. I offered him one of the drinks he had helped to pay for. Charity comes easy to the victor.

He jumped up. He seized my hand. He asked my name. He told me his own. He was an insurance agent and I was his friend. His *real* friend. 'Why is it?' he asked. 'Why have I no trust in what people say? I always imagine they tell me a lie. I ask you, M'sieur. What is this failing? *Qu'est-ce que cette défaillance?*' Tapping his forehead, he added, forlornly, 'Inside here there is something I do not understand. I don't understand it at all.'

The Disbeliever introduced me to the whole company. After trying to buy me another drink, he said *he* would get me a room immediately. It was his obligation. And out he walked.

'A curious one that,' said the *patron*. 'He thinks too much what other people think, and that is not good for a man.'

The youth returned with news of a room booked and supper ready in twenty minutes. After that he would like to take me out in his car, for he had a friend at the *Perroquet Vert*, a good woman who knew every clergyman in the neighbourhood.

He opened his car door. I said I preferred to walk.

He stared at me incredulously, but at any suggestion of disbelief on his part thereafter – and I was in his company until early in the morning – I merely looked at him and tapped my forehead. His eyebrows went up, but he grinned.

About the *Perroquet Vert* there was an air of mercantile efficiency. It stood out from the eerie lighting, the smell of perfume and musical wallpaper. The place was packed. The phone rang. The till tinkled. The men drank. The girls (three) were pretty but sullen, their smiles mechanical. They switched them on and they switched them off. Only Madame, the one who knew every clergyman in the district, seemed wholly human. Perhaps rather larger than life.

'Who's next? Who's next? Why *you*, of course, M'sieur Valois. My God! I shall forget my own name next. What a busy night we've had to be sure. Yes! She is ready and waiting upstairs. Waiting *anxiously*, M'sieur.'

And upstairs he went, a tubby little man, still arguing about that stock. It would recover. Of that they could be certain. He paused on the landing, slightly out of breath, still searching for the exact phrase. *Au fond*, they still owned the Congo. It was their *right*. A matter, was it not, of defending their beefsteak? And his companions nodded. If not entirely convinced, they could argue about it later. They had plenty of time. The latecomers had to wait for nearly an hour. Madame went on talking to the Disbeliever.

We had gone out with the avowed intention of finding Lisette, the girl he referred to repeatedly as his fiancée, but after visiting several houses that night I couldn't be sure if they were really affianced or if he merely wanted to renew acquaintanceship with a cut-price whore.

He knew about everyone around the place. He knew their jargon. To hit the carpet (*faire le tapis*), those girls (*les putes*) had to be pretty tough. With them you had to watch yourself all the time. Behind her back he referred to Madame as *la taulière*, the gaol-keeper. He had known her for three years. But what he didn't know or, rather, what he wouldn't accept, was there could be no arguing about the current market price. Those girls cost a thousand francs each, flat.

Madame was clearly shocked by his efforts at bargaining. It introduced a sordid note into what she referred to as 'the accepted custom'. He might have been asking for a reduction in the current mortgage rate or a foreshortened form of the mass.

'Ask your friend there,' she said. 'The English respect tradition. He will confirm what I say.' He wandered off, moodily, leaving me to chat to our ample hostess.

She wore an almost transparent evening dress. Her underwear had been doped with something that glowed under the fluorescent lighting. No, she couldn't recall the name of Father Leo, but then the priests came and went so often that it was difficult to keep track of who was about. Her own sister had taken the veil. As for herself, she had a great respect for the Church and invariably closed a few minutes before midnight on Saturday. It would not be seemly to do otherwise.

From that little house of hygienic sin we went off to two or three others. They were all alike. A bar downstairs and two or three rooms above. They opened at dusk and closed at two in the morning. From the front they were indistinguishable from any of the brick houses in that suburban estate except that everyone went in through the back door.

The Disbeliever got nowhere. *Les putes* were booked up hours ahead, by telephone. Some had standing dates with regular customers who, for the standard rate, got about twenty minutes of their time. A hard life. For the price of a very expensive beer, I talked to one or two lip-biters and matchstick breakers. But the response was meagre. Their eyes were constantly on their wristwatches. In me they saw an inquisitive non-consumer; I felt like a Gallup pollster or an unsuccessful welfare officer. For all that, one rather jolly girl, a big brunette from Düsseldorf, enlarged my vocabulary by one memorable word.

I asked her where her 'friends' came from. The middle-aged, she said, were mostly locals. They turned up regularly. It was like a club. But the old ones might be from anywhere. She thought it a little sad to be old, especially when they suffered, as so many of them did, from *Torschlusspanik*. A curious word. I made her repeat it twice. It meant the fear of the closing of the door.

On the way back, the Disbeliever insisted on looking once more into the *Perroquet Vert*. Most of the cars had gone. Madame sat behind the bar alone, sipping a cup of coffee. She wasn't particularly pleased to see us. But this time my friend came straight to the point and clinched it by putting down a thousand-franc note.

Madame looked at it and looked at her watch. She shook her head. 'No,' she said. 'You are too late. If you want, you can have me, but I must be down again in ten minutes. We close at two.'

If the Netherlands can be vulgarly likened to a cow, her udder is the rich province that hangs down under her belly, that is between the legs of Belgium and Western Germany. I slipped into Dutch Limburg and slipped out in one day. The province has a complicated history which I don't propose to go into, but it contains at least one town, Maastricht, which I reckon among the most attractive in Europe. It seems impossible that such a joyful little place can blossom within five miles of the stench of the Meuse coalfields.

The heart of the city lies in the cafe-lined *Vrijthof*, but you catch the spirit of the place from the street cries and the sound of laughter. I liked the face of the lop-sided buildings, the clip-clop of piebald ponies that draw vegetable carts through the narrow cobbled streets. There is piety in the great bronze image of the Virgin, simplicity in St Anthony who preaches to a congregation of fish in the *Boschstraat*, and a sense of the ridiculous in the statue of the *Mestreechter Geis*, the genie of good humour. I wish I knew more of what they chatter about in the markets, but they speak a language of their own. A friendly waiter translated a sliver of conversation between two old women at a café table. He said: 'They say they've got a new priest from Leyden, a young man. They think he'll do well. The children seem to like him, and so do the bees.' Offhand, I don't know where else you might hear talk like that.

Where all the amiability comes from is difficult to say. Maybe from putting up with a lot of trouble. The place the Romans called *Trajectum ad Mosam* lies on the most convenient crossing of the Meuse. The ramparts have been knocked down and built up at least a dozen times. For centuries the inhabitants grew accustomed to the domination of two lords, the Bishop of Liège and the Duke of Brabant. With admirable tact, they built a town hall with two opposing staircases so that both dignitaries could enter together without any argument about precedence. The arrangement doubled the administrative machinery, but it meant the people could elect to serve under whichever did most for them. If they wanted to, they could change their nationality, but only once. Yet the arrangement seems to have gone pretty smoothly, for, as they used to say: 'One lord, oh Lord! Two lords – good!'

During the course of an ample lunch in the open air I bought companionship easily by feeding fan-tailed pigeons with bits of a delicious tart they call *vla* and got no more than a mild remonstrance from my friend the waiter, who suggested that bread might be cheaper.

He advised me against walking to Aachen where I had a mind to see the tomb of Charlemagne. He could see no way of getting there except on busy roads, and nor could I, so I settled for the direct route to Liège, which is by way of the Albert Canal and what the guide-book calls the Hill of the Huns and the Monsters of the Meuse.

The monsters are mososaurs, the prehistoric lizards of the sea. The remains of those fierce-looking animals, the size of whales, have been dug out of the hill of chalk to the south of the town. From the map it looked as if I could reach the caves where they were found by following a cheerful little river, the Geer or Jeker, but I forgot that in a walled city space is extremely valuable and for most of the way the Geer gurgled underground. None the less it led me to a handsome little museum in the Bosquet Plein where I fell among good company.

Speaking about a journey across the United States, John Steinbeck said he often wondered why it was that when he planned a route over-carefully it usually fell to pieces, but if he blundered along in blissful ignorance, aiming in a fancied direction, he usually got through in fine style. This has been my experience too often for it to rank as coincidence. I arrived at the museum by accident. A local schoolmaster happened to be there. He saw me looking at the mososaurs and asked if I would care to meet two neighbours interested in prehistory. He slipped out and within ten minutes he came back with a university lecturer and an amateur geologist who had done a lot of digging for fossils in Britain.

The place that Pliny called the Hill of the Huns is St Pietersberg on the map. The chalk has been sliced open so deep by quarrying that from Wolder or thereabouts the twin hills look like a pair of breasts sticking up in the air. On my friends' advice I took to a track and breathed deep on the first hill climbed in nearly two hundred miles of walking. On the platform halfway up, the crowds had gone home and the janitor wasn't too pleased to let me in, but with credit from the name of the museum and an extra guilder I had the caverns to myself for half an hour.

St Pietersberg is an immense underground labyrinth which has been mined for its stone since pre-Roman times. The underground galleries extend for about ten miles. They wind about in such a convoluted way that only trained guides dare venture far from the main arteries. In remote workings they have come across the pathetic remains of those who lost their way. The skeletons are usually huddled together, showing how the unfortunates tried to keep warm during their last hours in the dark and terrible silence. One inscription on a wall reads: 'Four men of God gone astray found death here in the year 1640.'

In times of invasion by the armies of France and Spain the local people fled into the caves. There are records of underground battles and how the sound of musket shots echoed among the galleries. One group of refugees who had been living in a remote tunnel for months was betrayed by the crowing of a cock they had brought with them. Their attackers blew the roof down and sealed them up alive. Nowadays, the caverns are populated only by large flocks of bats and tourists and the few who come in each day to tend the chicory and mushrooms they grow there.

In a pub on the banks of the Albert Canal that night they told me a strange tale about the nearby fort of Eben-Emael, reputedly the strongest in the world. The Belgians built it high above the canal in 1933. They installed artillery and a curtain of outer defences designed to resist attack from all sides. It guarded the roads and bridges to the west and at the outbreak of the Second World War the Allies reckoned that sector as safe as anything military ingenuity could devise.

They were curiously optimistic. German storm-troopers destroyed the place in a quarter of an hour. It was the focal point of their attack on the west. After months of preparation a fleet of gliders released over Germany floated down on to the fort, silently, in the half-light of the dawn. They encountered neither mines nor barbed-wire entanglements on the top. Sappers threw bombs into the ventilator shafts and blew up the gun emplacements. As the troops swept on into Holland, the defenders were reduced to the position of captives in their own fortress. This is a matter of military history, but the story as they tell it in Lanaye is rather different.

They say that a colony of Germans who had been working on the canal were given secret instructions to settle there. They married local girls. Under cover of growing chicory in the galleries they began to pile up tons of high explosives. When the Germans decided to attack they simply pressed the button.

'Pouff! Up it went,' said my informant. 'What can you do against people like that? We hadn't a chance.'

Into the Ardennes

I remember walking through the night for hours and hours, towards Herstal, where Charlemagne, that King David of the Dark Ages, held high court and put his seal to all manner of important decrees. Now Herstal, I knew very well, has become an industrial slum. In a letter Burgomaster Andrien had warned me that: 'Of that great period, alas, not a vestige now remains.' The foundations of the palace lie under the gasworks. But as I trudged along that canal it pleased me to think of those who had walked that way nearly twelve centuries ago.

I saw myself in the company of Paul the Deacon, Peter the Grammarian and Godescall the Illuminator. I wondered what I might say to that great scholar Clement the Irishman and Dungal and Durcuil. All holy men, all hastening towards Herstal at the king's command.

But I never got there, at least not that night. When the stars were about their middle turning I grew unutterably tired. My feet ached. I looked around for something softer than the towpath to lie on and God alone knows where I eventually pitched down.

At first light I thought for one exquisite moment that God had clothed my fantasies with a sung eucharist in *son et lumière*. From across the water at six o'clock came a sound that rose and fell, as in liturgical response. And I heard the clear sound of a bell ring and ring again, twice, and the murmuring ceased as might be at Elevation. And I tell you, I thanked God and said a prayer and swore I'd do better and write to my mother that very day. God is not always in sanctified places. That bell hung from a little engine that chuffed up and down in front of an enormous steelworks. *Deus ex machina*. The bell rang out once; it rang twice, and at that second *tang-tang* a mechanical hopper

75

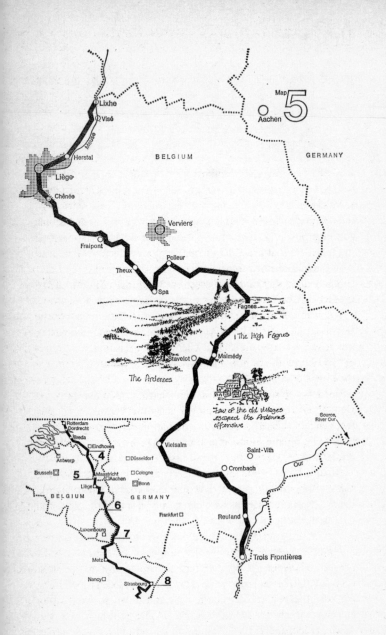

Map 5

Aachen

BELGIUM   GERMANY

Lixhe
Visé
Herstal
Liège
Chênée

Verviers

Fraipont

Theux   Polleur
        Spa

                              Fagnes

                          I The High Fagnes

        Stavelot   Malmédy

The Ardennes

                Few of the old villages
                escaped the Ardennes
                offensive

                                        Source,
                                        River Our

Rotterdam
Dordrecht
Breda
        Eindhoven
                    4
Antwerp

Brussels   5   Maastricht
                    Aachen
            Liège   Vielsalm   Saint-Vith
BELGIUM   6   □ Düsseldorf
                                                    Crombach
                GERMANY   □ Cologne
                                □ Bonn
        Luxembourg 7   □ Frankfurt
                                                    Reuland
        Metz
Nancy □   Strasbourg 8   Trois Frontières

began to haul coke out of a moored barge with a sound you could have sworn came from holy choir.

I got up and dressed and packed and walked on slowly, for, as I say, my feet were sore. When that bell clanged not twice but three times, I stopped. Was it an omen? It may have been. I hold with De Quincey that not to be at least a little superstitious is to lack generosity of mind. Perhaps my feet were worse than I thought.

About feet there is something that few but infantrymen and long-distance walkers know: that is, by continuous pounding they become flattened. They splay out, plantigrade, like the feet of a bear. In my experience the process is most evident after about two hundred miles, the distance across country from Land's End to Bristol, where, some years ago, I thought a walk through Britain had come to a full stop. Now it so happens I had again walked just about that distance from the sea and it was about time I took the cure.

A simple matter. You bathe your feet. I dangled mine in the canal for about ten minutes. You dry them, carefully, and put on thin socks, or none at all. Sockless and comfortable, I walked on to Herstal and Liège, slowly, praising that bell until I heard it no more.

Herstal makes heavy gear, including guns and atomic equipment, and the people live in affluent squalor under skies stained by splotches of smoke the colour of diarrhoea. It comes from the blast-furnaces. The miners are known as coal-heads and the bargees something I have forgotten, but wholly to their credit, I hope, for nicer people would be hard to meet.

At the point where the canal joins the river under a statue of King Albert the size of King Kong you may find brightly-lit villages of barges companionably roped together for the night. The crews go aboard each other's craft; then off they go in the morning to link up somewhere else.

I waved to a man reading a newspaper on his foredeck and Captain Lamartine waved me aboard to take breakfast with Madame and three little Lamartines, all from Huy downstream. His job was to dump iron-spoil in the sea, but that day *La Grandeur* might have been done up for a regatta. Bunting hung from the television aerial and Madame had put a cake in her press-button cooker. It was the birthday of the smallest m'sieur.

With quiet pride she showed me the oil-fired central heating and the bathroom shower. With its fitted carpets and teak furniture, the sitting room might have been a luxury flat. To judge from the almost new Mercedes battened down amidships, barge masters are not short of money. According to Maurice Lamartine, the problems were getting crews, finding a school for the kids and keeping Madame *contente*. She was always talking about settling down somewhere. As for himself, he implied that if he never saw Huy again it would be once too often. He paid neither rent nor rates. No need for holidays. They travelled everywhere. There was nothing else quite like it. *Il n'y a que ça*. But he worried about recruitment.

The Germans, he said, were tackling the problem by mooring superbly got-up show-boats in the Rhenish river ports with the biggest senior schools. The youngsters were invited to come aboard and see whether they fancied a life of touring Europe in their own homes. But with eight thousand barges afloat he reckoned that even the Germans were desperately short of crews.

Outside, in that transient camp on the canal, the captain's neighbours were doing nothing much except hang about, waiting to cast off. They took it easy. I thought what hooting and indignation there would have been among car drivers held up for an hour and a half. But those amiable fellows seemed wholly unperturbed. Some dozed on deck. Some gossiped with only an occasional glance over their shoulders to see whose turn it was next, and then one by one, in the most leisurely way imaginable, they slipped away through the lock with no more than a jolly toot to show they were glad to be off.

For a bargee, time is the interval between a stop and a start, between eating and sleeping. The rest is largely contemplative. Somebody has remarked that if adequately fed there is no reason why a bargee would not live for ever.

That city called Liège in French, Luik in Flemish and something else in Walloon has been described as a priest's paradise, a man's purgatory and a woman's hell. They work hard, they go to bed early in sheets changed twice a week and pay their dues on Sunday. Of the reputed hundred spires, only a dozen or so were visible that smoggy morning. Far beyond, seen over what looked like an air-borne bank of rather dirty cotton-wool, rose the flat roof of the Ardennes.

On a pair of feet miraculously come back to life, I strode in through that great riverside bird market, the Oisellerie, pausing only to marvel at more kinds of curious-looking pigeons than a caricaturist could have imagined. Here you may buy grotesquely frilled blondinettes, bluettes, satinettes, English croppers, rollers from Central Asia, barbs from the Barbary Coast and knock-kneed pouters with a feathered balloon in place of a breast, all cooing and preening and seemingly incapable of flight.

In a hotel marred only by an enormous juke-box, I met my friend Gaston, the biologist known from years ago in the Congo. We took a drink together and might have had another, but the box began to jangle infernally, so off we went to look for the tent that had been posted on to Liège.

The chase lasted about two hours. If I hadn't been accompanied by a man who would have gone far in the diplomatic service it might have lasted much longer. At the post office they assured us that no doubt the parcel had been lodged at the railway station, and there we trudged, shaking hands successively with the enquiry clerk, his immediate superior and the departmental chief who referred us to a customs officer in a distant part of the town.

At this I shook the fellow's hand with diminished warmth and turned to find both our referees waiting with hands half-raised in the ritual gesture. It is perhaps churlish to dispraise the custom, but in Belgium it has an obsessional flavour. With a muttered M'sieur or Madame everyone seems obliged to shake somebody by the hand at intervals of about half an hour. In government affairs there is a complex system of protocol about who raises his right hand first, thereby establishing where the shakee stands in the estimation of the shaker.

Liège lies at the centre of an immense web of water, road and rail-borne traffic supervised by little kingdoms of *fonctionnaires* who seem to work as far apart from each other as they can. In addition, you are up against separately-housed *douanes* from whom clearance chits can be obtained at the expense of credentials, small duties and a lot more handshaking. I would not go through that rigmarole again to reclaim my soul.

In a particularly dreary part of the town we located someone in what looked like a glass sentry-box who incautiously admitted that a cylindrical parcel from Holland bearing my name had arrived about two days ago. Could we describe it? I held out my hands like a fisherman. About that size, I said. But thick and wrapped up in bright yellow paper.

At this the *douanier* nodded. He remembered it very well. But, alas, there was a little problem. Unfortunately, it would have to be cleared by yet another authority since it had arrived *via* Aachen in Germany. Indicating that as far as he was concerned, the matter was closed, he held out his hand.

Before I could splutter out what I thought of him and in particular the whole damned bureaucratic system, Gaston stepped forward, adroitly, and grasped the proferred palm. Shaking it slowly, and looking the man straight between the eyes as if trying to recall a half-forgotten acquaintance, he said surely they had met somewhere before. Could it not have been in Brussels where they had both enjoyed the hospitality of his good friend, the Chief Inspector of Customs? Somebody had just received the ribbon. The *douanier* nodded, cautiously. Yes, that might have been the occasion, he thought.

Brightening up as if he'd got down to the very heart of the problem, M. Gaston said why then, *that* must have been nearly twelve years ago. My God! how affairs had changed. Inefficiency everywhere *and* political corruption, due, in his opinion, to people who had no conscience, no sense of operating a good public service. Now as to the little matter of the tent, about that affair he could tell a droll story. Incredible as it seemed, his friend there had managed to walk all the way from Holland in the time it had taken that parcel to arrive in Liège by rail! Now why was that? He would tell him. Because it had come through the hands of certain *socialists* in Germany who were out to discredit Belgium and her government. Need one say any more? And the *douanier* said he need say no more at all. He understood perfectly. He lifted a phone. At a few sharply spoken words of command my tent slid down a chute like a sausage from a machine. I paid a few francs duty. More handshakes all round and we walked back to the hotel with the juke-box.

* * *

That evening we got down to what we really came to talk about, the Congo and its people and the great days we had spent there. In the course of a story about the highlands of Kivu, Gaston grunted loudly in the manner of an old male gorilla and several guests looked round, nervously, and moved their chairs back. A priest shrugged his shoulders. Not to be outdone, I recall giving a pretty fair imitation of the talking drums by hitting the edge of a coffee-cup and a half-empty bottle with a spoon.

The talking drums are a very sophisticated form of bush telegraph. Around what is now Kinshasha, the local people, the Lokele, slit a carefully-dried log in such way that a sharp blow on one side produces a high note called the woman tone, whilst a blow on the other side makes a much deeper note called the male. By putting the local tonal language in terms of high notes and low notes, like dots and dashes in morse code, a message can be tapped out in the stillness of the night and picked up within a range of six or seven miles. On the analogy of morse code, the word for swamp, phonetically rendered as *li-sar-kar*, can be transmitted as *dot*, *dash-dash*. To avoid words that sound much alike, the Lokele have made up a lot of compound phrases. Thus White Man is the 'Spirit of the Forest', whilst a chicken is the 'Little bird that calls *Kee-oo*, *Kee-oo*'. Both Gaston and I knew a bit of the language, and to show that I had not forgotten those nights we spent together in Yangambi, I rattled away enthusiastically with that spoon.

The priest leaned forward with a pained expression. 'M'sieur,' he said, 'it is almost impossible to hear the music.' And he leaned back.

Up to that point we had managed to ignore the juke-box that boomed away in the corner, emitting drum music which I suppose came from the swamps of Merseyside or Manhattan. We apologized and left.

After much back-slapping and toasting at the inn door the next day, I set off for those gracefully clothed hills that lie between Liège and the Grand Duchy of Luxembourg. I carried a lot of extra weight in the shape of my tent and a litre of superb Corton, but, wine being what it is, I trod the lighter the further I went and it was good to get away from the stench of industry. Holland had been fair enough, but I wouldn't wish the Lower Meuse on a dog. Hopefully there would be about two hundred miles of open country before industry re-emerged in the vicinity of Metz.

Some are born wanderers; some have it thrust upon them. A group of disconsolates in the second category sat by the roadside at an intersection, trying to thumb lifts to Aachen, to Luxembourg, to anywhere outside Belgium. They had been tossed out of town by no less than the police chief who, tiring of guitar twiddling long past midnight in the *Jardin d'Acclimatation*, had said if he found them in Liège the next day, he'd run them in. 'The bastard wouldn't let us sleep there,' said a girl from Springfield, Mass. 'Fine thing when you're jes' tryin' to be *sociable*.' Her companion, a young Dane, made a faint gurgling noise. 'He's got one helluva hang-over,' she explained. They carried two bed-rolls and a rucksack garishly placarded: LUXIMBERG – JUST MARRIED.

Belgium is not too well disposed towards those they call *les nozem*. For myself, I couldn't quite make up my mind. They are a wholly mixed lot. Young and unregretting. With hands in pockets, shoulders bowed and pavement-scraping steps, their gait is the very negation of my notions of pedestrianism. But, then, they are not walkers, or at least, I have yet to meet any. They seemed surprised, almost resentful, about suggestions that it might be more enjoyable to walk than hang about for lifts. They are confirmed *autostoppeurs*. As for their raggle-taggle garb, it's meant, I suppose, to draw fire from the squares of orthodoxy. For some folk a glimpse of bare flesh is as provocative as an Iron Cross or a bowler hat on an errant youngster unfit to have served his time in an international war or a take-over deal.

Back and sides go bare, go bare . . .

Nothing new in that. The *gyros* were castigated in the eleventh century, 'They go about naked in public', says the Council at Salzburg, 'lie in bake-ovens, frequent taverns, games, harlots, earn their bread by their vices and cling with inveterate obstinacy to their sect, so that no hope of their amendment remaineth.' As for their morals, for men anchored by vows, there is something curiously disturbing about a wench on the loose. The Blessed St Boniface of Devon, Wynfrith as some call him, has no doubts about pilgrimages on which the gravest minds in the Church had always some reserve. It should be forbidden entirely to women and nuns. 'There is not a town in France or Italy', he says, 'where there is not an English harlot or adultress.'

When I first cast about for a serviceable route to the Alps and beyond I engaged in much frustrating correspondence with ministries and the secretaries of rambling clubs in Paris, Brussels and Luxembourg. Apart from the networks of little tracks, I had been told of a partly-completed international cross-country highway for walkers that will eventually extend from Liège south to the Mediterranean. This is the *Sentier de Grande Randonnée*. The French sections are supervised by a *Comité National* with offices in the *Avenue de la Grande Armée* in Paris where they sell *topoguides* or walkers' maps with a bit of description of the parts that have been surveyed and lightly signposted. The frustration came from the discovery of evident gaps in the route, especially those in Lorraine and the Jura.

On the way out to Fraipont that bright morning I kept a constant look out for the *jalons* that mark the trail. These are two horizontal stripes of paint, a white one above a red which at varying intervals have been stencilled on rocks and walls, trees and gate posts. They employ a double *jalon*, one above the other, to indicate an unobvious change in direction. All this sounds nicely reassuring and easy to follow, but, as I soon discovered, in many places the marks have been defaced by landowners or weathered to such an extent that, when confronted by a choice of tracks in woods and clearings, the walker is obliged to quarter the ground like an anxious retriever. For this reason I usually plotted my own course and used the recommended route merely for general guidance. In a series of generous curves fit only for happy indolents, the *Sentier Ardennais* weaves around Banneux and Hautregard, Spa, and Vielsalm. With a notion to see those great upland moors called the Fagnes, I scurried through the beechwoods more directly, keeping to the watershed of that heavily scoured torrent, the Vesdre.

This is the country of the Walloons, a teutonic word meaning foreign, akin to *Waalsch* in Dutch and *Welsh* in our own language. They are a cheerful, impulsive, square-headed people, descended some think, from that famous Gaulish tribe the Belgae, with an admixture of Romans who fought them and found them a tough lot.

Towards evening I came down to a small pub in the vicinity of Theux where the resident genius turned out to be a cheerful mongrel that smoked cigarettes. They assured me it never took more than two a night and before I became anxious about how it put them out, the animal neatly dropped the half-burned stub into a cuspidor for which it got a biscuit and a scratch behind the ear.

A bed? Madame assured me she had the best in Belgium. She bought them herself in Brussels, and as for the food, I forget now where it all came from, but she spelt out the details and served a handsome supper in the bar.

In places where there is company I cannot abide solitary confinement at mealtimes, especially in those small, over-decorated rooms set aside for the occasional guest. Madame laid out a table and went back to the bar with her eyes fixed warmly on a man who played billiards supremely well. After a particularly good shot he held his upturned cue by the base and looked up, waiting for her nod of approval.

In another corner of that lively little place the white-whiskered patron sat at a desk, carefully writing down something from a pile of aluminium rings. They were tags from racing pigeons in the loft outside in the yard. During the evening a young lad, who I took to be his grandson, rushed in excitedly, carrying a bird between his cupped hands. At the old man's cry of 'Look here!' the whole company crowded round. Some writing in Indian ink on one of the wing feathers showed the bird came from Marseilles and had apparently lost its way. They speculated at length about the winds it had probably encountered and how it had flown there, circling the ruins of Franchimont before pitching down, exhausted, among the other pigeons in the loft. Eventually the old man closed his ledger with a decisive snap and shuffled up to the bar, asking why in the name of God the whole world had a drink except himself.

With simple affection Madame said, '*Mon vieux* – you are a fat fool. Have you not got a tongue in your head?' At this the old man took the proffered glass and shuffled back to his seat, breaking wind uncomfortably near the man who played billiards so well.

I should feel I had repaid a very real debt if I could relate everything those Walloons did to make me feel at home that night. They offered me drinks; they explained some of the jokes made in their almost wholly incomprehensible patois. They sang songs. And as local folk will, they got to boasting about where they came from. There was much argument between a carter from Namur and a flower-grower from St Hubert. The first asked what city could claim more than the heart of Don John of Austria who had saved them all from the Turks, but the florist stuck to his horticultural guns. From his home town came not only that St Hubert, the Apostle of the Ardennes, who, out hunting one day, had seen a stag with a crucifix glistening between its horns. It was also the birthplace of Pierre-Joseph Redouté, that Raphael of rose painters who counted all the pretty women in Paris among his patrons.

At half past eleven the mongrel trotted round with the last cigarette of the evening; Madame said it was time they all went home, and I wished her good night, asking how early I might have breakfast. She said if I was in that sort of hurry it could be prepared immediately, but she would prefer seven o'clock. And there it was, on a table in the bar which had already been swept out. I asked here what time she usually got up. She said mostly at half past five, but it had been a busy evening.

The word Ardennes comes from some Celtic expression meaning dark or obscure. From a hill-top, looking down on an apparently endless expanse of trees, you can sense something of what those forests of spruce and pine must have been like when they were heavily populated by wolves, bears and wild boar. They are still the home of a vast number of foxes which are now being systematically destroyed by the Belgians in a so-called control operation.

I set off that morning towards Spa, the town that gave its name to some hundreds of resorts which have been built around medicinal springs. As usual, I walked through the woods, striding along through gaps in the trees. The route could scarcely be called direct, but for once it didn't really matter. I had time to spare. A friend I had arranged to meet in Malmedy some fifty miles away had been delayed, and I had three whole days in which to get there. What made the going difficult were the blocked trails and the roped-off paths. Notices in two languages said plainly: 'Keep Out! Danger of Death!' The Ardennois were gassing foxes.

You could smell the cyanide. The partly-decomposed head of one animal leered from its earth, its jaws still horribly agape. Underground they must have died in thousands. They were still there, rotting slowly. The foresters were not even bothering to dig them out.

Proclamations in several market places said that the Mayor had the honour to inform the commune that cases of rabies had been confirmed by the Institut Pasteur. Henceforth, under powers vested in him by the Act of something or other, *all* dogs must be muzzled and the people warned that all vagrants would be captured and summarily destroyed.

Rabies flared up in Poland about thirty years ago and began to spread outwards in all directions, like eczema. Although all warm-blooded animals, including bats, can become infected, dogs are primarily responsible for passing on the disease to man, and one of the most important international carriers is the dog's wild relative, the fox.

Rabies is a fearful disease and almost invariably fatal in man. Once infected, the victim can expect to undergo agonies comparable only to torture and die within a month. As the viruses travel through the nerves to the spinal cord and begin to multiply in the tissues of the brain, the symptoms are restlessness and depression, rising to fever and uncontrollable excitement. The spasms are intensified by cold air or a drink of water, hence the old name of hydrophobia. The problem is how to control the disease.

A dog can be muzzled and leashed, but the fox is a notorious wanderer. The pairs raise a family and the progeny wander off in search of new homes. In an operation which seems fundamentally misguided, the Belgians are trying to destroy all their foxes in a broad *cordon sanitaire* across the Ardennes.

This policy is likely to have the very reverse of the effect intended, for as soon as the territory of an animal is left unoccupied new tenants quickly move in from outside. The empty fox earths of the Ardennes will attract hordes of animals from where they are most numerous and probably most heavily infected. This is the Vacuum Effect. If the animals were left alone, the chances are that the disease would stabilize itself and eventually die out, or become a rarity. But here we are getting into that intricate system of equipoise which, for want of a better phrase, we call the balance of nature. Conservationists are not merely concerned about the extinction of rare plants and animals; they know better than anyone else that in the absence of competitive variety, some species become grossly abundant, especially those which are no longer being kept down by their natural enemies. In the case of the fox, the increase is probably due to the decline in the popularity of fox furs. The animals are no longer being killed off in large numbers for their pelts. Essentially, the problem is how over-abundant stocks can be judiciously and humanely controlled. A little country on the edge of a fox-full continent can never hope to keep its woodlands fox-free. I put this point to the chief exterminator of Staneux, who said I couldn't show him evidence of a living fox within a radius of twenty miles.

'But won't they come back?' I asked.

'Perhaps so,' he said, 'but we must do *something*.'

Spa used to be called the Pearl of the Ardennes. The setting is magnificent. A compact little place in a claw of high and wooded cliffs, but through much handling the pearl has lost its lustre. Since the aristocracy of Europe flocked there to take the cure and play *biribiri* for roubles, thalers and francs, it looks as if it has been in and out of the pawnshop a few times. The paint on the mansions is peeling. Junk shops sell the worst of junk and the smell is of anisette, fried potatoes and petrol fumes. Cars were thundering through the town for the Grand Prix at Francorchamps.

Somewhat dispirited by the sight of an open-air beauty contest in the rain, I wandered off to the Springs of Marie-Henriette where nowadays they sell more beer than medicinal water. Eventually I pitched my new-found tent down on an island in a caravan park and slept in the company of four indignant swans and several loud radios. The open-air life can be something of a disappointment.

After a bad time on Dartmoor during my last long walk, I debated whether to take a chance among the great bogs of Baraque-Michel, but they assured me it had been a dry year. The Fagnes, they said, were quite safe. And being country folk I assumed they knew what they were talking about. In fact, I have rarely seen finer moorland, nor walked more easily on moss and cotton grass. But what the Fagnards didn't mention is that this mossy source of half a dozen rivers is ringed by forests as tangled and as impenetrable as any you may find in western Europe. You get there *via* the Vecquée, a deep-cut swathe through the trees beyond Baronheid. On that old boundary between West Prussia and Belgium the silence among the silver trunks of beech is that of a cathedral, broken only by the downward-falling cadences of willow-warblers.

The track runs on, rising almost imperceptibly into tall stands of spruce. Here are blue-green pagodas of trees with their branches curved and feathered like a retriever's tail. And on I went, unworried by path-finding until high sun. Under that thick carpet of pine needles there is, I suspect, a Roman road, probably from Spa to Aachen and, as if wholly confident in the heading, the compass needle barely shifted more than two or three points in six miles of brisking along.

How I strayed in pursuit of a big black woodpecker is rather hard to explain to those unmoved by the sight of a big black woodpecker, but I'm not to be put off easily by what I am intrigued by.

If you include the dowdy-looking little wryneck among the company, there are ten woodpeckers in Europe and at one time or another I had seen them all except that black fellow, as big as a crow and handsome to look at in his scarlet skull cap. Thus it was that when a fine specimen flew out of a larch and plunged down into the trees below the track, making a derisive cackling noise, I scrambled after him, not much caring about how I got back. It flew on to the limb of a dead tree where it began to drum with a noise like one of those rattles they use in sports grounds, but more hollow and sustained in duration. To my intense delight, another bird appeared and the two began to chase each other round the trunk of that tree, but whether out of anger or love I cannot say. They were as nimble as Spanish dancers, an illusion heightened by what could have been the noise of castanets. I watched this performance for several minutes, marvelling at their agility.

Throughout Europe this woodpecker has been associated with a number of curious folk-tales, most of them associated with rain and fertility. One is about how the Lord ordered all the birds and beasts to dig holes for water in a time of drought and all obeyed except the woodpecker, who flapped from bough to bough, chattering away to himself. When reproached the bird said he had no mind to dirty his feathers in such menial work.

'O vain creature!' cried the Lord, 'henceforth thou shalt wear nought but a garment of sooty black, neither shalt thou quench thy thirst from brook or stream. Raindrops falling from the sky shall be thy drink and thy voice shall only be heard when other creatures are in hiding through fear of an approaching storm.'

The legend of those red-capped sprites that lure travellers to their doom might have been more appropriate, since I followed those birds down to a stream. They flew off, still cackling derisively and I spent several hours there trying to find my way back to the Vecquée.

With a bit of food and ample shelter on your back there is nothing particularly hazardous about getting lost in a forest, but you can waste a lot of time. Scratched and thoroughly irritated by the situation, I felt pretty tired. When the stream began to fall down from what looked like a wooded cliff I took to a deer track in a quite different direction, but that, too, became too steep to follow. At this I plodded upwards through any gap I could find, doing my best to avoid all scrub, particularly the larch and juniper which harboured ambitious patrols of small black ants.

By sundown I had tried about every trick I knew. I had climbed a tree on what seemed to be a substantial knoll. But from the top I could see nothing but trees. I had tried to keep on a north-easterly bearing, hoping I should come out at least somewhere near where I wanted to be. But it led me into a swamp among the trees.

Feeling thoroughly dispirited, I sat down on a log and debated whether to go back – which wouldn't be at all easy – or spend the night there and see how things turned out the next day. Before I could make up my mind, from somewhere upwind came a faint trill that sounded vaguely familiar. I listened intently. Though far away, it rose and fell in a musical curlicue and when I realized what it was I thought that noise more beautiful than anything I had heard that day, for it was the call note of curlew, those birds that breed on open moors.

A bird had led me into that forest. There seemed a fair chance that a bird might lead me out. On an encouraging if wholly unexpected bearing to the west, I stumbled through spruce until I came out on the very edge of the High Fagne. The trees ended abruptly. There was neither scrub nor undergrowth at their feet. I might have emerged from an immense crypt upheld by columns of conifers.

The Fagnes are barren places, the haunt only of birds and peat-cutters. They are among the tundras of western Europe, a relic of those days when the Ardennes were the outermost wall of the ice-sheets that crawled down from Scandinavia.

In that half-light the hummocky tufts of cotton-grass stretched out as far as the eye could see, but I didn't venture among them. I felt enormously tired. I ate a meal and before it grew too dark to see, I spread out my sleeping bag on the floor of a wayside shrine and slept through what seemed centuries of night.

In Malmédy the altar of the cathedral had been dressed for Ascension-tide, that day on which God's son is proclaimed triumphant. Bells boomed. Pigeons tumbled in the clean air, and all the world and his wife were out and about in their Sunday best. By the time I walked in looking conspicuously dirty, about thirty children had already been led to the bishop. That great occasion over, the solemn little boys and their sisters in the garb of brides walked through the bunting-decked streets. They walked slowly, hand in hand, paying their respects to their elders but no-betters. They were kissed and patted and given ice-creams and told to wipe their noses and run away. A band played in the market place and the mayor released a hundred balloons. That night everyone reassembled for the confirmation parties. There were three in the open air and at least a dozen in the hotels.

At the *Bristol* the head waiter brought in a dozen bottles of champagne. 'Another one?' I asked. 'No, M'sieur,' he said. 'A wedding this time. It happens sometimes, even here.'

Towards Stavelot and Vielsalm, the woods are lightly carpeted in those violets known to children in the west of England as blue mice. The landscapes are wholly pastoral. They have an air of standing slightly apart from time. But here and there by the roadside you may come across the blackened ruins of a farm-house and old trees shattered by the splinters of shells. For through this region clattered the tanks of the Sixth SS Panzer Army in that bloody affair in the Ardennes called the Battle of the Bulge.

For company I had my old friend Peter Elstob, a military historian, who wanted to see something of the terrain he was writing about. In general our talk was more of tactics than birds and botany, but with geography as common ground we got on hugely well, scarcely noticing the miles.

As he explained it, the marvel is that Hitler managed to scrape together eighteen divisions and some seven hundred tanks and hurl them against the immensely powerful Western Allies. It came as a surprise even to some of his generals, for in September 1944 it looked as though the Third Reich was very near defeat. The great supply port of Antwerp had at last fallen, shortening the Allied supply lines by hundreds of miles, and British, Canadian and American armies stood poised for what the military calls total investment. But the precious asset of time was lost, particularly by the quarrel between Montgomery and Eisenhower about who should get what in the race for Berlin. This gave Hitler time to organize and launch one of the most sudden and unexpected counter-attacks of the Second World War.

The objective: Antwerp. The hope: that the Allies could be divided, mauled and held long enough to switch German troops back to Russia. At this distance from events, the outcome seemed inevitable. But from the total surprise caused by the attack, it cannot have been apparent to the men of the American First Army. On the long night of December 15, 1944, they were mostly asleep in a sector reckoned to be dead quiet. Before dawn that morning they were struck by the spearheads of two hundred and forty thousand German troops, tanks and guns, the biggest force that had been thrown against the Western Front since the war began.

Like international chess champions, army commanders can usually determine their opponent's strategy by his preliminary tactics. Although Allied Intelligence had been deplorably weak in failing to anticipate the attack, it soon became known that, for the sake of morale, the old but still much respected Field Marshal von Rundstedt had been persuaded to come out of retirement and command the offensive. What puzzled the Allied commanders was that Rundstedt seemed to be up to a series of tricks that were quite out of his known character.

German commandos dressed up in Allied uniforms drove captured vehicles ahead of their main forces, giving false orders to the Allies to retreat and spreading demoralizing rumours. Those captured were summarily shot. Necklaces of searchlights directed on to low clouds at night created artificial moonlight under which hosts of tanks crawled like bed bugs on a white sheet. In the worst winter for forty years, parachutists floated down on the High Fagnes. Snow-bogged vehicles were supplemented by thousands of horses withdrawn from the Russian front. But the orders were not being given by Rundstedt. It gradually became apparent that Hitler had taken command himself. And through the enormous confusion and panic, his Panzers drove on deep into the Ardennes. They came to a stop only when they ran out of petrol.

But Hitler miscalculated one vital factor. Far from dividing the Allies, the strength and violence of his attack brought them more closely together than ever before. Not caring about whose toes he trod on, Eisenhower gave command of the northern half of his broken line to Montgomery and the southern one to Omar Bradley.

On the German side the divisions of the new People's Infantry, the *Volksgrenadiers*, were stiffened by veterans. From the Russian front came SS troops used neither to giving nor expecting quarter. In their dash to the Meuse they refused to be delayed by the taking of prisoners. Nearly a hundred disarmed

Americans were slaughtered in a field near Malmédy. Another fifty who had been forced to fill the tanks of Germany's toughest Panzer leader, Joachim Peiper, were dispatched in the same way. The news of these massacres stiffened resistance.

German tanks, panting up a hill towards a petrol store, were met by a river of burning fuel. Nobody – not even Peiper – managed to reach the Meuse. Deprived of air support and worn down by the stubborn counter-attacks of the Americans, the offensive collapsed.

Casualties on both sides were enormous and the people who just happened to be living where a battle flared often got shelled by both sides. Thousands died. Those lucky enough to escape in time came back to find their towns and villages reduced to rubble. By an error which has never been satisfactorily explained the old town of Malmédy was bombed by the American Air Force on three successive nights in the quite mistaken belief it was held by the Germans. This, you might think, could happen once and, by a remarkable perpetuation of error, perhaps twice. But not three times. Yet that's how it was. On the third occasion soldiers and civilians came out to welcome the high-flying planes which, they imagined, were out to redress what they had suffered and they were met by yet another dreadful shower of bombs.

Malmédy, like Bastogne, Vielsalm, St Vith and other places thereabouts, has now been almost entirely rebuilt. Though the architectural styles of many centuries have been carefully repro- duced, the foundations and the internal structure including the plumbing and drainage are entirely modern. This caused a lot of resentment in towns where houses were merely patched up to remedy a gaping hole in the roof or the walls. People want to know why they can't have the comfort of those who live in Malmédy and Vielsalm. The reason, they say, is tourism. That's where all the money has gone.

Peter and I said goodbye in Vielsalm and I walked on into that ever-narrowing no-man's-land between the borders of Belgium, Luxembourg and West Germany. Unless you take to the high plateau of forest and bear down on the little place called Trois Frontières, the open country is as undistinguished as a plate of boarding-house vegetables. There is nothing particularly offensive or ill-tended about those thin strips of farmland, but the feeling is one of utter neutrality. The people seem to have no kinship with their country or with each other. They want nothing more than to be left absolutely alone. They are as elusive as field mice, their cottages overgrown with creepers. If it wasn't for a pile of fresh-cut stakes at their doors, you might think they were uninhabited.

Those stakes intrigued me. You see them everywhere. They were too thick for supporting crops of peas but too thin for timber. What on earth *were* they for? I put the question to an innkeeper near Crombach and he looked as surprised as if I had asked him why his customers drank.

Out of the thick patois came the words *héritage* and *patrimoine*. Through the tavern window he pointed to a field where three lines of stakes marked the holdings of four men. In Belgium the laws of succession are rigid. The widow and her sons have inalienable rights of inheritance, which often result in bits of land being divided and divided again until they resemble the small-holdings of Norman serfs. So great is this hunger for independence that in some places the stakes are used to uphold stands of electrified wire even though it keeps tractors off the land and interferes with the drainage. What I couldn't understand was why the people continued to collect more stakes when they couldn't expect to inherit a bit of property more than once or twice in their lifetime.

The innkeeper nodded. He conceded the point, but, as he put it, 'One can always hope.'

Luxembourg

On a bright morning in May I walked down into the Grand Duchy and liked the place from the start. The frontier guard shouted '*Moien*', and went on playing cards. They don't bother overmuch about passports in Luxembourg. And the villagers couldn't be more friendly. Far from scampering back into their houses, they came to their gates just to say that polite *Moien*. They all say it. It means good morning, or just hallo, and is near enough to that clipped Mornin' you hear in the North of England to make me feel at home. '*Moien*,' I replied, exercising my command of patois to the full, and ambled down to the river, feeling on top of the world.

No need to hurry. In Echternacht on Whit Tuesday they dance in the streets in honour of my fellow-countryman St Willibrord and I had a mind to see them at it. This gave me three whole days to make less than forty miles.

I took to the Our, which at the frontier is a mere *schlinder*, a rivulet, but as pretty as a maid in a mini-skirt. And as slim. In places you can jump from one bank to the other, but after a few miles she deepens and begins to take her frontier duties more seriously. I clung to her with affection and felt sorry when she lost her identity, first in the bosom of her sister-stream, the Sur, and then in that sadly polluted waterway, the Moselle. With those rivers for guides I trod the length of the frontier from just below Burg Reuland to Mondorf-les-Bains.

If you look at that line on a map, the impression is of the head of a ferocious dog with jaws agape, ready to bite the backside of Germany. It looks as if the creature could turn round in a wink and assail France. Or ward off any threat from the north by a fine display of teeth. The Luxembourgers have good reason to be on the alert. They are the most trodden underfoot of all the

95

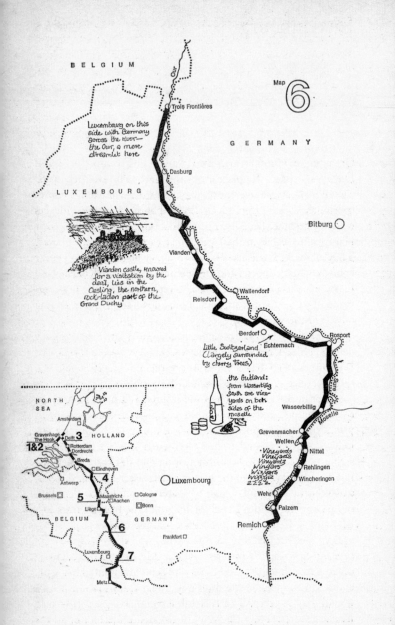

BELGIUM

Map 6

Our

○ Trois Frontières

GERMANY

Luxembourg on this side with Germany shares the river— the Our, a more dreamlit here

○ Dasburg

LUXEMBOURG

Bitburg ○

Vianden ○

Vianden castle, renowned for a visitation by the devil, lies in the Oesling, the northern, rock-laden part of the Grand Duchy

○ Wallendorf

Reisdorf ○

Berdorf ○   ○ Echternach   Rosport

Little Switzerland (largely surrounded by cherry trees)

the Gutland: from Wasserbillig south are vineyards on both sides of the Moselle

NORTH SEA

Amsterdam ○

HOLLAND

Gravenhage
The Hook   Delft   3
1 & 2   Rotterdam
        Dordrecht
        Breda   ○ Eindhoven
                4
Antwerp ○

Brussels □   5
        Maastricht   □ Cologne
        Liège   □ Aachen   □ Bonn
BELGIUM   6   GERMANY
        ○ Luxembourg   □
                □ Frankfurt
        Luxembourg □   7
Metz ○

○ Luxembourg

Wasserbillig

Moselle

Grevenmacher ○
Wellen ○   Nittel ○
Vineyards Vineyards Vineyards Vineyards Vineyards
        Rehlingen ○
        Wincheringen ○
Wehr ○
Palzem ○

Remich ○

communities of Europe. No major war has left them unscathed. They have been under the domination of Burgundy, Spain, France, Austria and Germany. Despite oppression, or maybe on that account, they are resilient, good-natured, unpunctual folk whose motto is *Mir woelle bleiwe wat mir sin* – we want to remain what we are.

The patois, or, as they properly call it, *their* language, sounds a rough mixture of French and German in which specialists can detect echoes of half a dozen old tongues from pre-Roman Celtic to what you might have heard in the courts of Charlemagne. Thomas Henry Passmore says it 'leaps from High German to Dutch and back again, and plays arpeggios of large compass upon the whole gamut of Grimm's Law'. That may be. The language is wordy and so devoid of inflections that even simple ideas have to be paid out of a bag of small change.

Much of the official business is in French. You see it in the names of streets, on shops, on hotel menus. In church they mostly speak German. The newspapers are printed in German, and sometimes good black-letter stuff too, but with the cultural articles written in French. In a police court they speak three languages, the judge and counsel knowing full well that the case for the defence will rest heavily on slowly-spoken testimony in Luxembourgeois. There is a smack of English about many words. To gabble is to *gabber*; something nasty is *knaeschteg*; there is *cabbage* and *shabby* and you pull up a horse by shouting *Woa!* But, when you get the hang of it, it's disconcerting to discover that the language changes as you move south.

The upper or northernmost part of the Duchy is reckoned harsh and called the Oesling, a rocky place deficient in calcium and phosphorus, the portion of Esau. To the south is the *Gutland* or *Bon Pays* which has much in common with the neighbouring orchards and cornfields of Lorraine, a land of abundance fit for Jacob.

I ambled along, admiring the placid pools and the flash of kingfishers, but had gone scarcely four miles when my little rivulet cast off her clothing of willows and plunged naked into a towering gorge of schist and slate. Here all seemed dark and hostile. The sun shone fitfully through streamers of cloud. No sound there except rushing water, the shrill of titmice and the cat-like call of buzzards circling high, like mobiles, above sullen cliffs.

The trail is blazed by yellow blobs of paint. I followed it closely, outflanking the promontories, turning aside only to look at rough crosses and heaps of fallen stones that mark ancient shrines. They were dedicated originally to those dark gods of the Celts, perhaps Cernunnos, the horned one, or Epona who was both a great queen and a riggish mare. When St Willibrord walked that way 'to wake up the soul of the world' he ordered his missionaries to plant crosses among those pagan shrines. They remained upright for centuries, for the priests knew there were always those who preferred rites associated with the older and lustier gods of heathendom.

What was left of the rich legends of the Celts was transformed by court bards into highly moral tales in which Christian virtue invariably triumphed. They weren't going to risk their necks in front of a pious lord-bishop by describing the bull dream, the *tarbfeis*, the initiation of maidens or what had to be done to avert infertility at the right hour of the right night. But by turning the whole story round, they could substitute the Devil and his works for any old brand of ritual and eroticism, and if the story sounded thin they could always bring in the names of a few unpopular lords to give the narrative some sort of credible background.

There is, for instance, that Euphrosyne, the fair daughter of the Master of Falkenstein, who was awakened at midnight by a gentle tapping on her window. It may be coincidence that it happened about the time of the summer equinox. Looking out she beheld whom she thought to be her suitor. He motioned her towards his saddlebow. It was not until they were high on the cliffs above the Our 'near an oak' that a shaft of moonlight revealed the face of the very Prince of Evil, and because of what he tried to make her do there – and by all accounts it was no straightforward rape – she threw herself down on the rocks that still bear her name. The inference is that it wasn't the first time this daughter of an oppressive lord had been out on her own. Moreover, she had been formally spoken for by another.

They also tell how, by a clever trick, the Devil was trapped in the vaults of Vianden, a castle lower downstream, but as I went to see if he was still there that story must wait awhile.

With the possible exception of the Vosges, I found no place where legends sprout more quickly than among the cliffs of the Oesling. There is scarce a cave, an isolated rock, a lone pine tree or a pile of stones without supporting folklore. Why is this? It can't be put down to the imagination of the Luxembourgers who are a matter-of-fact sort of people, not given to crossing themselves at the wink of summer lightning. It goes back thousands of years, certainly before anyone went there merely to look at the place.

It could be that here is a physical and cultural divide as marked as anything this side of the Alps, a place where the hordes that flowed down from the north and the central steppe clashed with the people of the Mediterranean. The Nordics and the Mongols introduced the horse; the Armenoids the plough. Pastoralists fought farmers and, centuries later, charioteers the Roman infantry. Christianity gradually replaced paganism, but the struggle for the great plains around the Rhine went on to the great distress of those who lived thereabouts, and in times of sustained trouble there is comfort in the supernatural.

In a little riverside tavern between the hamlet of Ouren and the bridge at Dasburg I became a bit of a supernaturalist myself. You must judge whether it had any effect on those big black cats who were up to something I couldn't quite make out. Or whether by coincidence they scampered off, terrified. You can never be sure about cats.

It seemed a friendly place. To the enormous consternation of an old retriever who had been forbidden to move, chickens walked into the bar. He sat under a table, stretched out, twitching, trying to pretend they were not there. I sat outside in the eerie sunlight, munching bread and sausage enlivened with a glass of Mirabelle, that distillation from little yellow plums about the size of marbles.

The first cat walked up and arranged itself, tidily, without so much as a miaouw. But it stared at me intently. Apart from thinking it was one of the biggest cats I had seen, I tried to ignore the animal. But when, a few moments later, two more cats of the same size strolled up and sat down, I thought rather differently of the matter.

Either you like cats or you don't. Whole nations have been divided on what people thought of an animal that mates openly, walks in silence and keeps it own counsel. As most people know, the Egyptians venerated the animal, going into mourning, shaving their own eyebrows when they died and burying them in hallowed ground. But not so much is known about the cat-stealing and counter-cat-stealing which dampened relations between the Egyptians and the catless Greeks and helped to precipitate the war that eventually ruined them both. And thus it was the venerated protector of granaries went to Rome.

Cats and Christianity spread throughout Europe together, but for some reason the animal fell into profound disrepute about the middle of the fifteenth century. Some blame the epidemic of fear aroused by the witch and her feline familiar. It may be that in western Europe, especially in those forests between the Meuse and the Rhine, Christianity lapsed temporarily in favour of the old cult of Freya, that goddess of love and fertility who went about in a gleaming chariot drawn by a leash of cats. At certain times of the year, lusty women took to worshipping her by yowling and behaving like queens on heat. Unattached young men were much in favour of these practices, but not so those who found their beds empty at night, and certainly not the priests who persuaded Pope Innocent VIII to put an almighty malediction on all forms of cat worship. And things went hard for the animal thereafter. Cats were tortured and walled up in new buildings to assure the fitness of the foundations. Cat-hating became a cult and cat-killing a sport. That's why cats stare. They *know*. That's why those cats were staring at me.

And then a remarkable thing happened or, rather, a series of happenings which may or may not be related to what I wrote on the table with my forefinger. Glancing behind, I discovered that two more cats had crept up and were staring from just about the same distance as their fellows in front. Now if three cats are disturbing, five are positively unnerving. Recalling that certain fruit juices possess strange qualities commended by no less than Dioscorides, I dipped my finger in the glass and drew a certain sign.

Call it coincidence. Call it what you will. The fact is that almost immediately there came a frightful screech from the bar. Out flew a white cockerel with that old and sorely-tried retriever hard on his tail. The pair raced into the circle of cats who turned at bay. At this commotion, a man appeared and threw a brick at the dog. The cats vanished. They just disappeared. The cockerel escaped by flying up on to the tailboard of a cart. The dog slunk back for a beating, and I wandered back to the Our, musing on the power of signs and what it is that cats know.

Like Urspelt and Urhausen, the word Our probably comes from some old association with the aurochs or ur, that ancestral mother and father of most of the domestic cattle we know today. With its huge horns and black skin, the aurochs must have been one of the most spectacular animals known to the early Europeans, but after lingering on in the forests of Poland, the last old cow went the way of the dodo in the seventeenth century. From those place-names, it looks as if bears were once common in the forests around Bereldingen, Berweiler and Berdorf. No doubt they killed beavers in Bivels and Bivingen, wolves in Wolverlange and Ulfingen and perhaps the lynx, the *louswolff*, in Luxembourg. For myself, I saw no animals larger than roe deer in the woods of the Oesling, but for hours that night I listened to as fine a chorus of owls as ever I heard. I heard it from the topmost turret of a forest fire-tower where, with bed spread out and supper laid, I looked down on an immense sea of larch.

That bird we call the tawny owl and the French the *hulotte* went out hunting at dusk. I saw but few, but they spoke to each other throughout the night and from what I know of their language, I had a pretty shrewd idea of what they were up to.

Tawny owl talk can be reduced to three phrases. There is that high-pitched *kewick* which, however sharp it may sound, is homely talk in owldom. The females don't much mind if their mates go off on their own, but they expect a pretty smart *kewick* in reply to that 'Where are you?' Sometimes I thought the response sounded a bit petulant. With his hearing aid focused on a fine fat field mouse, you could imagine the old man thinking that if she didn't shut up there would be only beetles for supper.

The call note most people associate with the creatures is that long-drawn-out *hoo-hoooo* with sometimes a briefly stuttered *hu-hu* ahead of that wailful *hoooo*. It means 'Get off my land!' The tawny is sending out his personal call-sign. He knows where he's going and he expects others to respect his own territory. If there's any trouble he screams.

From the top of that tower I heard converging birds becoming increasingly agitated until, from a series of frenzied cries, you could imagine the row they were having. Twice during the owl concert I heard a deep guttural note from that eagle of the night, the *hibou grand-duc*, a huge owl that can tackle a hare, but I may have been mistaken. It came from afar and was overlaid by a lot of local chatter.

The bridge at Dasburg is closely guarded by a smartly-got-up German official on the east bank and largely ignored by the Luxembourger on the other side. I asked this man if I could wander on to this common property. What he said I don't know for he spoke with his mouth full of *sterzelen*, a sort of fried porridge made from buckwheat, but with an airy wave he implied that as far as he was concerned, the bridge was mine. Not so the German. As soon as I put one foot over the halfway mark, he marched out of his little house and stood there, staring at me. I paused for a moment and walked back a few paces. The German retreated, but not without an ominous look over his shoulder. By taking a few paces forward I found I could entice him out again, but he stopped reacting to that childish sport and stared at me from his doorway. I shouted '*Moien!*' and went on my way.

Downriver, the banks were busy with fishermen, especially in those places where it said the sport was *wholly* forbidden. I asked a man with several fine trout in his basket if they ever got into trouble. With curious logic he said they weren't fishing on their side and to show what he meant he flicked his float under the banks of West Germany.

It began to rain, lightly. But there were puddles at the side of the road. An open sports car raced past perilously close, splashing me with dirty water from head to foot. I saw the driver. He wore a black beret and both he and the girl by his side seemed vastly amused. They shouted something ribald in German. Before I could think of something to shout back they passed out of sight and I trudged on, boiling with indignation.

This sounds a trivial matter, but, as I know from experience, a day's march usually takes on its colour from what happens early on. The car incident meant undoing my whole pack and putting on a dry pullover and oilskins and walking on, trying to take an interest in things that merely looked extremely wet. By dint of more will-power than enthusiasm, I tuned in to the argument of a few birds. There were spider orchids in the ditch and galaxies of large white daisies in the meadows, but until I came within sight of Vianden I never quite managed to take my mind off those hoodlums.

Vianden was called Vienna or Viennense long before that place on the Danube was even heard of. The word means rocky and very appropriate it is. The impression of those higgledy-piggledy houses standing one above the other is of an avalanche. They might have fallen down the cliff on which the ruined castle stands. I had a mind to see the view from the battlements, but before I got halfway up the hillside it began to rain with tropical violence.

From the doorway of a shed I became aware of a curious whine high up in the air. It came from the moving wires of a cable lift. The double seats of the cars were completely exposed to the weather. They were all empty except one, on which, to my surprise, sat the car driver in the black beret and his girl-friend. They didn't see me and I didn't shout. But as they slowly disappeared into the grey clouds, I felt that with some help from on high a small account had been largely settled, the more since it would take them at least twenty minutes to reach the top.

From Vianden came the House of Nassau, the ancestors of the Dutch royal family. The town charter goes back to the fourteenth century. Somebody has described the place as an amphora which has never quite lost the fragrance of its vanished wine. But it's very noisy. I took lodgings near a bridge chronically blocked by lines of cars and diesel coaches bringing yet more tourists into a town that already seemed overfull. Yet at dusk all became strangely quiet and I wandered about talking to farmers and innkeepers who make a point of not drinking in their own houses after the last coffee has been served.

Their custom is to tell stories against themselves, emphasizing their indolence and stupidity, two qualities which are the very reverse of what you are likely to find. Their climate, they say, is fit only for wild boars and Luxembourgers. It makes the skull grow at the expense of the brain. They recount how, during the last stages of the German occupation, the house of a certain burgomaster was hit by a shell. As he staggered towards the door the main beam fell on his head, but far from killing him, it merely gave him flat feet from which he still suffers. They are grateful to the Allies who came to their rescue, but claim that when the troops pulled out there was scarce a virgin left over the age of twelve to take part in their Christmastide play. As for that great castle on the hill with a Knights Hall large enough to feast five hundred men-at-arms, whole books have been written about its ghostly inhabitants, but with the exception of the eternal dice game in the vaults they are not in broad character unique.

That story concerns a boisterous fellow, a famous count, a descendant of the Master of Falkenstein whose daughter Euphrosyne had been seduced by the Devil. After a crusade and a campaign or two in Rhineland he fell back on local sports, hunting wild boar, bargaining with bishops, feuding with his neighbours and drinking and gaming in between times.

One night, after a feast in the great hall of Vianden, he went down into the vaults with his host, the Count Siegfried, and began to throw dice for fifteen tuns of local wine, some potent stuff known as the Kneecracker. They gained and lost by turns, throwing in a fief and a vineyard to raise the odds, but as one account has it, 'with neither sat fortune for long and they grew warm'.

Hours passed. Siegfried tired of the game and wanted to call it a night, but in an incautious moment Falkenstein shouted: 'May the Devil take the man who leaves the table first.' The outcome is in part predictable. The Prince of Darkness appeared in an operatic roll of thunder. 'Gentlemen,' he said. 'Pray let the game proceed, for I have all the time in the world.'

They say they are still at it, that late at night you may hear the *clink-clink* of dice on a marble table. Being true knights they will not break their word, but the Devil, who is not a gentleman, declines to believe them and there he sits, watching the play in a state of diabolical patience, for he has much to do elsewhere. He is part of that power that always wills evil, yet sometimes procures good. Those who do his handiwork nowadays go about in the guise of Progress – or national growth.

Before I set off that morning, Madame said the *patron* would be honoured if I could spare a few moments in his office. In that cosy parlour he introduced me to the deputy burgomaster and somebody else. He offered me a brandy. He coughed discreetly and started a little speech. As soon as he mentioned the great mountain I knew what I was in for. A case of mistaken identity. When he had finished I said that flattered though I was, there had been a small misunderstanding, *malentendu*, and in imperfect French I tried to describe how it had happened once before in the Congo.

Two of us had walked over that range called the Ruwenzori or the Mountains of the Moon. It had been an easy haul in the company of porters and an efficient guide. All that remained was the eight-day voyage downriver in a dilapidated stern-wheeler to what used to be called Leopoldville. Unfortunately, due to some breakdown in communications between London and the *Banque du Congo Belge*, I found myself in a second-class cabin with next to no money and a ticket tardily issued on credit by the not inaccurately described *Office d'Exploitation des Transports Coloniaux*.

On the second night out Captain Vanmessen called me to his cabin. Handing me a huge drink he congratulated me on climbing the mountain for, as he put it, it was a feat the whole world recognized. When I protested that it wasn't particularly difficult, that we hadn't in fact, got to the top, but had walked round the Margherita glacier, he became inexplicably angry. So it was all lies! he said. Why did the newspapers print such things?

It came out gradually, that I had been put down on the passenger list as Hillary who, the previous year, had climbed to the top of Everest. When the matter had been straightened out, Captain Vanmessen laughed uproariously and offered me the best cabin on the ship.

They made the same mistake in Vianden, and I must say they were very nice about it. They pressed another drink on me, saying at least it was an excuse for a little occasion. After more handshakes all round I set off for Echternacht by way of Little Switzerland.

Beyond Wallendorf the Our falls into the Sur, a river that drains the whole of central Luxembourg and marks the eastern frontier as far as the Moselle. Undecided about how to get round some riverside cliffs, I fell into tortuous discussion with a pleasant old roadmender who spoke only the local language and a little German. He sensed the problem, but I couldn't think of anything that meant 'across country' except that I didn't want the road. *Keine Strasse.* I was a walker. '*Ich laufe lieber,*' I said. Pointing to what seemed a likely trail through Little Reisdorf, he trudged off, wishing me a warm good day. A British car pulled up. I didn't altogether like the way the driver turned to his wife and said: 'Let's ask this old boy.' I certainly resented his imperious 'Hey you!' and strolled over rather truculently.

'*Sprechen französisch?*'

'A bit,' I said. 'What's the problem?'

'Oh you speak some English?'

I nodded. It seemed obvious.

'Well, I tell you what. We're lost. *Nous sommes perdus, vous comprenez?* We're trying to get to Vianden. But they say there's an obstruction – *une obstruction* – at Wangerton. Don't quite see how we can get round.'

'Go back to Bettendorf and head north. It's a main road.'

'I say, that's a very good idea. Y'know you speak English *awfully* well. Where did you pick it up?'

'Thank you,' I said, 'as a matter of fact I was a prisoner-of-war at Eton.'

'Oh *were* you. That's *most* interesting. *Au revoir, M'sieur.*'

'Goodbye,' I said.

As they peck at the buds in the orchards of Hessenmuhle, the bullfinches call '*Dieu Dieu*'. A godless practice, but pretty in effect, since at each light gust of wind the blossoms fall like snow into the waters of the White Erenz.

There are two rivulets called the Erenz, the White and the Black, and the land between is rugged and remarkable for a most muscular breed of men. Stripped to the waist that morning, they were scything hay with great strokes that hissed more than half-circle through the soft fescue. These *Erenzvolk* are reckoned to be descendants of that gallant tribe the Treveri, who fought so fiercely against Caesar that after subjugation he declared them a free people. Some were granted rank in the Praetorian Guard, where their great height and ample display of limbs must have caused a flutter among the nursemaids of Rome.

From that stock came a red-bearded pagan chief called Roderic of the castle of Zorodersbourg whose courtship of a Christian maid has been so nicely put together by that most excellent biographer of the Grand Duchy the Reverend Thomas Henry Passmore in his book *In Further Ardenne* that I prefer to let him tell it largely in his own words.

Now there was a noble German maiden, Schwanhilde, who dwelt with her younger sister Vallida in a great country house near Christnach. Both, having made a trial of persecutions, had given themselves to Christ. It came about that the fierce Roderic cast hot eyes upon Schwanhilde, and would make her his. But the Christian lady hushed her answering heart, and made reply that this could never be, save only if he should give up his low gods and be a Christian. Then Roderic swore a great oath by Odin or such, and took the brave girl and shut her up in a dark dungeon, where she languished for months; but though he came every day to the door and coaxed and threatened, she swerved not a hair's breadth from her former word.

In the manner of the times, Roderic was eventually converted in rather a miraculous way, and asked the maid to marry him. Then comes the surprise. Up to that moment he did not know that, far from seeking deliverance, she had been praying night and day for his soul. She loved him with all her heart.

Passmore says: 'This touch of nature about Schwanhilde makes me prefer her to the general run of old-time saint-maidens whose prude hearts were ice turned towards their pagan wooers. Those unnatural ladies had no temptation to conquer.'

Little Switzerland, that wild country beyond the Black Erenz, is far too dark and deeply fissured to deserve the name. All is chaotic. Rocks perched on vertical cliffs have been sculpted by ice and water into the shape of dragons and gigantic toads. Streams percolate through cracks hundreds of feet in depth. In places you can just manage to squeeze through, but if the walls closed by no more than a foot you would be crushed to death. Seen from the height of the Falcon's Rock, people walking about on the floor of the defiles look like cheese-mites in the ruins of a rich Stilton. But they pour in from Berdorf and Vogelsmuhle, anxious to see the Breeches of the Devil, the Gorge of the Wolf and the Pillars of Hercules. One signpost offers the choice between the *Werschrumschluff* and the *Zickzackschluff*, and make what you will of that.

Little Switzerland is a platform of weathered sandstone pushed up by side pressures into an enormous arch. The topmost rocks were unable to withstand the strain and cracked open. In poured rivulets that scoured out the softer sediments, leaving behind a rock garden on the Cyclopean scale. I didn't take too kindly to the place, but it may have been a touch of indigestion.

Late that afternoon a storm broke over the Gorge of the Wolf, but with plenty of shelter from those overhanging rocks I rather enjoyed the echoing barrage of thunder. All is humid there. Ferns droop, mosses glisten and water weeps from the rock face. Underfoot are liverworts, adder's-tongue, a pallid sort of garlic, and orchids with minute green and white flowers.

The storm passed. About five hundred paces beyond the gorge the track slipped out into the bright light of a belvedere where, a mile below, is the little town of Echternacht on the edge of a far-reaching plain.

The streets that night were thick with tourists and other sorts of pilgrims with here and there a skull cap and touch of priestly purple. Outside the rebuilt basilica, the crowds were noisy and the smell of *fritures* tremendous. If I record all this somewhat dryly, it is because I walked into the town with my stomach barking, an upset brought about, I suspect, by an incautious drink from a stream infused with mica, a mineral that can induce something close to dysentery. Madame recommended *un Buff* which, according to the label, is an elixir highly spoken of by a once-dyspeptic Prince of the Blood who is now reported to be living comfortably near Neuchâtel. I took one cautious gulp, toyed with an omelette and went to bed, hiccuping gently over the life of St Willibrord.

In the seventh century that fearless Northumbrian, the man they called the athlete of God, walked the length of Europe with eleven companions, venturing into places where he was often unwelcome. Yet thousands were converted on the spot. Hundreds asked for more instruction. A few had doubts. There was Radbot, king of the Friesians, who, with one of his august legs already in the baptismal font, asked, cautiously, where he could hope to meet up with his illustrious ancestors. 'In hell with all other scurvy heathen,' said Bishop Wolfert, a prelate unremarkable for his tact.

'Oho!' replied Radbot, promptly removing his leg. 'Then I prefer feasting with my forbears in Valhalla to singing hymns with your starveling crew,' and another soul was lost to God.

For all that, the twelve gained footholds in half a dozen kingdoms and set up a great mission station at Echternacht, where in those days it was unusual for an assertive foreigner to die quietly in his bed.

Well past his sixtieth year, Willibrord sent for his old companion Wynfrith Boniface and said: 'You are the better man. I grow old. Take my crook and tend my sheep. Let me seek my cell and scan that account I must render soon.' Boniface shook his head, gently. But that night the old man quietly slipped away in his sleep.

In Echternacht on Whit Tuesday they parade through the streets in his honour and dance until they can dance no more. The *Springprozession* is a very old ceremony, but nobody can say how old, or how it started. The legend concerns a hypnotic tune played by a man condemned to death. It's likely that the dance began as a kind of homoeopathic litany used to ward off epidemics of chorea which were common centuries ago. There may be a tenuous link between the two since nervous disorders, such as St Vitus dance, were thought to stem from sorcery and the man on the scaffold had been charged with dabbling in the black arts. The story is that for his last wish he asked to be handed his violin. He played a jaunty tune that set everyone dancing merrily until they discovered they couldn't stop. Even a bishop had some difficulty in exorcising what was clearly a misapplied art and by the time he had finished a fearful malediction, the man had slipped away.

In Echternacht that morning they were out in the streets at first light. The fortunate sat on chairs and behind them the crowds lined the procession route in thick ranks. They leaned out of windows and stretched in a double row across the bridge. Under the flags and streamers you saw signs of festival everywhere and yet among the people you sensed serious waiting, as for a solemn thing about to happen.

The ceremony began on the authentic note of anti-climax. As it does in crowds, the word went round quickly that four bishops hadn't turned up. Perhaps a flat tyre, a missing mitre or a minor dispute over precedence. But they couldn't start without them and the crowds had to wait, which they did with no impatience for the bars had been open since dawn.

Towards ten o'clock, or perhaps a little later, the chief of police raised a cheer by cycling round perilously fast, announcing through a loud-hailer that all was well. The missing prelates had been found. The great bell in the basilica began to toll. From somewhere above the Church of St Peter and St Paul came the deeply-intoned litany: *Sancte Willibrorde, stella lucida, patriae nostrae, ora pro nobis*. And down they swept, the hierarchs of Christendom. First a cardinal, and then an archbishop with his morse blazing on a cape of woven gold. And then at least four bishops with their choirs all chanting. *Sancte Willibrorde, almae pater pauperum, ora pro nobis*. Coblenz or it might have been Metz looked pale as he limped ahead of his retinue, his right leg stiffened by arthritis and prayer. He blessed the crowds and they lowered their heads and crossed themselves, murmuring the familiar chant.

As they walked past, still chanting, there came the sound of a distant band. In that solemn atmosphere it sounded strangely out of place – as a street trombonist might have interrupted an open-air prayer meeting. The notes were vulgar and brassy, but there's no denying the jauntiness of the tune. The Echternacht dance goes *Dah-dah di-dah; diddy dah dah dah*, borrowing heavily from the *Silver Fleet* or that old German air *Adam hatte sieben Söhne*. Behind the band came the dancers who danced and danced with such resolution that you had the impression that if anyone fell down, he would have to be dragged out of the lines quickly or else those behind would dance over him.

Linked by lightly held handkerchiefs, they held up their arms, gracefully, in the manner of a Highland fling. Some seemed too old by far for that sort of exertion. But on they came, old men and old women and young bucks and mothers with little children who hopped about looking rather puzzled by it all. I saw a dancing soldier with his arm in a sling and a dancing matron with an enormous pair of breasts with a fascinating rhythm of their own.

Pious fathers of the Church have done their best to stamp out the festival, an irrational idea since religious dancing is older than history and at Echternacht the sacred is nicely intermingled with the secular. One moment your ears are blasted out by the cornets of Luxembourg fire brigade. Then come rank upon rank of dancers. But almost before the noise has died down to a gentle roar you hear *Sancte Willibrorde* chanted by yet another bishop and his train.

It takes almost four hours for the whole procession to wind out of the basilica and return by way of the *rue des Merciers* for the busy organizers are constantly pouring more companies in at the starting point. The object is to let everyone of repute join in behind one of the church groups. And even when the affair has officially come to an end there are bands playing at street corners and late-comers dancing under the flowering lilacs. Some of the choirs wander round the town still chanting as they collect alms. *Sancte Willibrorde, alma pater pauperum.*

For this town this is by far the busiest day of the year. Many visitors make it an occasion for an annual holiday, and back in their villages no doubt they relate how in the streets of Echternacht that morning they saw the whole of life whirl by. And death too.

Just outside the town a small group stood around a car with its wheels in the air. A priest knelt beside a shape almost entirely covered by a gendarme's cape. *Sancte Willibrorde salus infirmorum.*

Down the rocky track that leads to Grevenmacher you come to the riverside port of Wasserbilig. It means 'cheap water', the place where most of the rivers of Luxembourg join the Moselle. When the grapes ripen, the whole village is up to its knees in wine: Riesling and Sylvaner, Auxerrois, Pinot and Traminer. This, as anyone can see, is the *Gutland* with soft mists in the morning, a rich soil and not a bit of schist in sight.

What with the warmth, the faint thunder of pigeons and that great river for company, I might have sung a *Mosellied* had I known one, but some fool of a truck driver knocked me into the ditch and the kind of day I had hoped for lay in ruins. Looking back on the incident, I don't think he meant to scrape past quite so close, but something protruding from his tailboard caught the edge of my pack and over I went. I picked myself up, unhurt, but angry. The blind anger of fright. I pounded after him, for he had turned into a quarry at the side of the road owned by a man called J. Schmuck.

Now in Yiddish, *Schmuck*, as I know, is a very rude word. Vituperation is difficult in a wholly alien tongue. Seeing the driver, I bore down on him and shouted 'You *bloody* Schmuck!'

At this he looked puzzled. '*Nein, nein*' he said. '*Josef Schmuck, Zementwerk*', and imagining, I suppose, that I knew the boss, he insisted on shaking my hand.

At the top of the Calvary steps at Grevenmacher is a bone-white chapel where martins nest under the outstretched arms of Christ on the cross. Far below the Moselle curls round the town. The air that afternoon was heavily scented with hawthorn and lime and there I slept, stuporous with wines from the *caves* of Bernard Massard, St Laurent, and I forget who besides. Somehow they got the idea that I wrote about wine for the press, and the owners of those cellars offered me their best. One invitation followed another. They explained how rather more than half their crop went to Belgium, a third to Holland and quite a lot to Germany for intermingling with sparkling Moselles. But they had their mind on the British market and notwithstanding my weak protests that I could do nothing about it they charged my glass again and again.

I would have given much for a pint of light ale when I awoke, but it was not to be had. Back in my lodgings the company had been looking with quiet satisfaction at a dozen bottles of Pinot left in my name and it was close on three o'clock before we got to bed.

On the German side of the river the air is grossly polluted by saffron-yellow smoke from the chimneys of yet another cement works owned by Joseph Schmuck. Into that murk I strode, marvelling that it hadn't already blighted the fringe of the finest vineyards on the Moselle. In a spirit of pure inquiry I sampled a glass at Wellen and found that light Moselle infinitely preferable to what my friends had pressed on me. This is unfair on the Luxembourgers, who are producing inexpensive table wines. The Germans, on the other hand, are not general practitioners, they are specialists. They have developed the special qualities of grapes grown in a cold climate. By ruthless viticulture, they have created some of the finest wines in the world. The wonder is that the difference is so marked on opposite sides of the same river, particularly since in terms of sunlight the Moselle thereabouts flows only slightly towards the Germans' advantage.

The vineyards stretch out as far as the eye can see. On one of the service tracks a tractor chuffed past, slowly, hauling a cart-load of jolly Moselle maidens on their way out to work. With their hods held high, like pikemen, they hailed me heartily and lustily, too, or so I took it, for one massive wench shouted something incomprehensible and lifted her skirts high above her knees. They can't have understood what I shouted back, but it appeared to please them hugely.

Above the music of skylarks that morning came the fearful clatter of helicopters. Spindly machines like dragonflies were constantly in the air, spraying the vines with a pesticide. The Moselle carried a scum of small dead fish, the food of a host of buzzards and crows. They had died from an overload of one of the organo-chlorines carried down into the river from the vineyards above. In time, the birds that fed on them would either die or lay infertile eggs. This is the infection of a whole chain of organisms on a scale never experienced before, and it sickened me to see that lethal mist floating down from the sky. This is not to suggest that modern viticulturists should go back to mixtures of wood ash and cow urine as they did in the old days. But they could do better than employ a series of poisons which are almost indestructible, polluting the very depths of the oceans.

I put this to a chemist employed by one of the syndicates in Grevenmacher. He agreed but shook his head. 'The oceans,' he said, 'are a long, long way from Luxembourg, and this is a highly competitive business.'

If those Moselle maidens – the ones who had passed me in the vineyard – had known they were dancing with a man who had been harbouring a rather irrational grudge against their country and its people for the greater part of his life, they might have been less cordial, but, looking back on the incident, I don't think it would have made much difference. The two world wars that prick my skin of prejudices probably meant no more to them than the Crimea and Spion Kop does to me. And drink is democratic stuff, and it certainly wasn't their first that morning. They recognized me as soon as I walked in to the tavern. *Ach mein Liebchen! Der fabelhafter Engländer!*

My German is, in fact, largely limited to entomological terminology and things like: 'A white wine, please,' and 'Where is the lavatory?' But I didn't get the chance to say much. Somebody shoved a coin in the juke-box. One of the biggest girls I have ever seen began to wriggle like a belly dancer. She seized my hand and we spun round together to something extraordinarily noisy.

After a bout or two with her friends, Massive Mitzi came back for more. But I shook my head, wearily, and pointed to the bar. I meant to give the impression that I wanted a drink. They took this to mean they were all getting one, and they shouted loudly for the Herr Ober, who, I suspect, had taken refuge in the cellar.

He came up the stairs, cautiously. What they said I don't know, but they pointed at me, proudly, as hunters might point at something unusual they had just captured alive. He smiled, and in warm idiomatic American said: 'Good morning. Zares no need to buy dese dames a drink if you don' wanna. Zay got a heap o' dough.'

Gallantly, I told him to fill 'em up.

'Four marks,' he said. 'Vair ya headin' for?'

I told him and, with the groundwork sketched in, I asked him where he had picked up his English.

'In the cooler,' he said. 'I did eighteen months in Florida.'

'How on earth did you get there?'

'In a submarine. Zay fished us out of the Caribbean.'

'Were you sunk?'

'Nah! Ve soonk ourselves. No fuel left.'

'Did you volunteer for the subs?'

'Volunteer *für die Unterseeboten*? You most be kiddin'! Zay scared de hell outa me. I wouldn't volunteer for nutting! Zay tried to put me into ze tank brigade, but I say I am scared of leetle closed spaces. I have the medical certificate to show it. So vair do I find myself? In a lousy submarine! Zose army guys, day got a *grreat* sense of humour, eh?'

I nodded. The same jokes. The same misery. The same war. I began to feel a lot better about the Germans. As one old ex-serviceman to another, I asked what he was doing in American waters.

With his finger he drew the outlines of the North Atlantic on the top of the bar. There were fifteen submarines. One after another, they slipped out of Kiel at night. To get down to the South Atlantic they went north to Norway and across to Iceland and Greenland and south to Labrador. They hugged the American coastline so close they saw the lights of Atlantic City and Nassau Sound. There were no patrols inside the three-mile limit, he said.

'How did you refuel?'

'Zare was supposed to be a tanker waiting off Curaçao.'

'*Supposed* to be?'

'Yeah! Zay soonk 'er before ve got zair. Fifteen leetle submarines and no Momma, eh? So ve soonk ourselves.'

The bar suddenly seemed enormously quiet. The Moselle maidens had gone. Before they trooped out, Mitzi gave me a smacking kiss on both cheeks and her friends pressed on me a glass of wine the size of a goldfish bowl.

Sipping it, I turned over my old store of prejudices. 'Did you hate the English?' I asked him. 'What did you think about us when you were in that submarine?'

'*Hate* you?' he said. 'By God. Ve hate nobody except zat crazy captain. He wanted to be an admiral. Ve had one great beeg idea. To stay alive.'

Out in the bright sunshine, I felt disinclined to hustle. The clouds seemed to be moving in badly superimposed pairs.

> *O Mosella*
> *Du hast ja so viel Wein*

The Germans call them Rhine wines. It takes an expert to distinguish a hock from a Moselle, which, in modest quantities, is less alcoholic and in bouquet and flavour more delicate than any other wine I know of. About a Dhroner Hofberg or a Bernkasteler Doktor there is something close to indefectibility, a wine such as Athena pressed on Penelope to ensure her constant affection. Of the two grapes that grow most commonly thereabouts, the Sylvaner is apple green and almost translucent, the Riesling more pale and lightly freckled with gold. Yet between those heavily-laden beneficent terraces flows a foul river.

In the restaurant above the bridge at Remich they offer *fruits de Moselle*, a plate of local fish. I looked out of the window and saw a bird of prey float past, dead, its wings pathetically outstretched like the eagle on the German flag. And I ordered something else.

Lorraine

Instead of trying to dodge the *Pays du Fer*, the ironfields of Lorraine, I walked through that blighted country, direct, mostly at night. As Metz sounded more attractive than Saarbrücken and Sarreguemines, I clung to the moonlit Moselle from Sierck to Sentzich, sleeping under a cart from midnight until near four in the morning. An hour later, the farmsteads woke up with much noise. At the barking of dogs, I cut a stout stick and walked on, sleepily but with more confidence. After a bout with a brute the previous day, I had grown nervous of curs that slunk round the back of my bare legs.

To the south there appeared gravel pits, a sure sign of a river deep in the urban way of life. Beyond them rose pencil-thin blocks of flats and steelworks as big as battleships under plumes of rusty smoke. On the outskirts of Thionville, I tossed the stick aside and put on long pants to look less like John the Baptist in a town where respectable folk are got up in blue jeans and a beret. There I yawned over a large pork chop fried in fat and whole peppers, and made for the Tower of Fleas, a wonderful museum, full of treasure. But I saw it through half-closed eyes. Unable to resist great waves of fatigue, I went to sleep with my back against the tombstone of Marguerite de Sierck.

The curator woke me up. He shook me by the shoulder, gently; he made it abundantly clear that I was not unwelcome there, but, alas, he said, they were obliged to close for lunch in a few minutes' time. Perhaps I would care to come to his office for a glass of wine. He had what he called a great feebleness for the English. A family in London had done much for his son during the war. Had I seen their armour, their jewellery and ancient glass? He poured some Bordeaux into a goblet used by the first Count of Luxembourg and talked about the tower. In his opinion,

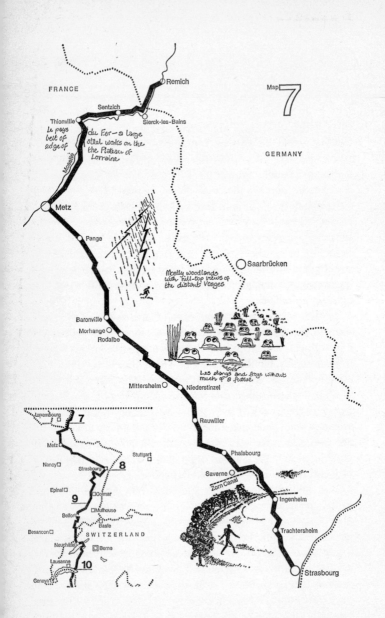

FRANCE

Remich

Map 7

Sentzich

Thionville

Sierck-les-Bains

Le pays
belt of
edge of

du Fer—a large
steel works on the
the Plateau of
Lorraine

GERMANY

Moselle

Metz

Panga

Saarbrücken

Mostly woodlands
with hill-top views of
the distant Vosges

Baronville

Morhange

Rodalbe

Les étangs and frogs without
much of a feature

Mittersheim

Niederstinzel

Rauwiller

Phalsbourg

Saverne

Zorn Canal

Ingenheim

Trachtersheim

Strasbourg

Luxembourg

7

Metz

Stuttgart

Nancy

Strasbourg

8

Epinal

Colmar

9

Belfort

Mulhouse

Besancon

Basle

SWITZERLAND

Neuchatel

Berne

Lausanne

10

Geneva

the keep of a medieval castle got its name not from fleas (*puces*), but from the deep well shafts (*puits*) into which the last defenders had been hurled. We spent most of that afternoon together and, on his advice, I set off for Metz on a road much quieter than the national highway.

To the west the sky glows from the light of coke ovens. You can hear the faint roar of industry. There is an acrid taste in the breeze, like a copper coin on the tongue. But to the east are woodlands, the home of nightjars and softly-complaining owls. Along that curious boundary I walked for five hours, stopping only twice.

In a seedy-looking bistro near the great ironworks at Guénange I thought I had incautiously walked into a fight. Two piratical-looking Algerians began to shout at each other, their faces scarce a foot apart. Several of the company joined in. I couldn't reach the door, easily, so I stayed. With contrived nonchalance, I untied my pack in search of a notebook. The effect might be compared to bringing a caged owl into a noisy classroom. The shouting stopped. Everyone swivelled round and watched intently as I fumbled about among jingling tent pegs and underwear in plastic bags. When, through sheer nervousness, I spilt a handful of sulfa tablets on the floor, they leaped about to pick them up, and even the Algerians smiled.

Outside in the warm night, the garish glow of the *Pays de Fer* sank to small rosettes of light. A few cars raced past with head-lamps glaring and horns tooting in dots and dashes. I listened with care, for a working knowledge of tootology is important to anyone foolhardy enough to venture on to an unlit road at night.

At the first toot you are obliged to decide quickly whether to leap for the hedge or wave boldly and walk on. Although the dots usually betoken affection and dashes animosity, the number of dots is critical. It shouldn't exceed three. As for the dashes, the more sustained the blast, the higher the degree of irritation on the part of the tootee. As some horns are predestined to raucousness at birth, the texture of the tone can be safely disregarded. I like best a couple of brisk toots – *staccatissimo* – and got several that night.

About eleven o'clock I walked into a very superior roadside restaurant with built-in music, a charcoal grill and candles on the tables. I sat down feeling somewhat like a coal heaver at a cocktail party. There seemed to be no place to park my pack other than under a table, an act which would have got me chucked out of almost any classy eating house in Britain. But the company looked at it with affection. Most of them bade me good night as they went out, and one sad-faced man pressed me to join the party at his table. I refused, politely, on the grounds that I had notes to write, but he wasn't to be put off that easily. Might he sit with me for a few minutes? Where had I been? Where was I heading for?

At the word Metz, he said he and his wife lived there. Would I spend the night with them? They could drive me there in about ten minutes. I went through the ritual explanations, but he brushed them aside. He said if I insisted on walking, why then, they would wait up for me. I protested that it was near eight miles. It would take me at least two hours to get there. Probably more. But he talked me into looking him up, a decision I regretted as soon as I got outside.

Moral cowardice, I thought. I had taken the easy way out. If I didn't want to see the man again, why on earth hadn't I put him off from the start? Merely to appear polite? I was under no obligation to him. Or was I? I debated the point and trudged on, seeing nothing but good camping sites by the roadside.

A long walk at light-infantry speed. The later it got the faster I went and the more ill-tempered I became. I don't know what would have happened in that large and wholly deserted city if I hadn't met a young soldier who slipped out of a house, pulling his jacket on, saying he ought to have been in barracks an hour ago. He left me at the door of a large mansion flat. A light shone over the porch and down came my friend in his dressing-gown. His wife had gone to bed.

He had laid out coffee, liqueurs and pastries and he talked and he talked until I was too tired to listen more.

All his life, he said, he had wanted to do something different, to explore something, perhaps to travel alone as I did. But somehow he could never find the time. There was always something that needed to be attended to. And he could never make up his mind what to do. Could I advise him? How did one start?

At this I sighed inwardly. Questions about what a walk costs in terms of time, exertion and cash can be answered quite easily.

I know something about shoes, clothing, equipment, and route finding. But at half past two in the morning I didn't feel like going in to questions of motivation and *résolution* and other fine-sounding words. At least not when I felt desperately tired. And when I discovered that among other business enterprises, he owned a travel agency, I didn't know what to say. It all sounded so sad. The long trips by plane. The company of other travel agents. The search for something new in Africa, the Far East and South America. He reckoned he had seen most of the world.

Quite unexpectedly, he said: 'Are we not all searching for something? And I have a little plan. Please don't laugh. Perhaps one day I will become a *valet de chambre* and write about what I discover. That will be an exploration, for who knows more than a personal servant about how people really behave?'

What would he discover? That all men are different? Or much the same? Or is this but another version of that man who went searching for happiness, that man of whom it was said Death followed on his heels until, finally, when he reached his goal, Death bent over his shoulder, curious to see what he had found?

Metz used to be called *La Pucelle* – The Virgin – and Messins claim that until the Prussians got the better of her in 1785, she remained wholly chaste. A pretty story but wholly untrue. When the Romans pulled out, Attila sacked the place and, through downright treachery, the Virgin fell into the hands of the French in the middle of the sixteenth century. Before that sordid affair, she ranked high among the free cities of Europe. It was reckoned an honour to be a descendant of the ancient Mediomatrici, and over their godsons at the font proud godfathers used to murmur: 'May you become Mayor of Metz or else the King of France.'

Metz today is a ruin of fortifications around a maze of streets and when the sun catches the curve of the river, the impression from the roof of the great cathedral is of a rusty sabre. Below is the Bridge of the Dead where criminals bound with leather thongs were unceremoniously tossed into the Moselle. By circling outwards from the cathedral, I found St Peter of Nonains, reputedly the oldest church in Europe, the Oratory of the Templars and much I can't remember. But I couldn't find that ancient ghetto, the *Jurue*, once the home of François Rabelais whose works I consider to be among the most amusing ever written. Metz, I think, does less than honour to the Oracle of the Holy Bottle and I have written to the mayor about it, pointing out that the little tumble-down alleyway below the *Place St Croix* is not even marked on the official street plan. Rabelais probably went to live there through sheer poverty.

In the words of a local historian, 'Charlemagne sought to domesticate the Jews by tolerant laws.' They were permitted to trade, but not in new goods. Eventually they were allowed to sell meat and became the butchers of Metz. But for all that, they were fearfully persecuted, especially during the Middle Ages when thousands were burned alive as propitiatory sacrifice in times of plague and famine. The *Jurue* remained a ghetto until the end of the nineteenth century when the community began to disperse.

The story is that when a tourist saw a priest in full canonicals entering a house, he said: 'Aha! So nowadays you are all Christians here?' And back came the answer. 'No, M'sieur, the place is infested by Protestants.' But, as I say, try as I did, I couldn't find the place on my own.

A car park attendant directed me to a synagogue nearly half a mile to the north where an old, courteous and very well-informed road sweeper insisted on leading me back, very slowly. With his brush over his shoulder, like a rifle, he pointed out the less-well-known sights of the town, making a slight detour to include a fire station and the Central Maternity Hospital. At my badly disguised impatience, he paused for a moment and said: 'Forgive me, M'sieur, but from what are you running away?' Feeling a bit ashamed, I muttered something about the time and fell back on a pace more in keeping with his years.

After what seemed like hours, we trudged down the open gutters of the steep *Jurue* where, outside the Chapel of St Genest, he pointed to a locked-up garden. 'The house no longer exists,' he said, 'but there it was that M. Rabelais lived.' It might have been but a few years ago.

Saying it was but a small service, he would not accept so much – or so little – as a drink. His dignity touched me. 'When people take the trouble to do dignified acts, it is worthwhile to take a little more, and allow the dignity to be common to all concerned.' Thus Robert Louis Stevenson. But, as he says, in our brave

Anglo-Saxon countries 'we do our good and bad with a high hand, almost offensively, and make even our alms a witness bearing and an act of war against the wrong.'

All you can learn of Rabelais in the *Jurue* today is what sort of people turn up, as I did, and ask questions which the local bakers and furniture makers admit freely they can't answer. Such people, they said, were usually writers and scholars, implying they were usually better dressed than I was. With a touch of piety, another asked what did it matter where he lived for though he was a famous man, he was not, as he understood it, a good one. At this, the master of opulent prose would have roared with laughter, for after fifteen years he threw his frock into the nettles and set about bashing Authority with as much gusto as ever Friar John flailed about him with that tremendous staff.

Rabelais came to Metz as a refugee and set up as a physician there. In Paris his protector had died and the sophisters of the Sorbonne wanted to slam a gaol door in the face of their runaway friar. For what had he called them? Those Sorbonagres, Sorbonigenes and Sorbonisans, 'Oddipol joltheads who in their disputes do not search for truth, but for contradictions only and debate.'

Why a man of such flaming vitality, a boozer and lecher unafraid of hell, high scholarship or the Holy Catholic Church, should have ranted against women at such length is intriguing. In all his wild tales about routs, harlotry and belly-bumping in general there is nothing to suggest even a tinge of homosexuality. But, aside from canting clerics and schoolmen, the harpies of the human race are of the unfair sex, 'well-skilled in the pretty vales and small fees of the pleasant trade . . . if the Devil will not have them to bag, he must ring hard the spigot and stop the bung-hole'.

Rabelais is the wandering scholar writ large; the intellectual anti-intellectual, the roistering phrasemonger, the acceptor of joyful reality who turns up unexpectedly, knocks back a skinful of liquor and climbs out of the back window before the bishop's men close in. Much of his life is a mystery. He appears and disappears. And after six years in Metz he vanished as surely as a flame blown out. Nobody knows where.

What happened? Did those whey-faced Sorbonisards catch up with him? Did he rot in gaol and die? Did he grease his boots for that last journey and recant?

I turned the questions over in the Café Matthis, the nearest wine-shop to the Master's house which is about the most that can be said for it. A dull place used by local tradesmen. But scarcely had I paid and made to move off when, from a distance, came the sound of martial brass. At that stirring *rumpitty-tump* the company brightened up as if touched by the wand of youth. Pushing their glasses and racing papers aside, they crowded to the door.

Down the *Jurue* swept a band led by a mustachioed giant who tossed a stave in the air. Somebody shouted: 'Look! There they are. At the back.' And a few paces behind the rest there marched two trombonists improbably got up in peaked shakos to pass muster among military musicians.

They looked out of place, and awkward fellows, too. The smaller of the two shouted something loud and abusive at the drum major, at which that man accomplished a marvellous feat. On a bend on that steep hill he swung round, and even as he marched backwards, still in step, he told them plainly to go away. They broke ranks at the door of the Matthis and strode in, bubbling with indignation and the band marched on bereft of its mutinous auxiliaries.

Both, it seems, were civilians, accomplished players who had won several prizes. For some forthcoming civic occasion they had been invited to supplement the military band. But the trial run had clearly not been a success. There had been a lengthy argument about the way they held their instruments, and one of them blew a brisk cadenza to show how it had come about.

On a march, the oscillating slide of a trombone is particularly obtrusive. Ideally, it should pass over the shoulder of the man in front without catching him one behind the ear. The angle depends on how the lips are applied to the embouchure. The short man had lost a front tooth. He was obliged to hold his instrument down, like a man shooting at a rabbit, and this brought him up against the backside of the tenor drum. But his companion liked to hold his instrument up in the air which meant he couldn't see where he was going. He tended to wander off on his own. The drum major had shouted at him and he had shouted back.

'A stupid man, that,' said the downslider. 'Does he think we are musical machines?'

Not a bit of it, they were assured. Without doubt they were the finest trombonists in Lorraine. Nobody could play quite like them. At this they wet their lips, liberally, and brassed out *Laissez les passer*, the defiant ditty about what the Messins thought of their conqueror, Louis the Sun King.

> *Lou Lou la, laissez les passer*
> *Les Français dans La Lorraine,*
> *Lou Lou la, laissez les passer*
> *Ils auront du mal assez.*

When they really began to whoop it up I slipped out quietly in search of an eating house recommended by the *patron*.

In Metz they say that had the pig but wings there wouldn't be a finer bird in the sky. They dote on pork – neck, spare rib, loin, belly, split head, chops, trotters or leg boiled or roasted. They enliven it with plums *à la Vosgienne*; they have their own version of *Schweinsschogel* and *Selianka*. Bacon is pushed into a tart *à la flamme*, and every eating house in town serves up a *Potée de Lorraine*, a huge broth of peppery beans, potatoes and cabbage from which you can fork out almost any organ or limb of the pig including a curly bit of the tail.

On that sultry afternoon I wished I had chosen lighter fare and, but for an encouraging belch from a fellow diner, I might have pushed my plate aside. At his '*C'est bon, n'est-ce pas?*' I nodded and tried to think of something polite. From the happy little chorus of grunts on all sides, I might have come out with 'Here there is certainly an atmosphere', but I thought of it too late and went on eating, slowly.

Some trace the Messins' addiction to pork to a story about the Mountain of the Gods, a curiously-shaped hill to the west of the town. It became such a holy place in the days of the Mediomatrici that priests planted groves of young oaks on the summit and forbade anyone to venture there except in orderly procession.

Now, as every ecologist knows, young oaks that grow in places undisturbed by man are much to the fancy of the wild boar, and within a few eclipses the animals had taken possession of the holy mountain. They rooted up the oaklings and scared people off. The priests tried out all the spells and incantations they could think of, but to no avail. For wild boars the mountain was truly heavenly. When it became positively dangerous to move about without spearmen at hand, the priests sought help from the chief seer of the Triboci, a neighbouring tribe renowned for its sorcerers.

An old man turned up with an amulet of boars' teeth and a distillation of *Heracleum*, a plant rather like the hemlock which some call hogweed or scabby hands. What he chanted during the whole of one night will never be known, but the story is that at his last great curse the scream of the hogs could be heard far down in the valley. And then it ceased, for a miraculous thing happened. Centuries before a Galilean re-enacted that incident in the country of the Gadarenes, the hogs plunged over the cliff and died in their hundreds on the reddish sandstone far below. The animals never returned to the mountain and the Messins never lost their passion for pork.

That afternoon I set off for Strasbourg, crossing the length of Lorraine in just over four days of hard walking, a distance of about a hundred miles. I recall this with quiet satisfaction since there are few tracks worth the name and I ran into some violent storms. To get through a network of *routes forestières* I drew an almost straight line on the map from Metz to Saverne and beyond and clung to it as closely as discretion and trespass allowed. If hurry is the resort of the faithless, I stand reproved. I expected little from Lorraine and what I found came as a bonus.

Borny lies to the south-east of Metz and you would be inclined to ignore it as I did. A quiet, unremarkable little place with potato fields among the brickworks. But walk on perhaps a mile, towards the handsomely named forests of Ars-Laquenexy and you may come across the Wood of the Dead. I ventured in on the trail of a golden oriole and remained there, intrigued at the sight of so many moss-dappled gravestones. There are no paths through that wood and some of the stones are almost wholly overgrown by briars and honeysuckle. With difficulty I made out the names of Werning and Bergman, Jurgen, Rommel, Hulst, Stuckmeyer, Widau, Fischer, Weinfloth and Gott. No inscriptions. Just names.

Almost hidden behind an immense beech is a statue to the Goddess of Victory. In her arms she holds a wounded soldier. The footstone is dedicated to the *Vestphalischer Infanterie*

Regiment XIII, a relic of the Franco-Prussian war. The oriole called again: *toodlee-oh, toodlee-oh* and in that quiet wood it sounded like a call to arms.

High up in the beech I caught a glimpse of one of the most striking-looking songsters in Europe, a bright yellow bird with black wings. Still trumpeting, the creature flew into a clearing where from a nest like a ball of hay there came back a somewhat sullen screech. The hen bird, a rather drab creature, seemed to be saying she had expected him back hours ago and, anyhow, he was a fool to be making all that noise. At this the cock became enormously excited. He plunged through the trees showing off every glint in his golden mail, and when she replied, still without much enthusiasm, he poured out every call in orieldom, as if utterly delighted at finding her alone.

From map and compass it looked as if Pange lay straight ahead on a bearing to Rémilly, but in a forest ride you can never be sure. A dip in the ground or a detour to avoid a patch of scrub and you are forty degrees off course. With some food in my pack I could have cheerfully ignored a small deviation, but I hadn't so much as a biscuit, and, as it grew dark, I thought often of soup, a lightly grilled steak and a pint of Bordeaux.

From the top of a high forest ride, I could see no lights, no friendly church steeple. Pange might have been unceremoniously destroyed and trees planted in its place. I had overshot that little valley by at least three miles. A woodman led me partway back and I must have completely misunderstood what he said, for I thought more and more about that steak.

They were friendly enough at the little pub, but they didn't serve food. Why should they? There was a hotel about six miles away and a bus would arrive in half an hour they said. When I shook my head, a young lad, who imagined, I suppose, that I was short of money, offered to drive me there. My explanation must have puzzled them for an old man said: 'Then what else *can* we do for you?' Before I got back to the subject of food, an ample woman beckoned me into the kitchen. Pointing to a bare wooden table she said they took their own meal there at nine o'clock. If I cared to join them, I could eat what they ate.

They served *potée de Lorraine*. If I'd had the sense to pitch my tent in the field at the back, I might have rounded off a good day, or at least dodged the storm that night, but I felt they'd done enough for me and set off after dinner to look for a site in the forest.

Towards eleven o'clock, an uneasy breeze arose and lightning flickered silently, like a faulty fluorescent tube. In that weird light I came across a stone tunnel no more than four feet in height and almost entirely overgrown with ivy. It led into a partly-buried cavern used, I suppose, for storing salt. I crawled in on all fours to find it reasonably clean and dry inside, though somewhat cramped. I dragged in a bed of soft willow branches and, with the tent for mattress, I stretched out, grateful for the shelter.

During the night I recall the crash of thunder and much rain, but slept on until a few ice-cold drops fell on my face through a crack in the roof. In an effort to stem that leak, a lot of earth and moss fell out and a lot of water gushed in.

Feeling unutterably miserable, I squatted under that shower with my tent around my shoulders like a shawl, uncertain what to do. The time: three o'clock in the morning. Should I make a run for it, or stay put? I should get wet whatever I did. Better perhaps to stay there, but when both tunnel and cavern began to fill up with water, I packed up my wet gear and went out into a storm of spectacular violence.

The lightning tore the sky open. I winced at each discharge, but stumbled on through bushes and low scrub, intent only on finding safe shelter. During one flash I saw the silhouette of a railway embankment ahead. Thinking there might be a hut on the line, I clambered up to the rails but found they were electrified. As I clambered down, hurriedly, another discharge struck a tree on the hillside.

Many years ago, as a newspaperman, I took a short course in the fundamental dynamics of lightning at the National Physical Laboratories. I recall the gunshot-like explosions as bright blue ribbons of light leaped between the outputs of the supercharged storage chambers. The physicist who pressed the button explained how, in an actual flash of lightning, the initial stroke, the one they call the leader, blazes a trail to earth. The flicker effect is caused by other strokes leaping up and down that ionized pathway.

I drew no comfort from recalling those facts during that wet and noisy morning, but when I managed to find the bridle-path that led back to Pange, I felt as though I'd discovered what pathways meant to those who first made them. Alone in the scrub I experienced blind unreasonable fear. The going wasn't difficult yet all seemed hostile. It seemed equally dark and lonely on that little trail through the trees. The storm crashed on, but there I had a sense of familiarity, of not being alone, even in the invisible presence of man.

Dogs barked behind farm gates, but on the outskirts of the village I broke into a shed only a little larger than the tractor it housed. Peeling off my clothes, I slipped into a shirt and pants less damp than the rest, and there with my head up against a mud-daubed wheel I dozed fitfully for a couple of hours.

That morning I prayed for a little draught of wind, for dawn stirred uneasily behind a mist of depressing thickness. I stamped about impatiently, feeling hungry and tired and at the first uncertain promise of increasing light I made for high ground, lugging a pack heavy with sodden gear.

No village marked that way through a great emptiness of common grazing and I shrink from describing what I saw on the ground. It seemed to be covered in bits of orange peel. They were brightly-coloured testacellid slugs. These creatures normally live underground, feeding on worms, but during the downpour they had been washed out of the wayside banks in countless thousands, and where a cart had recently passed by, they were industriously feeding on what remained of their down-trodden fellows. Turning off into the trees to avoid that sight, I sought food at the door of a cottage.

The old lady spoke a form of singsong German, yet with scarcely a dozen words between us we got on fine. As she bustled about making coffee and frying a large piece of ham I sensed that for a little while I had become her own son. As I sampled the first mouthful, she looked at me anxiously. Was it good? She touched my wet pack, indicating that if I cared to I could stay there and dry it out. Something more to eat, perhaps for midday? She held out a piece of rye bread and made as if to wrap it up. In this kind of inarticulate affection there is something close to poetry. I can't remember what coins she selected from the few I put down on the table, but I know them to have been small. Should I leave more? Recalling the crossing sweeper of Metz and the innkeeper of Pange and all that high and mighty stuff about dignity, I embraced her and left, thinking the morning looked much brighter.

Lorraine is a thickly-wooded plateau of relatively soft rocks nicely referred to in *Michelin* as *couches tendres*. They rise in a series of gentle undulations towards the hard shoulder of the Vosges which is made up of some very old stuff. So vast are the vistas that, through field-glasses at first light, I could sometimes see the hamlet where I hoped to spend that night. In between the sweeps of hills are the crowns of crew-cut forests, broken here and there by tumbledown farmsteads and much poor but carefully tended soil.

The German-speaking Lorrainers are warm; the French stock aloof, reserved. Before accepting your hand, they pause and say '*Sieur*' slowly, with a hint of a little interrogation mark as you may hear it from an English headmaster or a very senior Civil Servant, but, once said, you may take it they accept you, and I had straight dealing with all those I met.

There are good tracks to be found all the way from Rémilly to Les Etangs, that country of lakes, rushes and frogs around Mittersheim but I'm not going to say precisely how I got there lest I identify the garden of the contented fisherman. Although he is an outspoken man, I'm pretty sure he doesn't want anyone else to inquire about his affairs.

Late that afternoon, I spread my tent out to dry on the patio of his pleasant little wine-house and strolled into the bar where M'sieur polished glasses behind the till and Madame, an immense woman in a jaunty print dress, sat at a table, clucking over her accounts. Over the whole house there breathed a sense of peace. No customers except myself. No sound except the ticking of a clock and an occasional squeak from the budgerigar. I sat there, writing up notes about the night of the storm and the old lady and, above all, about how fortune changed, almost from hour to hour.

At length, Madame sighed. She put down her pen and said: 'Jules! A packet of blues.'

'Come and get them,' he said.

At this she smiled. She sighed again and waddled up to the bar. Before he handed over the Gauloises, the man held up his chin for a kiss. He got a warm one, on both cheeks. And as she turned towards the kitchen Madame received such a resounding slap on her bottom that even the dog looked up, surprised.

I scribbled a note about the unselfconscious quality of affection and got to thinking about what it must be like to live in a small pub, away from the discontents of city life.

Time ticked on. I decided to have another drink and invited the *patron* to take one himself. Pouring it out, he observed, conversationally, that he wasn't the boss. The *patron* had gone off for the afternoon. *Madame la Directrice* was in charge.

My turn to sigh. Adding an uncharitable commentary to my notes on the beatitudes of rural life, I strolled out into the garden.

A miniature Eden of flower beds and discreet rockeries. At the foot of the wall that screened off the kitchen, stood a log cabin of hand-hewn pine. It contained a lot of books and a fishing rod or two. Clearly a man's place. Over the door somebody had carved the words:

Pour chasseurs, pêcheurs
. . . et autres menteurs

The gate clicked. Up the garden path strode a spritely fellow of about sixty. A happy-looking man. I took to him from the start. With a fishing-rod and a basket over his shoulder, he looked on top of the world. The *patron* for sure.

Was I staying there? Alas, no! But a visitor, yes? Good! Would I care for a drink? I would, indeed, I said. And into the hut he went, and out came a bottle and glasses in his hands, and there we sat in that evening light, overlooking the valley, talking with an intimacy which springs up on rare and blessed occasions between two casually acquainted strangers.

Somewhere in the conversation I referred in all innocence to *cet homme-là*, meaning the barman. I had no intention whatever of prying into his domestic affairs. The *patron* leaned forward and smiled.

'Strictly between ourselves,' he said, 'I will tell you something, M'sieur. That man came to me nearly twelve years ago. I still pay him exactly the same salary, but now he does twice as much work. And I can go fishing.'

At this I bluntly referred to the cash register. Wasn't it perhaps a little dangerous to entrust his financial affairs to someone else?

'There is no problem,' he said. He paused, as if searching for the exact phrase and added, 'I can assure you, M'sieur, that Madame is not generous in everything.'

Lorraine lies across Lotharingia, once a part of the Middle Kingdom of the Emperor Lothair, one of the grandsons of Charlemagne. That narrow palatinate extended from the North Sea to the Mediterranean along the valleys of the Rhine and the Rhône. Attacked by the Northmen, by the Saracens and by Lothair's two brothers, Charles and Louis, who dominated the land on both sides of his territory, not surprisingly Lothair's kingdom soon broke up. He retired to the monastery of Prüm and died, miserably, a frustrated and entirely untrustworthy man. His immediate successors were an unruly lot, but by contrast with the Merovingians, the descendants of King Merovech, the line that eventually brought the illustrious if lecherous Charlemagne to power, they were as petty thieves to a gang of armed and utterly amoral highwaymen. By almost any standards, Christian or pagan, the general run of those long-haired kings – Childeric, Chlodovech, Chlodomar, Chlotar and that Caligula of his age, King Chilperic – were reckoned the enemies of God and man. They brought the customs of Iron Age tribesmen into the first stirrings of a much larger society, the rudiments of an empire lightly tinctured by Christianity and Roman law. Their history is of one gigantic family quarrel modified only slightly by the *Sippe*, the blood relationship, a tie more binding by far than wedlock.

They cheerfully poisoned their kith and kin. Not a few perished at the very baptismal font by the lightly disguised hand of their stepmothers. Large bits of the church roof had been known to fall on pious princes at their prayers. A sudden spear thrust at a royal hunt brought black blood from the throats of several in danger of attaining the throne, and to those who escaped royal disfavour there were constant perils from ambitious courtier-cousins, the ducal thistles among the young kingcups.

They rob, rape, and slaughter, force an entry into churches with drunken howls, abuse the bishops, mishandle the clergy, plunder the widow and orphan, and enjoy themselves generally. Duke Rauching caused persons who displeased him to be slowly buried alive and was accustomed when in festive mood to fasten burning candles to the legs of his slaves; Beppolen, created Duke of Angers, a man 'who never waited for the keys when he wished to enter a house', began his tenure of office by plundering the whole neighbourhood. Feeling with good reason that life was short, they were largely innocent of ethics, the more since in that Europe in embryo that curious thing called public opinion had not been invented.

Of all the horrors of that age, nothing is more nightmarish in retrospect than the blood feud between the two queens, Brunhilda and Fredegunda, a duel which lasted for three generations of Franks and Gallo-Romans. Elements of it are to be found in the sagas, in particular the thirteenth-century *Nibelungenlied* and what Wagner made of those stories in *The Ring*, adding a few gods and goddesses to give the whole thing divine authority, if not approval.

Bishop Gregory of Tours, the first historian of France, a pious father who knew the Merovingians all too well, seems slightly biased in favour of Brunhilda, the daughter of no less than Athanagild, king of the Visigoths in Spain. The facts are that Sigibert, King of Austrasia to the east of Frankland, fancied the girl and took her for wife. This brilliant match upset the pride of his younger brother, King Chilperic of Neustria to the north-west of Paris and Soissons. On the royal tit-for-tat principle, he gained the hand of Brunhilda's elder sister, the gracious Galswintha, and to show that he could cut a dash with the best of them he gave her a few cities in the south of France as a bridal portion. On the face of it, a nice balance of power. Two testy brothers betrothed to two classy sisters: bells pealed from the Loire to the Rhine. But Fredegunda bided her time.

By birth a mere serving wench who occasionally shared Chilperic's bed, she got rid of her lord's second wife as expeditiously as she removed his first. Galswintha was found dead one morning. Chilperic seemed curiously unmoved. There were those who said he had contemplated her demise himself. An investment in death was no more than a small insurance policy to a full-blooded Merovingian. This is not to suggest that he was wholly impious. With nothing better to do one dark winter night in Rouen he re-drafted the whole doctrine of the Trinity in such an uncompromising manner that, when he saw it, Gregory's hair stood on end all round his tonsure. Chilperic clearly loved Fredegunda. Brunhilda took the news of her sister's death with marked impatience and the vendetta began.

Her husband, Sigibert, invaded Chilperic's Austrasia so successfully that he might have been raised on his shield as *Rex Francorum* had not someone, seemingly at Fredegunda's instigation, run him through with a useful bit of sixth-century hardware called a scramasax. Brunhilda became a widow with yet another death to avenge.

To few people's surprise, Chilperic died in much the same way whilst out hunting one day. On the face of it, it looked like his sister-in-law's work, for Brunhilda had few reasons to love the Neustrians and, in particular, that woman who, some think, gave Shakespeare a few ideas about Lady Macbeth, assuming, of course, that he had read his *Gesta Francorum*. But others have it that Fredegunda did her liege lord in herself before he, in turn, did her when he learned, as he did, that she was having an affair with Landeric, his chief butler.

Deprived of royal support, for a time things looked bad for Fredegunda but, on the grounds that she was a poor hard-working and much misunderstood woman, she beguiled another brother-in-law, one King Guntchramn of Orleans, into acting as the guardian of her sole remaining son, the eleven-year-old Chlotar of dubious paternity. Yet that support once gained and her position strengthened, 'she altered her attitude and began to send out assassins to lie in wait for him in churches and other suitable places'.

Guntchramn died, peacefully it seems, but his heir, Childebert, King of Austrasia and Burgundy, had clearly been poisoned. No adult male of the long-haired dynasty now survived and, in the words of one of their chroniclers, Frans Bengtsson, 'the two old rival queens alone dominated the scene, and could devote their attention to each other with less interruption than ever before'.

Austrasian armies marched into Neustria. Fredegunda fought back, leading her men, employing several smart tricks that brought her victories at Laffaux and Droisi, but to everyone's surprise she died in a wholly uncharacteristic manner, that is quietly in bed, and Brunhilda shattered the Neustrians on the field of Dormelles in the Year of Our Lord 600. Although she won the day, Fredegunda's son Chlotar managed to escape and thirteen years later he exacted terrible vengeance.

By devious alliances, plots and counter-plots, Chlotar captured the aged Brunhilda at Renève near Dijon in Burgundy. He tortured her for three days. And near the end he tied her long hair to the tail of an unbroken horse. He thrashed its flanks and watched, complacently, as the maddened animal dragged his mother's life-long rival to a violent death. The vendetta was over. Against this sort of historical background, the underlying morality of the sagas and all that Wagner made and unmade of them are not quite as improbable as they sound.

From the top of a breezy hill near Baronville, I caught my first glimpse of the Vosges. No more than a violet-coloured smudge on a horizon nearly fifty miles away, but I put my tent down confident I should see more of those great hills the following day. Yet through some trick of light or elevation, or perhaps a dip in the ever-ascending steps of that plateau, the smudge disappeared. When another one emerged in quite a different place the next night, I began to get the uneasy feeling that the peaks of the Vosges were taking turns peering at me and sinking down again as giant brigands might at the approach of a nervous traveller.

I hurried on through a patchwork of woodland and villages all much alike, a place without signposts. The local folk seem to like it that way. As one of them put it: 'We know where we are, and our friends know where we are. So why should we bother about anyone else?'

Domnon-les-Dieuze is different. It looks as aristocratic as its name sounds. Among the fir trees are the fortified houses of lordlings and tenant farmsteads with a scampering of thorough-bred foals in their paddocks. If I'd worn a cap I would have doffed it with a flourish at the approach of M. le Général on a fine white gelding. Still I saluted him with reasonable ceremony and he returned my touched lock with evident satisfaction.

Speaking from the saddle, he assured me I had already walked through the finest part of Lorraine. The people there, he said, were poor but of good blood. Not mixed as they were to the east where you never knew who you would meet. They were neither French nor German with no respect for themselves nor anyone else. Nothing more than poachers and frog-catchers.

Far from lacking in self-respect, the people of the Etangs take pride in making their villages as attractive as possible. In the main street of Fénétrange you may see alternate window boxes of blue and white flowers. Around the *place* they have trimmed the acacias into the shape of floormops. The trees rise from little bowers of blossom in the pavement. The ironmonger has planted lettuce at the foot of the tree outside his own shop. They are very tidy lettuces and they look as nice as the flowers.

In Niederstinzel a blacksmith knocked a lively tune out of the better part of an octave of broken ploughshares and little boys carried stocks of new-made bread almost as long as themselves, but the lasting memory is of whole families engaged in frog-netting, which saddened me, for they are decorative and useful little animals which in many places are becoming rare. You can hear the chorus at a range of about half a mile. The sound can be crudely likened to somebody being violently sick in front of a battery of microphones, but at close quarters the bassoon-like belches are punctuated by the flutey notes of the females.

I have never eaten a frog. I have no desire even to see those little white legs on a plate, but a *gourmet de grenouilles* from Brussels once described the taste to me as 'somewhere between rather dry boiled fish and chicken', and, like much else, to English ears the description sounded better in French.

Across the marsh a single telephone wire provides a perch for innumerable finches and buntings, turtle doves and small birds of prey that use the poles as observation posts. By a subtle spacing arrangement, they all seemed to be getting on quite amicably and I walked under that avian thread of life for three or four miles, grateful for guidance and the entertainment it offered. The presence of swallows meant I was nearing a village and that afternoon I took my rest where I could watch the cosmetics of about a dozen birds spaced out like notes of music on a stave.

The first scratch is usually about the neck and throat, a brushing movement carried out so rapidly that, even through field glasses, the claw appears as a blur. This done, they extend first one wing and then the other, industriously pecking about for louse flies. These parasites are about a quarter of an inch in length and are so large in proportion to their hosts that a man similarly afflicted might well have lobsters scuttling about in his underclothes. The swallows pick them out carefully. They finish off by combing their needle-like tails, and then with an exultant shiver they plunge down about their business.

From Les Etangs I breached the Vosges by way of the Saverne Gap, tempering that day-long stage with a boisterous luncheon with the Baron of Phalsbourg and his friends in a tavern near that town. If I hadn't used a cloud as a sort of weathercock I might have slipped down into the quiet of the valley of the Zorn and bypassed all the traffic, but it rained hard, twice, during the morning and fearing another downpour I put my faith in crude divination.

If the cloud that towered over Bourscheid airfield blew towards me I decided to keep to the highroad, but if it veered north I would take a chance in the byways of the Zorn.

To my consternation, a bright thread of lightning unzipped that swirling mass of water vapour from top to bottom. Although it took me less than ten minutes to scuttle down to the tavern at Mittelbronn, I arrived there soaked through. Peeling off two skins of fabric inaccurately described as waterproof, I greeted the company somewhat churlishly. Somebody made a sympathetic comment. I thanked him, and since I couldn't remember the word for wet (*mouillé*), I observed instead that it was *un peu humide*. This I took to be passably good French but it brought the house down. Ah! They were droll, those English, they said. They diminished everything.

'A drink?' inquired a man with a curly moustache. He spoke English fluently. We talked. From his use of one or two expressions such as 'Good show!' I might have guessed (but didn't) that M. le Baron, as everyone called him, had flown with the RAF during the war. In quick succession he introduced me to the Deputy Mayor of Phalsbourg, one or two municipal councillors, the chief of police and several other citizens of distinction. They invited me to join them for lunch. What that celebration was about I never discovered, but the meal of creamed trout, braised wild boar and much dark wine went on for nearly three hours.

I did what I could to join in the local gossip, relying largely on slow judicious nods for, around a French dining table, there is little room for neutrality. The trouble was I often didn't know what they were talking about.

Someone said: 'I tell you, he has brought this on himself.'

'He means he's always getting boozed,' said the Baron.

'But where is he now?' asked the man.

'Probably in Metz,' said the Baron, quietly.

'And what else could you expect with a woman like that?' asked the man, turning to me. I sighed and shook my head, trying to give the impression that no doubt she came from foreign parts, perhaps even Strasbourg.

On the subject of womankind in general, the Deputy Mayor reckoned there were certain things they should never be allowed to do, such as pouring out drinks. 'For they do not understand proper proportions,' he said. 'Except a small one when it's for you!' And he looked at me, directly and I nodded, vigorously. 'And after all, who paid for it?' asked the postman. At this everyone nodded and banged the table until the bottles tinkled.

From drink the talk veered towards shooting at which I brightened up, venturing one or two remarks on the habits of African guineafowl and sandgrouse. They listened politely but said nothing. I switched to antelope and might have claimed even bigger game if they had shown interest in anything beyond the local sport.

'We hunt wild boar here,' said the Baron. 'Ever done any? No? A pity. They put up a good show. But you've got to hit 'em fast.' And to show what he meant, he snatched up a long roll of bread and put a shot clean through a waiter at the far end of the bar.

From their stories about how wild boar have fluctuated over the years, I gained the impression that the animals are naturally undemocratic. They flourish best under lordlings with land and time to squander on blood sports. They flee at the mere sound of the word Republic for the peasantry have no scruples about shooting pests that destroy their crops.

After much talk about the best dogs, the best rifles and the best shots in town, the company drove back to Phalsbourg where I incautiously agreed to meet them for a farewell drink. We met in the *Bar de Vosges*, a liquor house owned by the hospitable man with the courtesy title of the Baron. We moved off to the town hall and with some difficulty I said goodbye before the *confrérie* left for an informal inspection of a place at the back of the fire station.

The first two or three lines of the notes I wrote daily logged the state of the weather, the time and distance between successive halts for sleep together with a phrase or two about how things went that day or night. What follows that summary is largely commentary, long or short with bits here and there which now seem irrelevant, petulant and downright incomprehensible. Now and again I managed to wrap up a great deal of activity in a couple of sentences. Thus:

> 1 June: walked thirty miles through the night from Saverne to Strasbourg via Zorn Canal and Trachtersheim. No joy in Goethe and *Götterdämmerung*, but stars wonderful.

The canal lies between the Marne and the Rhine. If I'd kept to it as I intended to, it would have added another eight or ten miles to the stage, but near Ingenheim it became too dark for towpath walking and I struck off into the Alsatian plain through a lot of little roads. What the note doesn't make clear is that, aside from the stars, I scarcely saw a thing worth recording for more than eight hours. During that time I walked on, sustained only by one thought stream after another. As this is the vital stuff of a lone walker's entertainment, I'm trying to recall accurately a few of the themes and how they arose.

The canal luminous. No moon, but reflected chips of starlight wiggled like tadpoles on the surface of the water. Here, I thought, is a screen for thoughts as changeable as a pattern of clouds. I looked to it for support throughout the night. The name Saverne conjured up Sessenheim and Goethe's walks in the woods with Pastor Brion's gentle daughter, Frederika. A passionate affair, but the poet turned his back on the love she gave him. Had he any feelings of guilt towards her? Did she become the sorely-wronged Margarita in his tale of *Faust*? Or was I confusing the opera with Marlowe's version of the story? With Strasbourg in mind I had done a fair amount of homework on the life of Goethe, but none of it seemed of much value that night. Mephistopheles kept drifting in and out of my thoughts. I saw him in the scene where Faustus asks: 'How comes it, then, that thou art out of hell?' And remembered the answer:

'Why this *is* hell, nor am I out of it.'

Not comforting at that hour. Before I could get back to Sessenheim an owl called from the silhouette of a tree. I called back, blowing through cupped hands and in the course of that duet I completely forgot about Goethe.

A breeze sprang up. A smudge of cloud wiped out the stars as effectively as a blackboard duster. It grew very dark. Reluctantly, I turned my back on the canal and worked out a more southerly route from a torch-lit map. Where was I? Hopefully near Ingenheim on the D67. Better get off that road, I wanted a peaceful night. I found a side lane and trudged on for two hours without seeing anything I much cared about.

Near the bridge over the Rohr a signpost pointed to Hagenau, the domain of Hagen, that wicked son of Alberich the dwarf who forswore all love for the sake of the Rheingold. With some difficulty I tuned my private orchestra into the last act of the *Götterdämmerung*, but couldn't get away from those rather morbid drum rolls in the last great *sforzando*. The theme faded gradually and I trudged on through Trachtersheim and Pfettisheim, feeling pretty low.

Thought streams can be turned on and turned off, but given the chance to wander off on their own they tend to flow into the murkier parts of the subconscious, stirring up stuff best left undisturbed. The wind rose again. When lightning flickered in the east I began to worry. Eight miles still to go. I thought of that storm at Pange and where I might sleep if another broke over me that night. I thought of the Vosges and the Alps and what a storm must be like in the mountains. At a point where I began to feel thoroughly despondent the clouds parted to reveal an enormous freckling of stars. Merak and Dubhe, the two pointers of the Great Bear, hung over my left shoulder. A crude fix on Polaris gave me an encouraging bearing of south-east by east, and I walked on a little faster, pleased at being able to make even slight use of stellar navigation.

> A starlit or a moonlit dome disdains
> All that man is,
> All mere complexities,
> The fury and the mire of human veins.

I have often wondered how those circumpolar stars between the Dragon and the Lion came to be known as the Great Bear. The ancient Egyptians called them the Unwearied Ones or the Rowers of the Ships of Ra. I prefer the Plough or the Wain or even the Big Dipper. The name of the Septriones, the proud walkers, grips the imagination, but the Great Bear is a plain misnomer. The animal has lost its head and the tail would look more appropriate on a fox. But that goes for most of the star clusters. Unless you can pick out the two front legs and the mane, Pegasus is no more than four bright stars, Cygnus a crucifix and Cassiopeia the letter W nailed to the sky.

I walked on, mentally ticking off the names of the few constellations I could recognize, but without help from a star map I began to feel lost, overpowered by the thought of untold numbers of galaxies stretching out into what for want of a better word we call infinity. What did I know of their motions, their relationship to each other or what they stood for in terms of our own microscopic corner of the universe? The heavens seemed dreadfully cold.

And then a memorable thing happened. Glancing back towards Polaris, I caught a glimpse of Pisces far away to the west, near Aries and Cetus and I looked at that little group with affection. It triggered off a thought stream that made familiar at least a portion of the sky. In my mind's eye I saw a little point of light soaring straight up in the air and I went back in memory to a night spent in the observatory called the *Pic du Midi* high up in the Pyrenees.

By sheer luck I happened to be in Spain on a newspaper assignment when the Russians launched the first man-made satellite. The office cabled to say they had heard it could be seen from the *Pic*, and up there I went in an ancient taxi-cab, intent on an eyewitness report.

The observatory is French and the astronomers hadn't got much in the way of equipment beyond what they needed for their routine work, but they rigged up a battery of what looked like enormous theodolites to follow the satellite and work out its orbits.

At four o'clock in the morning we crowded together on the observation platform. The satellite rose out of the sea somewhere beyond the dim lights of San Sebastian. The first man to see it shouted: 'Ah, there she is. Look! Look! Under the Fish!'

As soon as he got a fix he called out the position to the others. But not in the cold mathematical language of inclinations and transits. He spoke in terms of constellations and in French it sounded like poetry.

From Pisces, the satellite brushed the hair of Andromeda. It touched the Lizard, passing between Cygnus and Cepheus, that great Ethiopian king, the descendent of Jupiter and Io. And on it went, into Draco and I forget where else, but I marvelled that star names used by the Chaldeans could still be of service to modern astronomers.

The memories faded. Another hour passed. I walked into Strasbourg by the Way of the Romans and only Venus shone through that pale blue light which is the mother of the dawn.

The Vosges

The *place Kléber* is no place for a quiet sleep at six o'clock in the morning. Shutters clattered, dogs barked and the sweeper-up swept to within three feet of my bench where he stopped and looked down with extraordinary compassion. 'M'sieur', he said, 'it is another day.'

I sat up feeling stiff, bemused, hungry and still extremely tired. Another day. Yawning prodigiously, I looked round. A large square of rather stiff buildings fronted by a row of cafés. Not quite the Strasbourg I had been looking forward to. Still, it was early.

In the Square of the Tripe Vendors I changed a shirt, greased my boots, rinsed out a pair of socks and washed under an open tap. The world brightened up a bit. By the time I had eaten enough bacon and eggs for two dragoons I felt fit to tackle the business of the day. This meant obtaining money from the *Crédit* and looking up people reputed to know the trails through the mountains. To that end I came armed with letters of intro-duction, but with one golden exception they all misfired.

They said that by good fortune Professor Louis Huck, the president of the *Club Vosgien*, happened to be in his office that very morning. An extremely polite man. He bowed and I bowed. We shook hands. I felt that at all times I could rely on his most distinguished sentiments, but on the matter of getting through the Vosges in one grand sweep from north to south he was a shade less than helpful. The club had published books and maps he said. I pointed out that I had already spent over a hundred francs on the best they had. At this he brightened up. He assured me they were very good. As for route-finding, that, surely, was largely a matter of choice. As he saw it, some preferred to go one way and some another. On that indisputable point we bowed

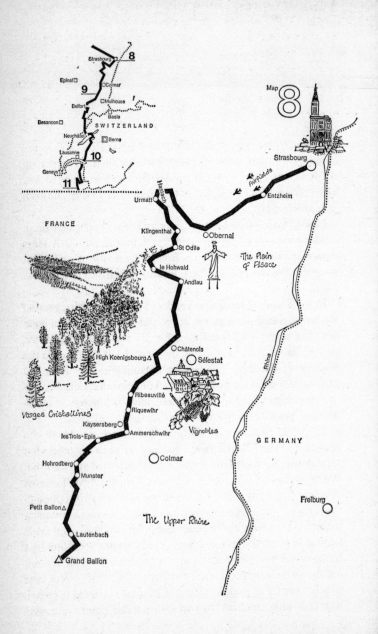

Strasbourg

8

Epinal □

9

□Colmar

□Mulhouse

Belfort

Basle

Besançon □

SWITZERLAND

Neuchâtel □

□ Berne

Lausanne □

10

Geneva □

11

FRANCE

Map

8

Strasbourg

Airfields

Entzheim

Hasiach

Urmatt

The Plain of Alsace

Klingenthal

St Odile

Obernai

le Hohwald

Andlau

Rhine

Châtenois ○

High Koenigsbourg △

○ Sélestat

Vosges Cristallines

Ribeauvillé ○

Riquewihr ○

Kaysersberg ○

Vignobles

les Trois-Epis

Ammerschwihr ○

GERMANY

Hohrodberg

○ Colmar

Munster

Petit Ballon △

The Upper Rhine

Freiburg
○

Lautenbach

△ Grand Ballon

and shook hands again, and like that young man in the *Rubáiyát* I came out through the same door as in I went.

Cities are reckoned to take a man out of the truth of himself. Those fine sentiments we cultivate in the open air are frayed easily by noise and petty wrangles with officialdom. For a walker the problem is one of chronic acclimatization, of settling down briefly to life in a different dimension. I should have liked to have wandered round the town, getting the feel of the place, but fate seemed dead set against me at the start.

At the tourist bureau the *chef* stared at my beard with a certain amount of curiosity if not distaste. He couldn't keep his eyes off it, and for good reason, for, as I discovered afterwards, it was richly dappled with fragments of eggs fried in butter. I asked about direct routes through the Vosges. Perhaps there was somebody there who could help me. He rang a bell and passed me on to a clerk who, after a long search through the telephone directory, handed me a slip of paper on which he had carefully written down the address of the *Club Vosgien*.

Behind the doors of a big French bank there is usually a tough-looking character got up in a frock-coat like an undertaker's mute. This is the *huissier* or beadle, a man who combines the functions of a doorkeeper with that of traffic manager, messenger and chucker-out. At Strasbourg the *huissier* and I got on fine. We spent hours together. Not for the first time, my credit had gone astray. A telephone call to London confirmed that the process had been set in motion weeks earlier, but the manager wanted it in writing from his head office in Paris. As Joe Liebling once put it: by the intensity of its addiction to money, a French bank establishes an emotional claim on funds in transit. You feel in the moral position of a wayward mother who has left her babe on a doorstep and returns to claim it from foster-parents who have come to regard it as their own. Through that gilded grille I argued. I gesticulated. I produced letters and a passport. But I got nowhere. Back I went to the penitential bench where the *huissier* told me how he had started out in life as a process server. And I could well believe it.

After an hour or two I learned that when a French bank manager says something can be attended to *almost* immediately you might as well come back the next day, which, in fact, I did, and it still hadn't been cleared up. But by then I didn't mind so much. I had met Moyshe and his friends and the city had become a warm, almost familiar place.

In a street behind the Kammerzell are two shops devoted to the sale of musical equipment. *Sonorisation appareils en tous genres.* The noise is terrific. In a basement under those shops is a bistro known as *Le Click*, patronized mostly by overseas students. I went there with a letter of introduction to the cousin of one of my Phalsbourg friends. A good fellow, he said. He knew everyone in town, including the burgomaster who, like the Baron, runs a bar. But he wasn't there and he wouldn't be there for about a month. As a young Nigerian put it in good basic English, he was in the clink. 'But we're friends of his,' he said. 'Sit down. My name's Moyshe and here's Fritz and Rudi.'

Moyshe had the God-sent gift of augmenting one's faith in the fundamental decency of human kind. If this makes him sound a bit too good to be wholly real, this opinion is not based simply on the few good turns he did me, although they were real enough. Everyone seemed to turn to Moyshe. When I made a few jokes about the morning's misadventures he immediately offered to lend me some money. Those dam' banks, he said, were all the same. The longer the delay, the more commission they got. As for a route through the Vosges, he knew someone, a professional botanist, who had walked from Strasbourg to Belfort, just as I planned to. He phoned him up and the result was some advice I had good reason to be grateful for. But, as I have said, it wasn't just what he did for me. Moyshe ran an unofficial advice bureau based on *Le Click* and among students he must have been the most sought-after man in town. Far from taking himself overseriously, he drank beer and knew a lot of pretty girls. They wandered up, anxious to be asked to sit down, and though he put them off with a whispered endearment, it was clear from the way they looked that the pleasure had only been postponed. When I got to know him a bit better and commented on his popularity, he said there were certain advantages in being black and Jewish *and* a Marxist. I think I know what he meant though I'm at a loss to explain it in a few words.

He came to Strasbourg to study economics and stayed on to lecture and gossip and drink. He reckoned ice-cold beer cooled his head, but, as he put it, he liked his women at room temperature. If he goes back to Nigeria may they make him Minister of Internal Affairs or maybe Lord Chief Justice, for I have rarely met a more generous man.

Fritz, a former air pilot and white hunter, ran a little garage for racing cars. Rudi claimed he was studying law in order to become an effective anarchist. I met many others in their company, but these were Moyshe's immediate friends, the Companions of the Prophet. We agreed to meet that night in my dormitory, the *place Kléber* and I wandered off feeling that in some miraculous way I had got hold of the keys to the city.

I recall those days as if on a film which has been speeded up. In between visits to the *Crédit* and *Le Click*, I wandered along the little canals, turning off into busy but still medieval-looking streets. I see the cobbled markets and whole oceans of strange fish on open stalls. I remember the barrel that rolled off a cart and crashed down into the gutter with a full-bodied thump. It lay there, ruptured, oozing a blood-red rivulet of wine. The carter turned it over with his foot, nonchalantly, before he picked it up and carried it down into a cellar with some rich stuff at three francs a shot pouring down over his leather pants. I can hear street cries and the boom of carillons. On that first day all bells except those of the doubting St Thomas in the temple of Protestantism proclaimed faith in martyrdom, for it was a saint's day and, needful of God's help as I often am, I made for the cathedral straight away.

The statues and bas-reliefs on the façade illustrate the whole bible from Creation to the Ascension. The figures in stone look wonderfully alive, their faces revealing sadness or joy, their clothing draped on visibly human limbs. Somewhere between the Romanesque apse and the Gothic nave you can sense the change in style; you can see how those fourteenth-century sculptors and cathedral builders changed the whole world of Christian art. Instead of trying to hold their viewers with stiff abstract patterns and dehumanized shapes of the eastern churches, they created space around figures that moved as the spectator moved. Faith became reconciled with the observable fact that all humankind, the strong and the frail, are kin.

From the great organ that afternoon came one long sustained drone as mechanics tried to remedy a fault in one incontinent pipe. A guide said the organist had gone home, unable, I suppose, to endure the noise. In former days the instrument stood below a hideous-looking mask called the Roraffe which used to make uncouth grimaces as the bellows went up and down. On great days, when the whole town swarmed in for mass, some wag might stick his face out of a hole in the mask during a solemn part of the service and, as the guide says, not always his face.

Up on the tower, from that corner of the platform where Goethe – who was afraid of heights – is said to have peered over the parapet daily to strengthen his nerve, I gazed down on the Plain of Alsace. It looked like a map. Clouds hung over the wall of the Vosges; the forests of Hagenau appeared dimly through smoke from the *raffinerie de pétrole* at Reichstett, but to the south, above the Black Forest, there arose the worn-down stump of a volcano, the Kaiserstuhl, a relic of the great rift or crack in the earth's surface called the Rhine fault or *Graben*.

Earth forces gradually pulled apart the plain between the Vosges and the Black Forest until the central portion cracked and fell down like the unsupported keystone of an arch. But when engineers began to bore a tunnel through a mountain near Freibourg they found a series of wavy structures known as step faults. In addition to side tension, it now looks as if that great crack in the earth has been caused by a tremendous thrust or uplift from below. Geologists tested the theory by making models of the movements of the rocks, some extremely complicated, some as simple as slowly inflating a rubber hot-water bottle carefully coated with layers of clay. The pattern of cracks that emerged showed with reasonable certainty what happened in that valley a long time ago.

The rift is still being wrenched apart, but the tremors they experience there can be likened to the last murmurs of a subterranean storm. At the height of the convulsions the sea poured into the fissure, while volcanoes such as the Kaiserstuhl and the Vogelsberg erupted violently. Even within historic time the Rhine has changed its course several times. The river once lapped the walls of Strasbourg and ambled round other Rhenish towns, trying one course after another in search of a permanent bed. It may be that in that last act of the *Götterdämmerung*, at that moment when the river rises and engulfs Brunnhilde's funeral pyre, there is a romanticized echo of an event which had become folklore in

Celtic times. Certainly, if the crack continues to widen, as geologists believe it is doing, the sea might once more gush down into the valley.

Strasbourg means the Fortress of the Roads. It guarded the riches of the Alsatian plain. Like Metz, the fortress suffered the usual run of invaders from Celt to Hun, but it emerged triumphantly as one of the Free Cities that existed from Hamburg to Venice. After a visit there in 1514 Erasmus wrote to a friend saying that never before had he seen a monarchy without tyranny, aristocracy without factions, a democracy without disorder, and happiness without insolence. Once a year all municipal officers were obliged to recite the great civic oath, the *Schworbrief*, a declaration of rights that ensured a series of checks and balances between nobles and commoners, and the guilds, assemblies, and administrators.

Horns were blown from the cathedral tower each night at dusk and all Jews were obliged to leave the city. Despite the great fairs, the carolling of master singers and the all-night dancing in the streets, the citizens were obliged to behave themselves. Heavy penalties were imposed for anything that smelled of impious conduct and censorship was heavy-handed. No book could be imported from France with the words *amour*, *fille*, or *madame* in the title. At the Reformation the censors abolished the Guild of Whores but allowed the girls to walk the streets if they abided by the dress regulations, which were extremely strict in those days. Everyone knew what a person did by what he wore. There were six categories of costume in Strasbourg. At the bottom of the sartorial scale were 'subordinate females', including housemaids, barmaids, and sempstresses. Then came day labourers, porters, woodcutters, and the like. Common craftsmen and notaries fell into the third category among midwives and music-teachers who could be relied on not 'to play for dancing'. Merchants conducting 'large reputable businesses' were allowed handsome cloth, but only magistrates, senators, legal counsellors and noblemen could put on what finery they liked.

Like Metz, the fortress fell to the forces of Louis the Sun King and it fell with scarcely a murmur. Under pretext of some manoeuvring in Italy, the Marquis de Louvois managed to surround the town with thirty thousand men and entered it almost before they could ring the great alarm bell, the *Mordglock*. Most of the burghers must have been comforted by the fact that the troops rode in with their lances at rest and their sabres sheathed. The majority of the inhabitants seemed more curious than alarmed. The city's old troop commander galloped about shouting directions in German to the French officers until Louvois told him through an interpreter to take the rest of the day off lest some Gascon or Picard became irritated by his caperings and ran him through.

The city became French overnight, yet despite a small army of proselytizing priests, the offer of bribes to converts and the declaration that all illegitimate children were to be declared Catholic, Strasbourg remained predominantly Protestant for over a hundred years.

One day, I tell myself, I shall go back to the Fortress of the Roads and spend a month of spring days ambling over those little bridges between the château and the *quai des Bateliers*. I shall walk under the grotesque overhanging gables in the *bain au Plantes*, looking leisurely at the old shops, the buildings, the intimate courtyards seen briefly on my way to the *Crédit*. Perhaps I shall meet Moyshe and his companions again. I hope so.

They were dancing in the *place* the morning I left or, if not dancing themselves, the news they brought inspired four West African girls to wiggle their shoulders and stamp excitedly around our table. As I understood it, there had been some change in government in Ghana or Togo which looked as if it might affect the grants of at least twenty students. Moyshe the fixer put calls through to their embassy in Paris; he had argued with somebody high up in the ministry and after much negotiation the affair had been settled. The grants were safe. A notice had been posted up in *Le Click*, but the girls knew nothing of the outcome until he reassured them.

At the height of that impromptu dance, the president of the *Club Vosgien* walked past. He looked a little surprised at seeing me there and, remembering what I said about wanting to get away as soon as possible, I don't think he regarded me as a particularly serious walker.

Bank managers possess the devilish gift of knowing precisely to what limits a client can be tormented before he grows belligerent and takes his account off somewhere else. Provoked beyond endurance, a friend of mine has twice managed to transfer a substantial overdraft to a rival establishment. But I'm less resourceful. If the *huissier* hadn't turned up that morning to say that all had been arranged, I should have telephoned London. As it was, we all trooped off to the *Crédit* where they still kept us hanging about.

I took slips of paper from one grille to another where they asked for credentials they had already inspected. I tried to be polite to frustrated genealogists who not only asked about my mother's nationality, but also her maiden name, and when at last they handed the bills over they said they were glad to be of service. I smiled, bleakly, recalling that 'a chagrin of love never forgets itself. One must not make bile about it.'

For the long-distance walker few moments in life are more exhilarating than setting out after an enforced delay. It's necessary to dress up, carefully, like a bullfighter. There must be no loose straps or badly-tied boots. Adjustments can be made when you get under way, but for the take-off the need is to swing forward with all lashed down, the muscles tingling in anticipation and the spirits high. For these heaven-sent occasions I stock a few marching tunes. I don't often sing them aloud, but from memory I can call up a complete orchestra and let the themes whirl through my head. A few are by Sibelius. When there are clouds ahead or I am unsure of the way I can make good use of the scherzo from the First Symphony, but it's stern Nordic stuff. You've got to walk fast. The percussion is furious and there's much torment in the air. I've had some good send-offs from Britten, Dvořák and Janáček, but of all composers give me Prokofiev for a fine day.

I strode down the *quai Turckheim* accompanied by that mischievous tune from the second movement of the Fifth, which contains fragments from *Peter and the Wolf*. The clarinet skips along pursued by the bass. The footfalls are light and irresistible. They contain the very stuff of motion, of controlled unrest. There is a gait, a going-forwardness in every phrase. The clarinets took me out towards the Island of Fishermen. They made light of that great highway to Selestat. They danced off west, down a little lane to Lingolsheim, and on I went, burning up the miles, glorying in larks and wonderfully clean air, for I had become a walker again.

Skylarks sing through most of the year, but after a climax in mid-March the gabble falls off during April and May when the pairs are preoccupied with mating, nest-building, and keeping off intruders. The June song may be reckoned a *Te Deum* or, in more prosaic terms, an assertion by the cock bird that he has done his best, that the youngsters are being provided for, and he has time for song. And what a song!

The birds are afraid of trees; they even shun hedges and over-hanging rocks that might harbour enemies, but with the sky for a watch-tower they sing:

> In crisps of curl off wild winch whirl, and pour
> And pelt music, till none's to spill nor spend.

The last I saw of Strasbourg was the tower of the cathedral, a rose-pink finger of stone in the sunlight but changing in colour with every cloud that passed. It slipped from sight near Entzheim, where that walk back to the Vosges so wonderfully begun became a miserable affair, since by chance I strayed into country where military aircraft are put through their paces at a height perilously close to the ground.

For two hours I walked on amid the mind-bewildering noise of engines and supersonic bangs. They came from jet-black fighter aircraft with swept-back wings. On the ground they screamed petulantly as if chafing at restraint. And then with an exultant howl they leaped into the air in groups of three, rising almost vertically. Once aloft they turned over on their wing-tips, banking and diving through cloud-rack, becoming more and more minute until nought remained but sound, the sound you might expect to hear for all time in the very depths of hell.

I made some ear-plugs out of moistened bread, but the sound got through. The planes came back at me fast, at ground level. I scurried along, nervously, looking round, never knowing where the next would come from. I likened those furies to Val-kyries. I tried to admire the way they were flung through the sky, but at heart I cursed them, feeling angry that human beings were obliged to endure that noise without being able to do any-thing about it. I remember thinking that if ever I came across one of those pilots I would give him a talking to he would never forget. But that's before I reached a little tavern near Obernai where half a dozen pilots lounged over the bar. And what did I do? I bought a drink and said nothing.

They were very young-looking men with the grave expression of seminarists, though from the sinuous gestures they made they seemed to be talking about girl-friends. I caught the word Odette and how Marcelle would have behaved, presumably in similar circumstances. But when one of them described a loop with his finger, it became apparent the names were those of their planes and the gestures had to do with how they performed in the billowy beds of the sky.

The warmth of that company completely defused my indignation. They invited me to take a drink. They were amused that I had thought of them as Valkyries and explained that, to avoid scaring livestock, they only flew low over certain parts of the plain. They asked me where I intended to walk. I said up to Oberhaslach and then, hopefully, down the spine of the Vosges, but everything depended on the weather. If it looked as dour as it did that evening I should head direct for the Höhwald.

They knew the Haslach intimately. They had lost a rocket there. There had been a court of inquiry and it took search parties nearly a month to find it. Heavily forested, they said. As for the weather, they thought it promised well. A high ceiling from eight o'clock the next morning. Perhaps a bit of *brume* on the hills at dawn when, as they put it, the trees began to breathe. But I should have confidence, for they had seen a weather report that very afternoon.

Outside, the hills were covered by a dirty tablecloth of cloud, but encouraged enormously by expert opinion I struck out for Haslach with a packed supper of rye bread and cold roast partridge.

Obernai is a medieval township with good timber which is as rare as silence on that tormented plain. From the frothy brown torrents that gushed down from the Klingenthal it looked as if it had been raining up there for weeks. I waded through a knee-deep stream that covered a road and climbed up into the forest. There I found good lodgings under a spruce and with only red squirrels for company I ate and leaned back against a stump, idly smoking and writing up my journal. It had been a full day. As I wrote of that long walk across the plain I paused on the word Valkyries, but in the silence they seemed but a memory of something heard long ago.

At dawn a thick white mist. The trees seemed to be breathing heavily that morning. Hoping fervently that the meteorologists of Entzheim knew what they were about, I struck up a trail that climbed a thousand feet winding around massive outcrops of smooth reddish-grey rock, the stuff of great cathedrals. The trees were most thickly branched Norway spruce that released a deluge of droplets as I brushed through. By seven o'clock the sun was no more than a lemon-coloured patch of sky, but the trail never wavered.

I praised that trail. I praised all trails carefully route-marked in red on those splendid maps drawn up by the *Club Vosgien*. They are numbered and the numbers correspond to encouraging directions on signposts nailed to trees that give the distance and the estimated time it takes to get to the place they point to. To the *col du Heidenkopf*, it said, and the walk took me two hours which is twenty-three minutes under par. Another pointed to Grendelbruch, a fine-sounding place I thought and no doubt hospitable too. But I never saw it. The old story. I struck out on my own for what seemed a more convenient bridge over the turbulent Magel and was soon lost in the wilds of Guirbaden, a place I hope never to see again.

Towards midday the mist became less opaque. The toppling clouds lifted or, rather, they dissolved into a thin cold mist that swirled down into the gorges like a waterfall in slow motion. Disconsolately, I trudged on, trying one path after another. But none seemed onward-going. They ended abruptly and twice I went back over ground I had trod before.

There is something pretty close to character in the archi-tecture of great forests. The feeling of being lost among trees is one of intrusion into another mode of being. The tangles of birch and spruce in the Guirbaden were rendered more oppressive by the eerie half-light and the low ceiling of branches. I had been lured into a cavern of vegetation haunted by something in-escapable. The undergrowth clutched at my clothes, holding me back and when, after much exertion, I gained a few paces the scrub seemed even thicker ahead. I reached a place where the ground fell away precipitously and ended, I suspect, in a vertical drop. Wet with sweat, I sat down feeling hopelessly tired. A harsh scream rang out and in the overpowering silence that followed I pondered whether to go on or turn back.

I had ventured there intent on seeing something of *les Vosges Gréseuses*, that land of legend beyond the Bruche, the river that flows down to Molsheim. To Haslach in the Grey Country came many a saint, including the great Irish missionary St Florian, a man of Willibrord's stature. Where miracles have been done legends flower and there were reputed to be more supernatural goings on in that region than anywhere else in the Vosges. But I sought no metaphysical explanation for the trouble I stumbled into that morning. There was more comfort in knowing something about natural history. That harsh scream was not a damned soul but a noisy bird I knew well, a jay, that colourful relative of the crow, the largest of the perching birds. Likewise, when I put my foot down on a foul mass of brain-like material, disturbing a cloud of flies, I knew it for a pink phalloidal fungus, probably *clathrus* and not something too dreadful to be thought about.

After about an hour the mist lifted and on trees there appeared the red and white marks of a track that clearly led somewhere. Far from being in any danger I had blundered on to the heavily-overgrown slopes of a spur, precipitous only for the distance an agile man might easily scramble down. With scant experience of high forest tracks, it took me several days to appreciate that although tortuous, the hard old rocks on which they stand are for the most part nicely rounded and reliable. The going is often steep but if you keep to the tracks never perilous, even in a mist.

With a torrent for assurance I clambered down towards the Bruche by way of the Bruderthal, a gentle defile where deer skipped through grass bright with gentians and mountain pansies. Before I settled down for the night I bathed my feet in the Hasel, the stream which Florian turned into a second Jordan.

How an Irishman came to that region is a tribute to the reputation of the Celtic Church, for although there were many monasteries in ancient Austrasia, it was to Ireland that the bishops turned whenever discipline grew lax or doctrine debatable. The story is that the wife of Dagobert, that ruler of the Franks, bore a daughter who was both dumb and blind. In despair the king sent for Florian who had already wrought great miracles. A messenger arrived leading a horse decked out in finery, but the old Irishman shook his head. That was not how God's servants were ordained to travel, he said.

The next day he threw sacking over his donkey and rode down to the court. At his approach, the girl who had never spoken before cried out: 'See! Here comes Florian and for the sake of his piety God has given me sight.'

Beside the Hasel, on land given by the grateful king, Florian founded a monastery and hundreds flocked for instruction there. Though his heart remained with the fraternity they pressed him to accept the bishopric of Strasbourg. Then began what his chronicler calls the blessed rule in that city. In the year 693 God revealed to him that he was about to die at a certain hour, and die he did. But not to rest. After much dispute about whether the right body had been buried at Haslach, Charles IV offered to inspect the corpse. For this pious office the canons presented him with the saint's right arm which was ceremoniously deposited in Prague. Five years later they were obliged to cut off the other arm to allay the jealousy of Rudolf, count palatinate of the Rhine. But there were doubts about whether the rest of the body was really that of St Florian, for robbers had thrown it into a ditch and made off with the coffin for the sake of its precious inlays.

It used to be the custom to invoke the name of the saint for protection against boils, cholic, gripe and conflagrations. Over their doors they wrote: 'O holy St Florian, guard thou this house. Set fire to others.'

My recollection of that saintly valley is ruffled by the thought of the huge dogs there. They are about the size of a Labrador but shaggier, the sort of animal you might expect to find at the heels of Orson Welles done up as Macbeth. Perhaps they are aboriginal Alsatians or the descendants of some breed used to pull down wolves. What I am sure of is that they didn't like me at all. This came as no surprise. There is something about my appearance that brings out the worst even in a normally well-mannered dog.

It may have to do with my hunched-up pack or rapid gait. Or the way I swing my arms. Perhaps dogs know intuitively that I dislike the sound of a bark as much as the cry of babies or Siamese cats. Or it could be that I just look and smell a bit trampish. Whatever the reason I view all dogs on the loose as potential assailants particularly when they come skulking up from the rear.

Two brutes that went for me on the way up to Haslach took flight as soon as I switched from defence to attack, but a third seemed disposed to fight. I could see no more than its feet at the bottom of a big gate, but they were huge feet and the bark was that of a huge dog.

To my consternation it appeared at a gap in a hedge where I had no choice but to bluff it out or turn back. With nothing to hurl I shouted and made a pretence of throwing things, a bit of pantomime which usually puts a dog off. But this one saw through the act from the start and came in low with its teeth bared. I caught it a glancing blow with my boot and it sheered off for a rear attack. I grabbed a stone, a solid bit of Vosgean granite, but before I could throw it an urchin popped his head over the hedge and bawled out something that cowed the brute on the spot. It turned round and slunk back.

That night I slept fitfully for it seemed as if all the dogs for miles around barked at my ears, threatening that though I had slipped through once unscathed they would be at me the following day. The chorus rose and fell from dusk to midnight when it began to rain. At dawn the sun put more diamonds in the grass than you may see in a Bond Street jeweller's. There wasn't a sound from the dogs, but I rose and walked back towards the Bruche, tired of saintly detours.

An inglorious sequel emerged from my bout with the great dogs of Haslach. Although I never carry a walking-stick, holding that arms are meant to be swung to increase momentum, I felt much in need of protection that morning. Long before I came within sight of the same gate which failed to protect me from the Cerberus of the night before I broke off a bone-dry piece of Arolla pine, near six foot in length and towards the base as thick as my arm. On a fancy I called it Willibrord and with that fine staff in hand I strode down the stream with enormous confidence.

The brute I intended it for never appeared. No doubt it saw me coming or heard me singing dog-battling songs from afar. And slunk off. A coward I thought. Big dogs often were. And to show what I thought of cowards I gave that gate such a tremendous thwack that Willibrord tingled and all but leapt out of my hand.

At that clout an apple-headed cur scarce larger than a ferret shot out from beneath the gate and scratched my left ankle. I fended it off. Had I taken a serious swipe I should have lifted it off the ground like a golf ball. It snarled and bit at the wood and might have set about me again, but a man appeared and shouted, and it was clear that he wasn't shouting at the dog, but at me. I don't know what he said, but I'm pretty sure he gave me a good talking to, making me out to be some idle dolt that walked about with nothing better to do than beat up small dogs. I threw Willibrord aside. Although I was attacked by dogs on three subsequent occasions, once pretty smartly, the burden of protection seemed greater than the hazards of walking unarmed, and I next to never carried a staff again, holding that a good walker is a biped not a tripod.

There is no map of the Central Vosges more easy to follow than one with the pretty name of the *Feuille de Mont Ste Odile*. It offers local tracks as well as a fine length of that international pathway, the *Sentier de Grande Randonnée*, which I had not trodden since those days in Luxembourg. The going is over well-clad hills topped by ruined castles. Around the famous convent of Saint Odile they lie like the outermost bastions of a fortress. Tourists drive up to the Chapel of Tears by a tortuous road, but pilgrims trudge through a natural calvary in the woods, some of them leading friends carrying white sticks, for the belief is that the saint can cure blindness.

The story is that, like Dagobert's daughter, this unwanted child of the Duke Aldaric was born blind and, but for divine intervention arresting her father's sword in a great flash of light, she would have been destroyed. After baptism her affliction 'fell away like scales'. She elected to become a bride of God and duly founded a convent that attracted the most noble-born nuns in Alsace.

Around the convent are hills described as *feu* or *fée* which I took to mean fire, thinking that there they worshipped Beltane, the sun god in whose honour enormous pyres were lit on May Day, giving rise to the festival called *Bealltain* in Gaelic. But legends tell of sprites in those woods and the word probably means the place of fairies.

From a promontory thereabouts I heard a series of belches and dog-like barks. Curious about the noise I scanned the ground below through field glasses and made out a herd of attractive little animals not much bigger than guinea-pigs, gingery in colour and vividly striped. They were the piglets of wild boar, perhaps a dozen in all, followed by three or four old sows, huge and hairy and plainly concerned about keeping their boisterous families together. They are busy animals, ranging far in search of food, but during the heat of the day they like to wallow in mud or cut a mound of grass into which they all burrow for communal comfort. In that dappled light the stripes of the piglets made them almost invisible.

On the way up to the convent I overtook half a dozen nuns in full habit and made a fine speech about resolution and how no doubt we should all meet again at the summit, implying it was as near heaven as we should get that day. Unfortunately they were Polish and didn't know what I was talking about, but they were very cordial and smiled, and I waved and strode on at great speed, wondering how on earth they had managed to get that far and what would happen if they met those wild boar.

In a wholly unsuccessful effort to avoid the bends of that zig-zag I climbed straight up through the trees and managed to lose my way for the second time in two days. A humiliating experience. It meant climbing down to where I had passed the good sisters an hour earlier. By following their neat little shoe-prints I reached the summit where the statue of the saint stands with her arms outstretched to God. I met the troupe coming out of the chapel and tried to give the impression I had been there for hours.

A very sophisticated place, this Saint Odile. In the refectory adjoining the convent a plump Sister asked if I would care to take an aperitif and recommended the *Coq au Riesling*. Outside, a choir of pretty little girls from Colmar sang plain chants; the ice-cream vendors did great business; diesel coaches rolled in and out and like a litany the guides intoned the story of the saint's miraculous life.

Out of a choice of several routes south I rejected only the one to Barr, the legend being that when Satan tempted our Lord and offered him all the cities of the world, he made an exception of Barr which he wanted for himself on the grounds that the stench from the tanneries put him in mind of home. Of the other routes, the Höhwald promised the most dense forests in Alsace, and Andlau the bones of yet another saint, the blessed Richardis. Much as I love a good woman I struck out for the forest assuming from the noise on that holy hill it would be quiet among the trees.

A pleasurable occasion and companionable too, since I fell in with an elderly German naturalist who brought out his flask and addressed me as *Sehr geehrter Kollege* as soon as he realized I shared his passion for what he called the *Tier- und Pflanzenwelt*. He was collecting beetles. Our linguistic bonds were slight, but, since I had once collected beetles myself, passionately, and the standard works on classifications are in German, we made do with a little Latin and what I could remember of the words for such things as antennae (*Fühler*), wing (*Flügeldecken*), wood-boring (*holzbohren*) and metallic (*erzglanz*). This served to distinguish a huge long-horned beetle (*Saperda*) found normally among willows (*Salix*) from a smaller relative less concerned about where it stuck its ovipositor (*Legerohre*), but it made for few subtleties of conversation. For all that, we got on marvellously well, pointing out biological treasure with the enthusiasm of small boys in a toy shop.

The Höhwald used to be renowned for its *bûcherons* and *schlitteurs*, that is the men who felled trees and those who pushed the timber down slopes on *schlittes* that resemble sledges, a difficult and often dangerous operation. They were at it that day, but not with the tools they used to use. The axe has been replaced by mechanical saws that howl like dogs, and instead of *schlittes* the woodsmen haul the dressed logs down chutes by a cable attached to a donkey engine.

The conifers, especially larch and spruce, are superbly well adapted to the senile soils of the Vosges and grow to perfection there. They are systematically felled and replanted in small blocks, a practice that leaves few large gaps wholly bare in the manner of Britain's woe-begone woodlands. Yet in the death throes of any large tree there is something agonizing, the feeling almost of being present at a public execution. One great spruce seemed reluctant to let go of the crest it had clung to for so long. With trunk all but sawn through it leaned over, quivering, until with that sickening crunch that puts you in mind of the extraction of an obstinate molar, the giant toppled and rolled over and over until it came to rest with its arms outstretched on the ground.

For company that night I put my flashlight under a handkerchief near the open flap of the tent and lay abed looking at the wonderful creatures that flew in out of the night. In a whirling circus of insects my guest of honour was the Emperor moth or, rather, his consort for I took that lovely creature with the owl-like eyes on her greyish wings to be a female. This is one of the moths that attract their mates by scattering subtle scents called pheromones downwind. I watched her as she clung to the canvas, fluttering so rapidly that the great eyes seemed blurred, and I wondered whether similar pheromones operate among people.

Some perfumers say they can detect differences in smell between different skin and hair colours. These aromas have been described as 'saucy and sometimes tiring' in brunettes and black-haired women, sharp and fierce in redheads; they are heady and pervasive in blondes like the 'nose' of some flowery wines: you could almost say it fits exactly with their manner of using their lips in kissing: firmer and more possessive in brunettes, more personal perhaps in blondes.

Medieval authorities recognized both the odour of chastity and its opposite, anchastity, 'resembling boiling starch', whilst Groddeck, that strange pupil of Freud, claimed that in reality our powers of smell are as sharp as those of a dog, but that we suppress them for psychosexual reasons. Maybe just as well, for if we smelled love and hostility we might become even more emotionally disturbed than we are in the presence of certain people we instinctively like or dislike. I had to get rid of my guests rather ungraciously by putting the light outside for it brought in a lot of flies.

* * *

At dawn came another mist so dank and so dense that I gave up all thought of storming the *Champs de Feu*. Any fires up there must have long since been put out. With kit wet and heavy I slunk down the road to Andlau, feeling thoroughly miserable.

No sound except the river that scampered along, gurgling under bridges and water wheels, bounding off briefly into the murk, but always returning to that little ribbon road as if unwilling to venture far into the trees alone. I rapidly overtook a priest who from a distance appeared to be saying office in the open air. When at close range I heard a second and higher voice, it seemed as if he were engaged in some curious dialogue between self and soul, or perhaps even with a higher power, though both voices, I discovered, came from a small radio he carried like a breviary and which at my approach he promptly switched off.

At his courteous good morning I said I didn't think it was good at all. I didn't like the weather in the Vosges. It couldn't be relied on. One day the sun shone. One made plans, hopefully. And then what happened? Down came either rain or mist. In a few sentences I managed to siphon off a lot of conflicting emotions. The truth is that at heart I felt a little ashamed of leaving a great forest for the safety of a country lane.

At this he smiled indulgently. Not really *bad* weather he said. Merely cloud. In summer it happened almost every morning and he pointed ahead to where the sky seemed miraculously bright over the church of St Richardis at Andlau.

Above the town the transition from heavy mist to bright sunshine became so marked that I turned round to look at buildings half obscured by the cloud. It was as if we had walked out of the still-open door of a steam room. We parted cordially, he for a baptism and I for my second breakfast that morning.

A stone effigy of a rather sorrowful-looking bear squats outside the Romanesque church of St Richardis. Another huge beast is painted on the south wall of the nave. In a vision the saint was told to found an abbey in whatever place she found a bear scratching the ground and she found such a bear at Andlau. For centuries they kept a lot of bears in the village in her honour. As most of them had to be imported from other countries, it may be that escapes from that holy menagerie helped to prolong their existence in the Vosges. It seems curious that although formerly married to that dissolute monarch, Charles the Fat, the grandson of Charlemagne, Richardis is usually referred to as the Virgin Empress. She walked out on her husband, but it looks as though, fed up with her piety, he tried to get rid of her.

Charles is said to have accused her of having improper relations with his chancellor, Bishop Luitgard. He sentenced her to an ordeal by fire from which she emerged wholly unscathed but, in the words of her biographer, 'saddened'. And off she went to found a community of women who were both virtuous and rich. She admitted nobody with less than half a dozen quarterings and only the Superiors were bound by vows of celibacy.

The bears were killed off in the eighteenth century but from the back of the altar on festal occasions there came such a grunting and snuffling that they brought them back, keeping up the bear garden until the abbey was closed down during the Revolution.

Below Andlau the stream dropped down into the broad Alsatian plain. When the sun began to shine I felt ashamed about scampering out of the mountains at a mere touch of cloud, but the walk, I argued, wasn't a penance. I wasn't out to storm every hill I came to, and I went off south, on the *route du vin*, rid of all path-finding cares until I came to Ammerschwihr.

The vineyards lie on the bosomy slopes of the Vosges. The air is warm and moist and feels enormously generative. The sound is of water pumps and bees and the screech of young starlings. High above are the wrecks of castles, once the homes of such as the Rappoltsteins who called themselves not barons nor lords, but simply *Herren*. They were *the* people. The others were only farmers or townsmen. Far below are walled towns like Dombach and Riquewihr, which dominated the old trade routes up and down the Rhine. Clinging to the hillsides, between the towns and the castles, are scores of little villages, today the homes of vine-growers. They are beautifully got up with flowers. In one village you may come across almost nothing but cascades of wisteria and clematis and in the next maybe a communal display of geraniums and begonia.

At Ribeauville at midday an untidy-looking gendarme cycled up and down the cobbled streets, brandishing a loud-hailer. ' 'Aloo, 'aloo,' he shouted. 'I have been commanded to say that the concert in the parish church tonight will take place one hour later, that is at nine o'clock. The Mayor has been called away on urgent business. Don't forget! At *nine* o'clock. Thank you, citizens of Ribeauville.' He paused and added '*Et bon appétit.*'

We met again in *l'Auberge Zahnacker* where the prime tipple is the pale green wine of that name. I asked if he'd care to take a glass, but he refused on the grounds that if he took but one more drop he would fall off his bicycle.

'Today, M'sieur,' he explained, 'I am fifty years old, an occasion when one has many friends and the morning has already been a long one.' He looked at the bottle a little wistfully. He sighed. 'But alas, for a man of fifty I have no resolution. No resolution at all. If you please, perhaps a little one.'

He sipped it with authority, admiring the colour and the bouquet. He clearly enjoyed it but it didn't brighten him up. Times were bad, he said, a situation due, in his opinion, to the insidious spread of Communism throughout the whole of Alsace. Those labourers now, they wanted everything. A franc here and a franc there. And where did those francs go? They went to Russia through the trade unions. Even the storks had left town. There used to be nests everywhere. But what was the situation today? Only one on the old tower. Where had the rest gone? The birds had gone to Poland and Rumania. And where were those countries but in Russia?

I asked about the *pfiffers*, the musicians and strolling players who had been coming to Ribeauville for their great festival, *Le Pfifferday*, since medieval times. They played and danced in the streets and handed out free drinks from the fountain in front of the *Hôtel de Ville*.

'*Pfiffers!*' he said scornfully. 'They are no longer *pfiffers*. They are organ-grinders. Is a man a musician because he can turn a little handle on a thing like a coffee machine? The real players don't come here any more.'

The wine-growers of Alsace are trying to popularize their Riesling and Sylvaner abroad, but as the district is sandwiched between the better-known vineyards of France and Germany they are obliged to lean heavily on local trade. Wolff, the nineteenth-century traveller, said some people drank between six and ten litres a day and kept a jug beside their bed in case they felt dry during the night. He found it 'rather plaguey stuff'. I prefer the term flinty. Ordinary folk still drink great quantities of the *ordinaire*. For those who want the hard stuff there is a range of liquors, including that tongue-tingling *marc* made from the husks of grapes.

Most of the townships on the *route du vin* offer something older or bigger or better or in some way more remarkable than anywhere else in the world. I took the aphrodisiacal qualities of the wines of Bennwihr on trust; I couldn't find the impregnable tower of Kientzheim, but I dozed under the six-hundred-year-old lime tree of Bergheim. The stump is partly filled with concrete and supported on crutches, yet the branches are heavy with leaves and when the bark falls off they nail it back. A notice says that there in the year 1300 the villagers held their first *fête populaire*. The great castle of High Koenigsberg is at the moment second only to Heidelberg for the title of biggest in Europe, but from the amount of rebuilding going on it may yet outstrip its rival.

To reach Riquewihr from that great castle I ventured down, briefly, on to the main road, where, on a traffic intersection, sat half a dozen *autostoppeurs* importuning lifts to various places from Salzburg to Belfort. Noise apparently means nothing to those who spend a fair amount of time in discothèques. Trucks roared, cars whined and to add to the devilish clatter, three shirtless fellows were boring into the foundations of a new traffic sign with pneumatic drills. One of the youngsters thumbing lifts looked vaguely familiar. He carried a rucksack placarded: COLMAR – JUST MARRIED. The girl from Springfield, Mass., recognized me and shouted 'Hi!'

'How was Luxembourg?' I asked.

'Pretty crummy,' she said.

'Why not walk to Hunawihr? It's across the vineyards.'

'You kiddin'? We're out to enjoy ourselves.'

'How long have you been married?'

The girl looked pained. 'Listen!' she said, 'I've told this jerk if he don't brighten his ideas up, we won't *get* married.'

What you won't find in the guide-books is that Riquewihr is an almost noiseless city. A tiny little place. A town from Lilliput surrounded by a huge wall. The sixteenth-century buildings are in a glorious state of preservation. They could be used for a film set for something by Dumas or Victor Hugo. The streets are so narrow that all cars are kept out. They are parked out of sight, beyond the city gates. Within the walls all you can hear is the heart-warming babble of human voices.

The crowds wander about talking, laughing, taking photographs and sampling free wine. There are a dozen *caves* in the one street that stretches from gate to gate and you can pace that little thoroughfare in five minutes. There I wandered, avoiding only the Tower of the Torturers, intrigued by how wrought-iron and dressed stone gave thoughtful individuality to almost every building in the place. Here is a town that can be proud of how it has handled its inheritance.

Not far from the *Obertor* you may find a tavern next door to a bakery where four or five locals are united twice daily in their common appreciation of *marc*. There is one serious wine-drinker among them. He looked at me anxiously as I sipped the first glass of a quarter casually ordered. It tasted a bit rough.

'Is it not good, M'sieur?' He put the question quietly, almost solicitously.

Falling back on an English platitude, I said, 'It's not bad. Not bad at all.'

'But do you *like* it?' he insisted.

I glanced round. The landlord had gone upstairs. The others were talking. 'No,' I said.

Having got to the kernel of truth, my kindly inquisitor leaned over the bar and picked up a bottle labelled *Traminer Réserve Exceptionelle* and poured out a generous measure.

'Try that,' he said.

A fine wine. Dry but rounded. To my taste better by far than the expensive *Zahnacker* I had bought earlier that day. But what had I been drinking?

'*Ordinaire*,' he said. 'From this region. As you say, it's not bad if you drink all day, like the postman. But it's not a wine. Good wines are produced in small quantities. It is a matter of time and attention and picking only the best grapes. Today they get as much as they can out of the ground, and what can you expect? The wine has no taste.'

He talked with such authority about *Spatlese*, the late gathering, and *Auslese*, the hand-picked bunches of grapes, that I assumed he was in the business.

'No,' he said. 'I am just a baker, but the problems are much the same. What makes good bread? It is a question of good flour and slow fermentation. In the old days we used to leave the dough to ferment for at least three or four hours, and it wasn't necessary to put chemicals into the dough. Today the farmers get much bigger crops from the same piece of ground, but the wheat has lost its taste. And to make it look nice and white – *comme un cadavre* – the millers grind it up fine and sift it, so you are left with very little except starch. The bread gives you wind and goes dry in three hours.'

In Riquewihr that evening I looked at my maps with some misgivings. I had dallied with the Vosges, turning my back on the forest when it began to look difficult. I had seen nothing of the interior. If the Alps were to be tackled with any confidence I reckoned it about time I did some mountain storming. That determined, I bought food; I slept for an hour and struck out straightaway for Ammerschwihr.

A word about sleep. There are certain rhythms within the mind and body that physiologists call circadian, that is – like a tide – they rise and fall within a cycle of about a day: *circa diem*. Sleep is one of them. Most people feel the need at intervals of about sixteen hours. If they get up at eight o'clock they usually begin to feel tired before midnight. My own intervals of sleep are much more brief in duration. No matter whether I'm engaged on a walk or sitting about at home writing, I usually sleep for about six hours at night with a supplementary nap after lunch. During those four days of rapid walking from Riquewihr to the outskirts of Belfort I fell into a different pattern of rest, sleeping only four hours at night and lying down, briefly at intervals of about five hours. In that way I covered near a hundred miles.

I went by the forest of Ammerschwihr and *Les Trois Epis*, climbing up to the ridge of the Hohrodberg with its tremendous view across the vale of Munster to *Les Ballons*, those twin peaks of the southern Vosges. The trails are decisive and for the most part high, winding in and out of defiles in boulder-strewn slopes, but I wrote down little about what I saw, being almost constantly preoccupied with route-finding, checking the distant features I could recognize against map and compass. On the way down through Luxembourg and Lorraine I had walked fast on several occasions, but never with such serious intent as this. The line of march became a training exercise, a dress rehearsal for whatever lay ahead.

Down in the valley of the Fecht, below the *Col de la Schlucht*, are weather-boarded chalets with high-pitched roofs of the kind you might see in any Swiss *vallée*. To this region in the eighth century came missionaries from Ireland and Scotland who left behind Highland names such as Magay and Waray. Some claim the word Munster is derived whole from that province in Ireland, but it would seem more likely to be a corruption of the great *monastère* they built there. But *Ballon* must surely stem from *Bealltain*, that festival common to all the Celtic tribes.

Above the trees on the *Petit Ballon* are high pastures called *chaumes*, in appearance much like the Downs of southern England. The custom is for farmers to drive their beasts up on to that rich grassland on the Feast of St Urban in May and drive them down again towards the end of September. That evening the cattle were browsing among cowslips, cuckoo flowers and bright yellow daisies, all spring flowers that bloom six weeks late on those windy heights. I slept among the cattle, comfortably, scarcely stirring until their bells tinkled again and the eastern hills were rimmed with faint blue light.

To reach Lautenbach at the foot of the *Grand Ballon* I clung to a path that swung about erratically, first to the west, towards the Steinberg and then back again, through the forest, gaining and losing altitude in a series of ample curves. And yet in *The Path to Rome* Hilaire Belloc says he breached those hills in a straight line by way of the Upper Moselle and the *Ballon d'Alsace*. This is puzzling. The Vosgean *sentiers*, the trails used by genera-tions of herdsmen, are invariably serpentine. They follow the contours, outflanking the steep places and skirting the thick and almost impenetrable scrub. How on earth did he manage to get through?

He answers the question himself. By faith he says, and when in doubt he recalled that the Faith is rich in interpretations. For authority he quotes Bacon to the effect that it's permissible and a pleasant thing to mix a little falsehood with one's truth. Belloc broke every vow he made, that is to walk all the way and take advantage of no wheeled thing; to sleep rough and cover thirty miles a day, and to hear mass in St Peter's on the Feast of St Peter and St Paul.

Belloc's route is difficult, if not impossible, to follow. It is no guide-book and that boisterous champion of Christendom would be amused that anyone might think it was. In what on the face of it is a record-breaking journey, he walked from Toul in Lorraine to the gates of Rome in just over three weeks, indulging, he admits, in several lifts and two train rides on the way. His business, he says, is with the feel of Europe undivided, and its people and where they live and what they believe in. He is pliant in contradictions and stiff with opinions; at times a moral bully. Philip Toynbee accuses him of using his church like a supporters' rattle at a football match, gibing at Jews, journalists, Protestants, spirit-drinkers and eaters of boiled mutton. The marvel is how he managed to get through the high passes without maps, wearing an old cotton suit and why, throughout the journey, he never saw a single flower, a bird, an animal, even a butterfly worth mentioning. He deals only in what he sees as the relationship of man to man. The rest of nature can go hang, an attitude which, some people think, is the fault of most if not all promoters of ethical systems in our western world. For all that, he has a keen eye for glimpses of character, for scenery on the grand scale and above all for the movement of light and air as you might sense it on the rim of the Vosges at dawn:

> The faint uncertain glimmer that seemed not so much to shine through the air as to be part of it, took all the colour out of the woods and fields and the high slopes above me, leaving them planes of grey and deeper grey. The woods near me were a silhouette, black and motionless, emphasizing the east beyond. The river was white and dead, not even a steam rose from it, but out of the further pastures a gentle mist had lifted up and lay all even along the flanks of the hills, so that they rose out of it, indistinct at their bases, clear

cut above against the brightening sky; and the farther they were the more mouldings showed in the early light, and the most distant edges of all caught the morning.

On the way down that day, just below the locked gates of the hostel run by *Les Amis de la Nature*, it began to pour down. I cowered under a tangle of juniper which for shelter is about as effective as a canopy of gorse. The storm passed quickly enough but it left me soaked through, and with pants and jacket gently steaming I made for a farmhouse below the forest of Rouffach.

I wanted no more than advice about the way down to the next valley, but the woman pointed to a chair and in strident German began such argument with her husband that I heartily regretted knocking on their door. The man went out. Ignoring my map, she held up her hand, indicating that I should have to wait. When the man reappeared with a bottle, she shouted at him again, even more loudly. Gradually it became clear that she had told him to fetch some wine, but he hadn't warmed it and I should have to wait again. And back the wine came, this time beautifully warmed and she gave me a glass with some oatcakes. And partly in mime she told me to take off my jacket so she could dry it properly.

The people of the Vosges are fussy and kind. Helpfulness comes easily to them, but they look worried, as bloodhounds do. In places where they speak French they took my small jokes at face value and looked at me as if I were completely mad. Even from fragments of conversations you gain the impression that on all the really important issues the last word is with the woman of the house. At weddings it used to be the custom for brides to feign reluctance. At the moment of espousal, they took care to bend their fingers so that the ring might not pass too easily over the first joint, and when the pair rose for the blessing the girl was customarily first on her feet. Perhaps they joke about these sorts of things among themselves; I should like to think they do though their humour is a bit macabre.

At Rouffach there is a story that centuries ago the villagers decided to build their own gallows at the crossroads, and very proud they were of it. A fine piece of mature oak, buttressed against shock with such care and ingenuity that at the critical moment of stress, that apocalyptic moment between life and death, the cross-piece scarcely quivered. But when the inhabitants of an adjoining parish asked if they could hang one of their malefactors on that work of art, the Rouffachers sent back an indignant message. 'Certainly not,' they said. 'This gallows is for ourselves alone, and for our children.'

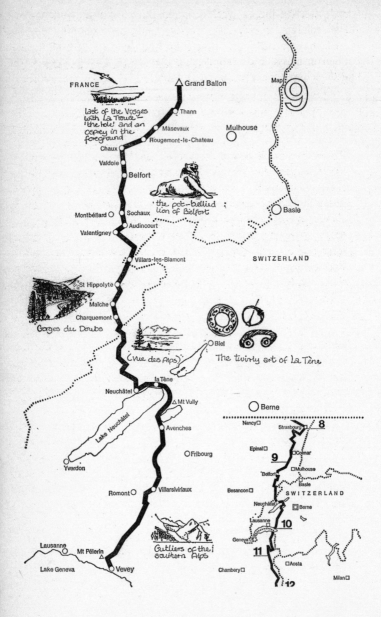

FRANCE

△ Grand Ballon

Map **9**

○ Thann

last of the Vosges
with La Trouée
'the hole' and an
osprey in the
foreground

Másevaux

○ Mulhouse

Rougemont-le-Château

Chaux

Valdoie ○

○ **Belfort**

the pot-bellied
lion of Belfort

○ Basle

Montbéliard ○   Sochaux ○

Audincourt ○

Valentigney ○

Villars-les-Blamont ○

S W I T Z E R L A N D

St Hippolyte ○

Maîche ○

Charquemont ○

Gorges du Doubs

Vue des Alps

○ Biel

The twirly art of La Tène

la Tène ○

Neuchâtel ○

△ Mt Vully

○ Berne

Lake Neuchâtel

○ Avenches

Yverdon ○

○ Fribourg

Romont ○   Villarsiviriaux ○

Outliers of the
southern Alps

Lausanne ○   Mt Pélerin △

Lake Geneva   ○ Vevey

Nancy □   □ Strasbourg   **8**

Épinal □   ○ Colmar   **9**

□ Belfort   □ Mulhouse
Besançon □   □ Basle
SWITZERLAND
Neuchâtel □   □ Berne
Lausanne □   **10**
Geneva □   **11**
Chambéry □   □ Aosta   Milan □
12

The Shores of Tethys

To the east the Vosges is drained by the Rhine; to the west by her tributaries, the Sarre, the Meurthe and the Moselle, and to the south or, more exactly to the south-west, by the Saône. In addition to those great rivers hosts of little cascades tumble off the shoulders of the *Ballon d'Alsace* with recourse to their only escape route, the Savoureuse. From some high bourne up in the forests of Lepuix they get hopelessly lost in the marshes of Rosemontoise, and into that depression I walked by way of the Rossberg, Masevaux, and Rougemont-le-Château.

Fine names and fine places. The meres mirror the sky. From a perch on a mooring post far out on the gently steaming water an osprey rose and made off on heavy wing beats, whistling plaintively. The villages are hidden away behind screens of reeds. With their well-stocked barns, good fencing and gaily-painted doors, they look prosperous enough, but some ill-humour hangs over the place like a miasma. The people are surly and clearly want no truck with strangers.

At the mention of food in a bar near Chaux, an old woman said she was *occupée* and went on sweeping up the floor. In the next hamlet the *patron* merely shook his head. I asked him: wasn't there a bakery or a general store thereabouts? He continued to shake his head. Then where did his own food come from? By the van, he said and that's all he said. No greetings, no regret, no farewell. Just that slow shake of the head.

I trudged on, reflecting that Rosemontoise lies in La Trouée, the great depression between the Vosges and the Jura, a gap through which the soft under-belly of France has been repeatedly assailed. I felt irritated and depressed, almost cheated by that incivility, since I had looked forward to the easy walk down from the *Ballons* as light relief, a short holiday before the more serious business of tackling the Jura. Two or three villages slipped by before I met the van coming up from Sermamagny laden, I imagined, with all manner of good things, but the fellow protested he had nothing to spare. After much argument he charged me an immoderate sum for some bread and pressed meat.

Somehow I couldn't avoid a clearly visible loop in the road from Thann. Even the blacksmith seemed unsure of the way. Rumbling dyspeptically, I entered Belfort through the slums of Valdoie, determined to ask no more questions.

Street names fascinate me. In my native north of England they give you an impression of what the old towns used to be like. From youthful days in that coal-black city of Leeds I remember Burmantofts, Boar Lane, Swinegate, Sheepscar and Kirkstall. Shopping centres nowadays, but they still conjure up a picture of a prosperous little township that handled wool and leather in the vicinity of a great Cistercian abbey.

In France you are up against civic pride and *amor patriae*. Most of the street names honour great men. If you know anything about who they are, that is if they are local or national heroes, you can often gauge how far you are from a city centre. Knowing the strong military flavour about almost everything in Belfort, I liked to imagine that *rue George Brulot* perpetuated the exploits of a little drummer boy at the time of the Prussian invasion: perhaps *Doctor Louis Chippre* became surgeon-general under Condé and *Jacques Bombard* invented a new kind of mortar. Passing the old roads to Colmar, Epinal and Besançon, I came at length to the *faubourg des Ancêtres* and there on surer ground came the classic succession of avenues from *Jeanne d'Arc* to *De Gaulle* by way of *Vauban*, *Clemenceau*, *Joffre* and *Foch*, all in proper order around the *place d'Armes*.

Belfort is what it says, an outstanding defence point in the most vulnerable part of the Gap. There in 1870, Colonel Denfert-Rochereau successfully defended the garrison against forty thousand German troops in what is reckoned one of the greatest artillery duels of the nineteenth century. The town was surrounded, cut off from the rest of France. Typhus and smallpox broke out among the defenders. For six weeks they were shelled at short range by near a hundred guns. But the Colonel showed himself a brilliant tactician. He made repeated sorties. From his bomb-proof emplacements he returned the fire with such accuracy that the Germans were forced to evacuate several villages they had taken. He was saved by a general armistice, and the artillerymen marched out into the ruins of the town with their cannon in train and colours flying. The action is commemorated by the enormous figure of a pot-bellied lion carved out of the rock face below the castle by Bartholdi, that same sculptor who made the statue of Liberty in New York harbour.

At sundown I sat on the bridge above the gentle Savoureuse, watching wagtails scampering about among snowy drifts of water crowfoot. Bells pealed, slowly, and when several homebound citizens wished me a cordial good evening, I decided that La Trouée was no more than a pocket of marsh air and sought lodging near the *Porte de Brisach.*

In that busy place the landlord, his plump wife and four children were already about their roast veal and salad in the bar. On his assurance that he would attend me almost immediately, I took a glass in the company of a bargemaster and his mate from Saverne.

We chatted comfortably. One advantage of an open shirt and a frayed jacket is that you can mingle among local folk without looking conspicuously foreign. A pipe is useful, too. It gives an air of self-sufficiency. I suppose a man on his own can look at ease, puffing away at a cigarette, but offhand I can't recall seeing one. But a pipe has something substantial about it and, like an open fire, it needs constant attention, giving you time to think about what you're trying to say.

With a polite little belch behind his napkin my host finished his meal. Still wiping his moustache he came over. 'M'sieur,' he said, 'now I am at your service *entirely.*'

He served me himself. A fine meal with a running commentary. Small jokes about that *vigorous* wine. It might be good for my feet, he thought, but not if I intended to walk far that night. What did I think of their country? At my expurgated account of the morning's adventures, he nodded. Everywhere, he said, good local folk were being ousted by uncouth foreigners. But I must understand he came from Provence where, he implied, their manners were as good as their food.

Towards eleven o'clock, at that hour when you are unceremoniously ordered out of an English pub, the bargemaster held court among the crews of five craft which had just come in, and we drank and talked until long past midnight. The subjects ranged among the commonplaces of travel, about how riverside towns were much alike, but as the wine grew more to my taste I recall telling immodest stories about voyages on foot, bringing in the thunderstorms and the dogs of Oberhaslach. I recount this dispassionately, holding that among strangers you get entertainment pretty much in proportion to what you give, and if my pedestrian chatter came out half as beguiling as their stories and good humour the night went well.

Belfort made ample amends for my brush with her marshmen. A woman in a bar refused payment for a coffee on the grounds that, years ago, her own son had set off on just such a walk as mine and, as I understood it, he had not yet returned. Before I set off again I discovered that of all things I had lost my passport. At the post office the *chef* seemed delighted to see me. He said one of his clerks had found the thing on the counter the previous night, but unfortunately the man had gone off for the day and it took us half an hour to find that valuable bit of cardboard carefully filed away under my Christian name.

The country to the south looked easy going as far as the Lomont ridge, the outermost wall of the Jura, but I failed to notice the words Chatenois-les-Forges and Peugeot on the map. Instead of the slopes I had looked forward to, I walked into mile upon mile of industrial squalor dominated by steel foundries and a huge automobile plant between Sochaux and Montbéliard. Thrashing about, venturing up side lanes in an effort to avoid the outerworks of a new motorway, I sought refuge on the towpath of yet another canal, a branch of the Bourbeuse.

The most that can be said for the local people is that, like the Rosemontois, they are not easy to get on with. This broad generalization is based on a few words with a seemingly deaf and dumb storekeeper, two or three cottagers, a road-mender and the fishermen I met on the canal. Perhaps they are not so much hostile as fugitive. They seem to shrink and curl up when you speak to them. The men don't talk much among themselves, at least not in the presence of strangers in bars, but their womenfolk chatter immoderately, kissing and embracing each other in the streets so warmly that I wondered what compensatory factors were at work in their fulsome displays of affection. A woman carried her podgy son into a café, an unresponsive child who looked embarrassed at being displayed on a table like a prize melon.

'Look at him!' she said to the company at large. 'The whole time he demands of me that I kiss him like this and like this. He is *never* satisfied.' And she set about him again. But far from looking gratified that youngster wrinkled up its face and began to howl.

Knowing something about their sport, I rank canal fishermen among the most friendly and philosophical of men. They are pensive solitaries, hardened to ill-weather and meagre reward. With nothing to look at except a tin of maggots and a red-tipped float, you might think they'd welcome a word from a stranger. But not in La Trouée. For the indisputable proposition that it was a fine day, I received stares so blank, so utterly lacking in lustre that I walked on, feeling they had fished existence by and I had touched the very heart of that depression. Choosing a quiet corner of that waterway, I stripped off and dived in, clutching a tablet of soap. In the purification ceremony I lost the soap and had some difficulty in clambering back up the steep bank, but I felt much better and slept for an hour in the sun.

According to *Michelin*, the Gap is about twenty miles in length, extending from somewhere near Sermamagny to Brognard where the canal swings off towards Mulhouse. I'm inclined to add a few miles, putting the outermost bounds of that grim place nearer Seloncourt or perhaps Bondeval where the country grows noticeably hilly and the people more friendly. There is nothing dramatic in the change of atmosphere, but you can sense it as surely as a hint of warmth in the wind. On I went, coasting along within a few miles of the Swiss frontier, entering forests that matched those last seen in the Vosges and close on sundown I came to an inn near Blamont at the foot of the great ridge.

As an inducement to stay the night, the woman of the place, a motherly soul, insisted on showing off a bedroom where no less than the winner of the *Tour de France* had slept with evident satisfaction. In the bar she described how he had taken a drink with them all, but somebody winked and to her indignation the company affected not to remember the occasion. Not to be outdone, I told how in two days I had walked down from the Rossberg and don't think anyone believed me either. With a reputation to uphold, I finished the bottle and went into a night as black as the pit. Unable to find the log cabin they talked about, I pitched down on an acutely sloping pasturage, not uncomfortable but rather like sleeping on the end of a seesaw.

Came dawn and what the Irish would call a fine soft morning, that's to say it pelted down. Stretching out I put my feet into a small but very cold pond. During the night, a little rivulet had trickled in and hadn't been able to trickle out. All my under-clothes were soaking wet together with several maps, a book on the flora of the Alps and the toe-end of a heavily quilted sleeping bag. I'm relating all this dispassionately as if it were the sort of thing I have grown accustomed to. It's what I remember when people say how nice it must be to sleep out in the wilds.

Under normal conditions I can usually pack up in about half an hour. This entails crawling out and spreading out something waterproof for a dressing table. After a good wash, usually in a stream but at worst in water from a cow trough, I stow away my spare clothing in plastic bags. These have to be pushed down hard into the rucksack with all the light stuff at the bottom and the camera and the books on top. Then comes the job of dis-mantling the tent and giving it a good shake and rolling it up inside the groundsheet together with the tent poles and pegs. That morning I packed up everything that could be packed inside the tent. Without so much as a bite or a wash, I went out into the downpour and pulled down my flimsy shelter.

For two hours I trudged on, climbing steadily with head down into the wind and the rain like a close-hauled boat. I argued, ineffectively, that it would be worse in snow, or if I were cold instead of merely being warm and wet. There's nothing remark-able about getting wet, but unless you can turn on some form of diversion, it wears you down, perniciously and quicker by far than almost any other form of physical discomfort short of outright exhaustion. But what have you got to think about in the rain at half past six in the morning except the rain? From almost forgotten lectures I dredged up what little I could remember of Stoic philosophy, but it didn't really help. As far as I could remember, the whole system had been demolished by Epictetus, or was I thinking of someone else? Who was the man who said he had never seen a real Stoic and never expected to see one? I didn't know and I didn't care. Better to do something practical about that large wet patch under my rain gear and I took off my shirt and jacket.

Instant relief. The rain slackened somewhat. Like air from a hair drier the wind felt warm. It bore down on me, steadily. I could lean against it, and in between squalls my clothes dried in a few minutes. This is the Föhn that sweeps across the northern Alps, melting the snow, the wind caused by deep barometric depressions in the hollows of those hills.

On the way down to Neuchâtel I saw the Jura in all her humours, silver-bright in the sunshine, black and menacing in storm and grey as a dove's wing at dusk, yet never more theatrical than she appeared from the summit of Lomont that morning. At first all seemed misty and obscure. Clouds hung over the gorges of the Doubs, but under the impact of the Föhn, they fell back, tumbling over each other to disclose ridge upon ridge of hills, a corrugation of limestone stretching out into infinity like the waves of a petrified sea. Geologists refer to those waves as a fixed swell, the swell of an ancient sea called Tethys.

In mythology Tethys is the daughter of Earth and Heaven who gave birth to the rivers. But during the Jurassic era, long before Europe took on her present shape, a sea now known by that name extended from the Pyrenees to the outermost Himalayas. Fossils show that the waters were dominated by giant marine reptiles. Dinosaurs roamed the surrounding shores and the lizards with umbrella-like wings glided down from the cliffs in search of fish and other smaller prey. The sea began to shrink about sixty million years ago. The hardened remains of the floor were pushed up into the shape of the Alps and other great ranges from the Atlas to the Hindu Kush. What remained of Tethys became the tideless Mediterranean.

The sun sneaked out, cautiously. It would have been good to spread out my sodden gear and bask on those warm limestone cliffs, but I felt ferociously hungry and coasted down to St Hippolyte on the banks of the Doubs.

In three days I crossed that wayward river three times. The Doubs rises on the Black Ridge of the Jura and flows north-east, cutting its way through some immense gorges, apparently intent on joining the Rhine. On the way there it encounters a head-on block at St Ursanne and swings round almost full circle, turning first west and then north towards the lakes of Rosemontoise. Near Montbéliard it runs into yet another obstacle and turns south for the Saône, a detour of nearly two hundred miles.

St Hippolyte lies on the floor of a gorge at the junction of the Doubs and the Dessoubre. A pleasantly dilapidated place '*situé dans un site pittoresque*', it says on the postcards. I recall an immense breakfast shortly before lunch and much argument with the village doctor, a smart young fellow called Prelot who beguiled me into a passionate defence of rustic life when it soon became clear that I didn't know much about it. He began with some provocative remarks about the need to brighten the place up. He would like to see a juke-box in the hotel and I forget what else in the one narrow street outside. If I hadn't caught the eye of the Mayor, M. René Guenot – 'just an entrepreneur' – I don't know what I might have said.

The doctor changed his tactics. Glancing down at my boots he said, 'If you will permit the expression, M'sieur, you are an anachronism yourself. Why do you walk about like a vagabond when you could get to the top of the *Combe de Goule* in ten minutes by car?'

'Because I can see much more by walking there.'

'But you are wasting a lot of time.'

'Instead of doing what?'

Dr Prelot sighed and then smiled, patiently. 'Listen,' he said. 'If you will allow me to drive you to Maiche this afternoon, I will show you something of our rustic life. But if you insist on walking, why then – *pouff!* – you will miss it all.'

Rather primly I said that I preferred to walk.

'Then I'll see you at the top of the *Combe* in about three hours.'

'How far is that?'

'About ten kilometres and *very* steep.'

Saying I'd be there in half that time, I set off after lunch with a great display of nonchalance. A stupid boast which I regretted within five minutes of leaving the hotel.

From the map it looked as if I could avoid the tortuous bends in the road by following a *muletier*, but it was far steeper than I thought. Mont Miroir loomed overhead. The track clung to the edge of the gorge. By keeping up a steady pace and breathing deeply and slowly, I reached the summit and sat down, feeling dizzy but still with a few minutes in hand.

Prelot didn't show the surprise I thought I was entitled to. Observing merely that, for the British, walking wasn't a sport but a form of masochism, he offered to meet me in a hotel in Maiche that night. I said yes, not knowing what I was in for.

Four or five old men sat round the bar of that unpretentious little place, watching the procession of late diners. When the girl strolled in, I may have been dozing or sunk so deep in thought that I had the momentary impression of a vision. She walked in slowly, as if in a trance. A beautiful girl. The Madonna of the sleeping car. She looked about nineteen. She wore a low-cut gown that swept the floor. She smiled and nodded to the locals who chuckled like starlings and raised their glasses.

Before I got an inkling of what it was all about, the door crashed open and in rushed a dwarf, a strange little man with short legs and the open-mouthed expression of a child. He ran up to the girl. He flung his arms round her waist, burrowing his nose between her partly exposed breasts and screamed, '*Je t'adore!*'

Far from looking shocked or even surprised, the girl bent down and kissed him gently on the top of his head. At this he shrieked and leapt on to a table where he began to dance, wildly, throwing out his legs in Cossack-fashion. From somewhere at the back of the restaurant came the sound of tom-toms. Two brigands had sidled in. They sat on either side of the door with the drums between their knees.

In to this company strode the Prince, a handsome young man got up somewhat in the manner of Hamlet. He came up to my table and held out his hand. 'Good evening,' he said in English. 'Dr Prelot told me you'd probably be here. My name's Wesman. Laurent Wesman of *Télévision Française*. We're shooting not far from here tonight. If you've nothing better to do, perhaps you'd care to join us?'

Mentally unstrapping a seat-belt, I stood up and met the director, Jean-Michel and eight or nine of the company. Christine Audhuy (the vision) smiled and said *halloo*. The brigands folded their arms and snarled. The courtiers bowed, and spies and a rebel chief made appropriate noises. The dwarf retired to a corner, sulkily, where to the huge delight of some youngsters he stood on his head.

'Jacques Kancellier,' said Wesman. 'Our comic. A fellow of *infinite* jest, but a little difficult at times.' Pedalling furiously with his legs, Kancellier began to howl like a dog.

Up in the hills that night they set fire to an old farm cart loaded with enough timber to burn a dozen martyrs. To get the silhouette effect of a camp-fire scene, they ringed the pyre with arc lights and threw on handfuls of salt for colour. Christine sat within ten feet of the flames, at the foot of the Prince, the part played by Wesman. As she gazed up into his eyes, perspiration dripped off her pretty nose. Her make-up dribbled, but without altering a long-sustained pose by so much as a flicker, she said her agent would hear more of it. There had been no talk of Jeanne d'Arc in the contract. 'I am not *La Pucelle saignant ou bien cuit,*' she said.

Safe behind the asbestos screen in front of the cameras, Jean-Michel tried to console her through a loud-hailer. She was their darling, he said. They *all* loved her, and what was a little roasting for art's sake?

I forget the serialized details of *Rendez-vous à Badenbourg.* It had to do with a bored prince of an exotic country who, tiring of plots and brigandage, ran off to Paris with a little seamstress and opened a highly-successful garage for racing cars. But I remember young faces in the light of that enormous fire and a nightingale that sang during a pause as if it had been brought in exactly on cue.

'A bird?' said a technician, taking off his earphones. 'Birds they are everywhere. No, we are not doing any background stuff. This, you understand, is a *facétie.* It has no great reality.'

Towards midnight I found Prelot sitting on a wooden box labelled *Poudre à canon.* He was drinking beer and discussing the elections with one of the cast. 'Aha,' he said. 'Our English friend, the vagabond. Tell us, M'sieur, what do you think of our rural life here? It has a primitive quality, eh?'

From Maiche I mounted the Sergnottes above Charquemont, scarcely pausing there, conscious of a dull pain in my right knee, the product, I think, of that imprudent scramble over the *Combe de Goule* the previous day. To the south, the cliffs of Tethys looked even more inhospitable beyond the Cendrée where the Doubs plunges into yet another gorge, the Côte du Grand Combe, a rift between France and Switzerland some twenty miles in length. When I stumbled, twice, on the way down into the gorge, I stretched out for half an hour on a warm white rock and wondered whether I ought to get that knee looked at, perhaps bandaged up, but from my notebook I saw that in all I had walked close on eight hundred miles which is a highly significant figure in my calculations.

I tackle a lengthy journey by breaking up the whole distance into parts of three or four hundred miles which is just about as far as incentive, the urge to reach a place, can be stretched, and then I rest for two or three days. My first goal had been Strasbourg, I hoped to be well within sight of the Alps that weekend, but it meant stepping out pretty nimbly for at least another sixty miles.

At midday or thereabouts the Föhn abated; a cool wind blew from the east and the shredded clouds reassembled, huddling together until one great thunderhead towered alone over a peak with the uncompromising name of the Staircase of Death. I looked at it with dismay. I knew that powerful gusts of warm air were surging upwards through that swirling mass of cumulus. I knew the droplets would freeze and fall down into the bottom of the cloud, carrying counter-charges into vapour already tortured in its search for equilibrium. All this, I say, I knew, and it scared me the more since there is little shelter on the roof of the gorge.

At the first tremendous crash I thought I had been struck and had somehow managed to survive. There was no perceptible interval between a blood-red flash of light and what sounded like a shot from a twenty-five pounder. The red colour came from seeing the stroke through closed eyelids. I felt both frightened and stunned. I crouched there for a few moments, feeling dreadfully exposed, and then I got up and ran through the pelting rain to an overhang of rock below the parapet. I have never been able to overcome my fear of storms.

A bad day that. For three hours the thunder rampaged up and down the gorge like a bad-tempered dog. At intervals it rained, hard, and when towards evening the sky softened, the woods of La Rass were wreathed in mist.

If the stocky little *garde* who searched me thought I was a smuggler he must have been very disappointed by what he found. He carried a gun and went through my pack with the skill of an old-clothes dealer. Out it all came, the disordered components of adventure: a sponge bag wrapped up in soiled underwear, medicaments and a few boiled sweets, a tin of dubbing and a flask of cognac, several maps and that most precious possession, a cloth-bound notebook. He probed and squeezed everything from sleeping bag down to a tube of toothpaste. Apparently satisfied, he asked me where I had come from.

'Holland,' I said.

'And your destination?'

'The Mediterranean.'

It came out pat. I had never said it before. I knew it sounded pretentious and I don't like to tempt providence. I ought to have added, 'I hope,' but I didn't. With nearly two-thirds of the trip done, I thought, To hell with it. Don't fool around. Say what you are really up to for once. The *garde* didn't look in the least surprised. He wished me a polite good night and made off. I might have been out for a day's stroll. I watched him climb back up on to the road with long strides taken with such deliberation that, from below, he seemed to be moving in slow motion. I wondered where his ancestors came from.

When I sketched out the ground plan of this trip I thought that by walking through several countries I might be able to distinguish some of the facial characteristics of Nordic and Celt, Alpine and Mediterranean. What I had overlooked was that in Europe 'pure' types are very rare and people on the frontiers of France and Germany, Switzerland and Italy are more mixed than most. Race is often used to denote a hypothetically pure stock which we assume existed in the past before it became mixed up with what we like to regard as 'foreign' elements. It's not just a matter of physiognomy or even skin colour. In southern India there are black Caucasians who seem related to Australian bushmen and possibly the hairy Ainu of Japan. Mongols range from yellow-skinned Orientals to the chocolate-brown natives of South America. The texture and the colour of hair are equally deceptive. People as wavy-haired as the Celts crop up among Negroes, and red hair is particularly common among Finns, the Jews and the Welsh as well as the Irish and Scottish highlanders. What it comes down to is that the so-called primary stocks of mankind, the Caucasoids, the Mongoloids and the Negroids can be divided up into scores of mixed or composite types and a few show clear traces of what are reckoned to be our earliest civilized ancestors.

From his heavy brow ridges and aggressive chin, the *garde* looked like a classic Alpine type, a survivor of those hunters who roamed Europe at the end of the last Ice Age. They were the cave painters, the creators of one of the most astonishing forms of art known to mankind. Man has used primitive tools for over a million years, but the hunters of the Upper Palaeolithic used them for supernatural purposes. What they left behind are not mere scratches or blobs of paint plastered on a wall as a child or a prisoner might plaster them to while away the time. They are vividly coloured frescoes that move as the torchlight flickers. They were carefully drawn and painted by people who lived constantly in the company of large herds of bison and wild horses, mammoths and reindeer, especially reindeer. The hunters knew every sinew, every bone of those animals. They watched them. They followed them. They slew them by driving them over the edge of cliffs or into deep pits dug into the ground. They cut them up. They ate their flesh, using the hairy skin for protection, for tentage, for clothing and the bones for tools. Never was a human society so thoroughly a part of its surroundings as those bands of reindeer hunters, and to ensure the return of their prey they portrayed them exuberantly alive, never dead. They painted them grazing quietly, head down or galloping away terrified, their nostrils high in the wind. The artists of Altamira and the Dordogne were so sure of the characteristics, the very essence of what they depicted, that they didn't bother to join their lines together. They merely showed the mountainous back or formid-able neck of a bison, a glimpse of a wolf or the head of a reindeer with its antlers spreading out like seaweed. They were propitiatory figures and among them they sometimes portrayed themselves, as spidery insignificant beings, crouching down, armed with a spear or running away from a charging animal. They portrayed their womenfolk with broad haunches and breasts and bellies broken down by maternity, but with warm flesh fulfilling desire and lulling their fatigue.

Art which expresses life is as mysterious as life. It eludes all definition as life does. By their use of art and fire the cave painters transformed the life of man by lifting him out of the brutish, the mere survival state of his existence. Through art they gained a sense of supernatural, that extra-worldliness which is the first stirring, the beginnings of religion.

The range of the Alpines, the descendants of those hunters, extended from western France to the Urals and beyond. But like all hunters they were thinly distributed. They were pushed back into the mountains by waves of invaders from the north and from the Mediterranean. The type is still recognizable. As I recall, the *garde* had a prominent thin nose and a long narrow face which are among the characteristics of the Basques, a race older by far than the Indo-Europeans. His hair looked almost black and his eyes and skin as dark as a gypsy's. Perhaps he came from the Italian Ticino or from Greek or Ligurian stock in Provence. Ethnological snap judgements get us nowhere. I decided he was a man obviously at home in the mountains and left it at that.

When I used to travel about Europe as a newspaper correspondent I kept a diary, jotting down notes about the people I met and the high spots of big cities, especially those places where they go in for international conferences. I don't think I ever re-read a word of what seemed memorable at the time, but the experiences helped to wipe out a lot of prejudices about so-called national characteristics stored up since childhood days. It may be that zoologists and physicists are quite unlike their fellow-countrymen. I certainly never recall meeting a Dane or a Swede more gloomy, a Dutchman more stolid or a Frenchman more disposed towards wine and women than the usual run of their colleagues from other countries.

But if one prejudice stuck it was that the Swiss will talk about almost anything except their private affairs and they will never invite you into their own homes. Perhaps the situation is different in Geneva, Zürich, and Basle, the places I visited most frequently, but I don't think so. When I come to think about it, I never tried to get to know the Swiss. But on this trip, that is between the Swiss border at Biaufond and right down through the cantons of Neuchâtel, Fribourg and Vaud to Vevey on the shores of Lake Geneva, I met people so hospitable that I can't easily describe what they did for me. In the woods that night Raymond Droz, a local wine merchant, and his wife saw me cowering under a tree, wet through, and insisted on taking me back to their home for dinner. They pressed me to spend the weekend there. When I slipped and fell awkwardly the next day, George Rufer, who grows gentians below the *Vue des Alpes*, almost carried me back to his chalet. And there were others, simple folk, who make me think of that little country's goodwill towards strangers with enormous affection.

In La Chaux de Fonds, the capital of the Swiss watch-making industry, they sell coffee as expensive as Scotch. You can buy bars of gold there, too, and anti-Föhn preparations to cure depressions caused by the wind that sweeps down from the Combes of the Doubs, but everyone depends directly or indirectly on the watches they turn out at the rate of thousands an hour.

The industry is essentially a remunerative by-product of the Reformation. John Calvin, the reformer, gave it a push when he forbade the goldsmiths of Geneva to manufacture crosses, chalices 'and all other instruments used for popery and idolatry'. When the French Huguenots began to make watches there the goldsmiths turned to the craft and within a century Geneva looked like becoming the centre of the industry.

La Chaux de Fonds acquired the lead when a local horse-dealer returned from London with 'a fat watch of curious design'. It may have been one of Tompion's famous time-pieces embodying the new idea of the dead-beat escapement, a means of regulating the movement with a notched balance wheel. The Swiss are a bit reticent about anything they haven't invented themselves. The story is that one day the watch that everyone admired stopped and when a local craftsman called Daniel Jean-Richard took it to pieces, he discovered what made it tick accurately. He improved on the mechanism and started to make watches himself. The craft spread to nearby Neuchâtel and Le Locle where they make more watches than anywhere else in the world.

If I had time to spare, and the zest to do the whole trip again, I should choose a far better, a far quieter place than *Vue des Alpes* for my first glimpse of those mountains. The Swiss want everybody to see the view in comfort. In addition to the tracks that lead up from La Chaux de Fonds, the national highway to Neuchâtel soars up to the very edge of the platform and there on a fine day, ideally about five o'clock in the afternoon, you may see hosts of alps and hosts of cars. For those who value a panorama in proportion to the number of peaks they can count, this must be one of the best, the most easily attainable spectacles in Switzerland. It's enormous. From Grindelwald to Mont Blanc the peaks stand out like the nipples on a sow's belly. But it's a far from peaceful sight. The viewers jostle each other to get at the best places to stand, and then they drive off, hooting wildly at other cars trying to enter. I tramped off towards the *Tête de Ran*, still on a road but a much quieter place, and there I sat down and wrote uncharitable notes about what the vista-seeker wants and why it never seems to satisfy him for very long.

On the *Vue des Alpes* the view is free and far from intimate. The mountains are about a hundred miles away. Even a professional geographer with a pair of field-glasses would be hard put to find much to hold him there. But when a visitor has spent a pound or two on being hauled up to a high place where he can wander about you might expect him to look at what he's come to see and not spend most of his time drinking coffee and buying postcards in the chalet at the top. But it's much the same everywhere. The plain fact is that it's rare to find anyone with any identification with the view. He is probably not interested in the birds and plants around the chalet. The whole atmosphere is far removed from his experience. After the momentary pleasure of surprise he is anxious to be off.

Perhaps I'm being a bit hard on those who are not particularly interested in natural history, but it comes down to the simple fact that if you don't know what you're looking at, you can't be expected to look at it for very long. With his affinities for what makes up the world, the naturalist is able to put a great deal between what he sees and that portion of his mind where boredom lurks. As a human being he's neither better nor worse than his fellows, but in the matter of deriving pleasure from the out-of-doors he is infinitely more fortunate.

Lake Neuchâtel lay far below. With every step I took the distant Alps sank a fraction more until all but the most obtuse peaks pierced the horizon, and then they too began to subside. I would have held them back. I would have soared across that intervening space as you can soar in the boundless stuff of dreams, and climbed those heights then and there, recklessly, forgetful of all else except mastering the outworks, the first wall of the range I had thought about for so long, but that's not the way of walking. There's no escaping the persistent ordinariness, the dull lengths of prolonged exertion, and I walked on the quicker, keeping to a well-blazed trail through hangars of fragrant birch and pine.

I forget what I slipped on. I remember thinking the wet grass seemed unduly slippery, but too late. With no grip left in smoothed-out boot soles, I rolled over like a shot rabbit and lay there sweating from a wrenched knee. When George Rufer hurried up I had all but written the whole trip off. I couldn't stand without a feeling of acute nausea, but that kindly man massaged my knee and with an arm firmly around my waist, he led me down to the chalet he had built among the trees.

There in his garden I lounged for half a day, propped up with cushions in a basketwork chair set down among bright clusters of gentians, listening to tales of the Jura in winter and of his work in the mountain rescue service. He had built the chalet for a dear friend, somebody who had died before they could share it together, but, as he said, that's the way things are. A man had to keep on living and he loved his flowers, especially gentians. I tried to describe those I knew best, those little trumpets more blue than the sky above High Teesdale, but in impoverished French it came out poorly. Yet he knew the name *verna*, the gentian of spring, and *nivalis*, the flower of the snows. They grew there in profusion. He showed me *ciliata*, which is delicate mauve in colour, and *clusii* that seems to grow straight out of the ground without a stem, and many more including a variety of *lutea*, a shaggy-looking plant as tall as a hollyhock from which they extract the medicinal dye and make a bitter liqueur, *Enzen-branntwein*. With my host's help, but much against his advice, I limped down into Neuchâtel that night.

The pharmacy lies behind the *rue de Seyon* in the old town. In all respects an up-to-date establishment with two young men in white coats behind a counter laden with modern medicaments by Ciba, Sandoz, Bayer, and Laroche. All packaged up in cellophane, looking much alike. These are faith cures for those with faith in a prescription and what the doctor thinks is right. But many continental pharmacies also cater for those who prefer herbs which have been used since King Gentius of Illyria treated his flatulence with a tincture of gentian, and this was such a shop. Hellebore for worms, hemlock juice for piles and anal fissures, valerian for hysterics, and an aromatic tisane of lime-tree blossom for the composure of a disordered imagination. For bruises and sprains I recall a choice between flowers of arnica and powdered slate which, when I come to think of it, looks rather like a bruise, but I had more faith in corticosterone. Remembering the rectal suppositories I bought by mistake in Strasbourg, I made sure they were made up in the form of an ointment.

A pretty young Algerian girl showed me how to roll on an elastic bandage, a cylindrical affair like a minature girdle. She offered to rub some of the ointment in, and as her gentle fingers slid around that painful ligament, I swear my knee felt better in no time at all. A bit of nature cure in its way. The knee played me up later on, but that morning I walked down the *quai Leopold-Robert* like a new man.

At the end of the fashionable *plage*, some two or three miles beyond Neuchâtel, lies Marin, a small port undistinguished by anything except the treasure that archaeologists fished out of the lake there about forty years ago. This is the La Tène hoard, a priceless collection of battle-gear including shields, spearheads and swords, and the complete wheel of a war chariot, all decorated with the deeply incised whorls and stylized florets of the La Tène school of Celtic art, an unsurpassed form of craftsmanship.

The *Keltoi* as the Greeks called them were the first nation north of the Alps whose name we know. They ranked among the four barbarian peoples of the known world, the others being the Scythians, the Persians and the Libyans. They are the earliest known Britons of whom we have written records. Celtic languages in the form of Irish and Scottish Gaelic have probably been spoken for over three thousand years. After Greek and Latin they are the oldest in Europe, but as a race the Celts are still much of a mystery.

They first appear on the scene in the Bronze Age, in about 900 BC, advancing up the Danube and Rhine, probably in search of precious metals. Under the name of the *Urnfielders* they cremated their dead, which means that nobody knows whom their skeletal remains were related to, but their successors, the Battle-axe people and the Hallstatt swordsmen, advanced across Europe wielding the first weapons to be made of iron. They attacked Britain, the two Pretannic islands they called *Ierne* and *Albion*. The contoured hill forts of Yarnbury, Figsbury Rings, Quarley Hill and Maiden Castle on the south coast are relics of those invasions. There is a beach-head at Lulworth Cove where trenches in the sand show how the Wessex farmers were driven back yard by yard by tall, loose-limbed warriors with lime-bleached hair. The Celts were great fighters. Strabo says they were war-mad. Herodotus had heard about them and Caesar and Tacitus described what they saw of the tribes in Gaul. But they were describing the Celts in their decline. The great period of La Tène art flourished three or four centuries earlier when they were the undisputed champions of western Europe.

They were a handsome people. Far from being dark and swarthy in the popular present-day image of the Celt, classical writers make much of their fair skin and long blonde hair. They wore flowing cloaks and *bracae* or breeches. In critical affrays there are accounts of how they drove naked into battle, screaming at their adversaries from the helm of their two-wheeled chariots. They loved bright colours and adornment, especially jewellery, and drinking and quarrelling and feasting. Banquets lasted for days. Strangers were always fed first whatever their business and the company afterwards in strict order of precedence though Diodorus says the champion's portion was often in dispute. This, he adds, sometimes led to fighting on the spot.

The precious objects found at La Tène are believed to have been thrown into the lake as votive offerings to whatever gods they worshipped, perhaps Cernunnos, the horned one, or Epona, the great queen-mother who assumed the form of a riggish mare. Nothing is left of the village they built there on piles except a bed of peat below the water. I walked round to Mount Vully on the eastern side of the lake where archaeologists were sieving out the tangible remains of what seems to have been a massive Celtic fort, but it was difficult to get any picture of the place. It had been pillaged long ago by the Romans.

On the way down through Luxembourg and the Vosges, I thought a great deal about the Celts, listening to legends and scraps of local history. In museums I looked at their beautiful gold torques, brooches, amulets and lengths of chain used for shackling slaves. On the sites around Neuchâtel and the Murtensee archaeologists described what they were doing, but they were specialists concerned about fitting together the fragments of one little corner of the cultural jigsaw. Nobody could say much about the larger picture of the Celts as a people. There is an air of uncertainty about everything. It's like looking at the wreckage of a volcanic explosion without knowing what the landscape looked like before the upheaval.

The word Celtic means different things to different people. In the strictly linguistic sense it means two related branches of the Indo-European language, the Geodelic spoken in Ireland, western Scotland and the Isle of Man, and the Brythonic which has survived in Wales, Cornwall, and Brittany. To many people the Celt is a romantic and rather superior type of Briton, dark and lean, the descendant of Cuchaillan and King Mark, the bearer of a culture far older than that of thickset, round-faced Anglo-Saxons typified by John Bull. Yet in both Great Britain and Ireland the invasions of Celtic Iron Age people brought in by far the largest single body of folk known, and the British of today almost certainly owe more in a physical sense to those fair-haired Celts than to any other group of invaders. They left their stamp on the whole of western civilization.

The Celts seem to have been imbued by some unquenchable vitality that came out in all their cultural and social activities. They were aggressive and reckless. They fought each other; they fought their enemies. They even fought Hannibal in his march through the Alps against their common foe, the legions of Rome. Yet in all their dealings they were reckoned a brave and honourable people, bound together by a closely knit social system akin to the *tuath* of the old kings of Ireland.

The *tuath* originally meant the people or the clan composed of a king, his nobles and free commoners. The king sat among his warrior-nobles. He led them into battle and acted as arbitrator-in-chief assisted, usually, by magician-sages or druids. The ownership of land was not held by an individual, even the head of a household, but by the kin from whom it could not be alienated. In a sense the kins ruled themselves. They were an intricate development of what held together the bands of reindeer hunters of Palaeolithic times. The system encouraged self-reliance and individualism. There was no public administrator or enforcement of law. The kins were bound by common loyalties and by common wealth in food and land and possessions.

But the system broke down. Like any other organism, a race expands or declines through processes of competition. The golden age of hunting and fighting and the haphazard acquisition of new territory came to an end. It lacked the purposiveness of their enemies. The loosely confederated kingdoms of Celtdom were split apart and conquered, tribe by tribe, by the highly disciplined and centralized power of Rome. And when Rome, the very mistress of the world, fell to the barbarians from beyond the Rhine, the only Celts that retained their identity were those who fled to Ireland and northern and western Britain. There in the twilight of their existence their bards described what had befallen them. Only a small portion of that great outpouring of literature has survived. The written word that superseded the oral tradition of relating history came to Britain late, and by then the Celts were beset by yet another foe, the Saxon invaders to whom, if we go back far enough, they were related.

The underlying theme is one of lament, of a once glorious company who had been scattered or slain. In the *Red Book of Hargest*, Heledd, the last of Cynddylan's kin, bewails her lot as she looks down on the smoking ruins of Pengwern, her former home.

> Cynddylan's court is dark tonight,
> No fire, no bed;
> I weep awhile, then fall silent.
> Cynddylan's court is dark tonight,
> No fire, no songs –
> Tears wear away my cheeks.
> Cynddylan's court, it stabs me to see it,
> No roof, no fire;
> My lord-leader dead, myself alive.

From the hill-fort of Vully I turned south through Vallamand to Avenches, once the great Roman city of Aventicum. *Michelin* says the old amphitheatre can seat at least ten times the present population of the town. I recall only the fountains in the main street. They spout from huge stone tanks as high as the armpits of a child, just the right height for sailing toy boats. The Burgundians fought the Helvetians around Villarsiviriaux and Estevennes. I remember only a cemetery and a white-haired old woman sitting on the edge of a gravestone, stroking the flowers, gently, as if they were clothes recalled with love.

Near Romont I began to feel curiously disembodied. I trudged on at the same speed, but I felt as if I were marking time in slow motion, like walking up a moving staircase that was for ever coming down. Woods and villages floated past as if painted on the rollers of stage scenery. Nothing seemed real except time and distance and the ever-rising rim of the Alps, that great barrier to the riches of northern Europe. From a hill-top that night they ringed the whole horizon. Through a rain storm at Palezieux they looked desperately grey and jagged, like the teeth of an old saw. And from Mont Pélerin near Vevey the enormous hulk of the *Dent d'Oche* and the *Cornettes de Bise* towered above the water of the death-grey lake.

Bleak Assault

The third and by far the most difficult part of the walk began at St Gingolph in the south-eastern corner of Lake Geneva. We came there by steamer. I make no apology for that brief lapse in avowed means of locomotion. My wife met me in Vevey. We had such a whale of a time there that, as loving wives will, she insisted on prolonging the affair by seeing me off at the very foot of the Alps, which, to say the least, she did not much like the look of. And nor for that matter did I. In between last-minute promises to look after myself and not do anything silly, the steamer whistle blew unnoticed, twice, and in a last-second effort to get ashore I was obliged to leap off the stern.

The trans-Alpine part of the *Grande Randonnée Cinq* starts behind the customs sheds at that little frontier port. In theory, at least, the walker can follow a trail marked by dabs of red and white paint for over three hundred and fifty miles. The *sentier* skirts the western outliers of Mont Blanc, dodging in and out of the Savoyan, the Graian, the Cottian, the High and part of the Maritime Alps by way of twenty or thirty passes. An artificial trail in the sense that the classic routes used for thousands of years by invaders, merchants and pilgrims are now super-highways, almost impossible to walk on. The GR5 winds through many of the less-well-known valleys and *cols*, a trail for those content with quiet and solitude. A wonderful trail if you can find the elusive markers and not be too depressed by the chronic mist and storms of late June and July.

In just under twenty days of hard going I ran into the worst weather I have ever encountered on a walking trip and if some of the moisture seeps into what follows I shall at least be giving a fairly accurate picture of what it was like in the mountains.

Map

10

The Massif of Mont Blanc

I set off at sundown, slogging up what, from across the water, looked like a hair-thin crack in the wall of the *Dent d'Oche*, wearing a pair of re-soled boots that creaked somewhat, but with ten new maps, scale 1 to 50,000, and a small collapsible umbrella, price forty francs, I climbed with something pretty close to confidence.

Novel is a little village on the face of a cliff some three thousand feet above St Gingolph. To reach it you wind through the larch and pine of the villas of the rich, most of them with a swimming pool and a large car hooked to a speedboat on a trailer in their driveways. Feeling something of an anachronism among tubby cigar-smoking men in bathing shorts and straw hats, I trudged on, glancing backwards occasionally. The narrow defile resembled the rear-sight of a rifle. High above, the chalets of Novel looked like cuckoo clocks on a shelf, and there I spent the night in luxury.

The guests chattered amiably. Most of them had come up there for the view back towards the lake. As to what lay ahead, they assured me that beyond the hotel there was 'absolutely nothing but mountains'. The *patron* had heard of a track over the *col de Bise* to Morzine. But who would want to use it these days when there was a good road up the valley of the Drance?

But surely someone knew the way. Were there no shepherds in Novel? Waving his hand towards pots of honey and the models of chalets for sale on the walls, he said: 'Here we are for the *touristique.*' As to the weather outlook, he shrugged his shoulders. Who could say? It changed rapidly up there.

Towards midnight the shutters clattered violently as a river of cold air poured down from the heights above. Lights were snapped on and in excited French a woman bewailed the loss of some underwear incautiously spread out on the window-sill to dry.

An early start in clear air that looked good but promised nothing. A few fluffy clouds and the whisper of baby breezes. Beyond the end of the road, an old man forking hay among some dilapidated hovels said he knew the path well. *Tout droit* all the way. *Et assez facile*, though a little difficult here and there. I had but to follow the red and white stripes. Like that! And he pointed out a crude dab on the corner of his goat shed. *And* that! Another had been splashed on a tree. A third appeared on a ruined wall. Some trailblazer had clearly enjoyed himself on the outskirts of Novel, but it looked as if he soon ran out of paint.

The marks, *le jalonnement des sentiers*, are usually thick on the ground near villages, but mighty thin and often difficult to find where you most want them, that is in open country, and for some reason which I could never fathom, the trailblazers have a passion for cutting off corners. In scrubby country the recommended route skips about like a goat, sometimes turning off a well-found path at right angles to gain a little altitude and at the expense of a great deal of perspiration. But I had no mind to disregard directions of any kind that morning and looked at those little stripes with enormous affection. They led through grassland and a wood, crossing a stream, the Morge, matching the written directions in the *Topoguide* – '*Le GR monte par prairies et une forêt, traverse le torrent vers le ravin de Vez . . .*'

But where was that ravine? The path led out into a rough pasturage. It extended as far as the eye could see. As I couldn't expect to pick up another mark in that grass for at least a mile, I strode on, but with diminishing confidence in the *Comité National des Sentiers*.

During a pause for breath I looked back towards the heights of Grammont to find that a tongue of mist had almost completely blotted out the trail up from the village, and worse, from the thickening vapour that swirled ahead, it looked as if I shouldn't get very far in that direction. Taking a fix on two recognizable peaks, I sat down on a rock.

I have been caught in a mist too often to worry much about what to do. The remedy is depressingly simple. If it gets too thick to see for more than thirty yards in terrain liable to fall away steeply you sit down and wait for it to lift. The problem is to put up some effective shelter without unstrapping the whole tent, which takes time. I squatted there with the outer fly wrapped round my shoulders like a cloak and stared bleakly at the map. Why no marks on those rocks? Had the paint washed off? In places you can detect only a vestige of what had originally been daubed on. But not there. Not a speck in sight. Yet from the compass and the pitch of the slope, the bearing seemed right. Maybe a bit too far to the west, but not much.

When the gloom thinned somewhat I plodded on slowly, for perhaps half an hour. The ground began to rise steeply on a westerly bearing. On a crest I came out on the surface of an ocean of vapour. Far below, in front and to the rear, it hung about as thick as smoke. Immediately to the west rose the dark walls of a cliff with the nose of a peak behind. Far ahead lay a snow-draped *col* with a miserable-looking farmstead in the foreground.

There I talked long and earnestly to an old man and his young wife and learned almost nothing at all. It came out eventually that they had moved in only the previous month. They knew nothing about any place in the vicinity except where their supplies came from, Novel and St Gingolph. After a glass of warm goat's milk, I hastened on to the distant crest, anxious to see what lay beyond.

From a distance, the bow-shaped *col* appeared to lie between a jumble of little rocks, but at close quarters they turned out to be massive blocks of limestone far too steep to be climbed, and I tackled the snow.

Moist, dirty-looking stuff and so incoherent that in places I sank in up to my hips. It took three-quarters of an hour to surmount that slope of slush, and if this fact seems of no merit among better-known Alpine records, I claim that by using a piece of fence post for support and leverage I discovered for myself the principle of the alpenstock.

On the rim of that *col* I looked down some three or four thousand feet to as dispiriting a view as ever I saw – the western end of Lake Geneva. Instead of breaching the outermost wall of the Alps, I had worked along the grain of the ridge to a platform on the heights of the *Dent d'Oche*. In terms of distance not a bad stage, considering the weather, but far from where I hoped to go that day and almost entirely in the wrong direction.

With visible bearings for guidance it became clear where I had strayed off the trail. It might have been more prudent to have stayed there, but I wanted to keep moving. I felt cold and had no mind to venture back into that ocean of vapour. I decided to try and work round the neck of the peak and strike south into the valley of the Dranse. It turned out to be a foolhardy strike, since it entailed climbing on to a ledge from which I had some difficulty in climbing down.

The *Dent d'Oche* appeared as an almost vertical cliff of ash-grey rock surrounded by a broad collar or platform of scree and grass, in places lightly patterned with snow. Up there the going looked easy, yet such are the distortions of aerial perspectives that it took the better part of an hour to reach a corner that seemed scarcely two hundred yards away. Around that projection the platform narrowed considerably and, worse, the drop below had increased. Where there had been a comfortable slope and a view of the hamlets down below, there appeared only horizons and an emptiness of air. I scrambled on, hopeful that around the next projection there would be some easy way of getting down.

To get round a small *arête*, I clung to the face of the cliff and kicked into the soggy earth for a toehold. To my consternation a substantial portion of that earth fell away. I managed to scramble on to what was left of the platform only to discover there was no apparent way of going on or going back. Around the next projection the ledge had all but disappeared.

I recall feeling both alarmed and extremely indignant. In that sense of indignation, of being let down by the unexpected, there is perhaps a spontaneous antidote to fear. I had done what I vowed I would never do, that is scramble up to a place where I should have some difficulty in scrambling down. I stress that word scramble since I am a walker, not a climber. The older I get the more I dislike heights, shrinking from the sight of verticals narrowing in perspective.

What remained of the ledge stood some thirty or forty feet above another platform, rather wider than the first, but with flanks that plunged down to some immense screes far below. An unendearing prospect, yet I reckoned if I could reach the second step in the cliff I could work back to the *col* without much difficulty. The problem was how.

Rolling over on to my stomach, I sought footholds in an oblique fissure. After one incautious glance over the edge I carefully avoided looking down, knowing that if I did the scenery appeared to be in motion, swinging sickeningly, momentarily, as it does when a roller coaster begins to plunge down. Climbing is no game for beginners. Play it cool, I thought. Play it *real* cool, slowly.

With good support for my left foot on something an inch or two wide, I found something else two or three feet below.

Handhold followed foothold. Seemed easy enough. All a matter of confidence. But the rock steps petered out about a third of the way down. O dear God, what now? Daren't jump. I'd fall off the platform below. Daren't let go. Daren't think of climbing back. *Deus miseratur*. God be merciful unto us. By God, I'm a bloody fool. Lead kindly light. Keep thou my feet. I do not ask to see the distant scene: one step enough for me. All a matter of confidence? Balls! Lead thou me on.

I slid down the last ten feet grazing my nose, but landed in deep snow where I sprawled back against the broken frame of my rucksack, feeling slightly sick.

For ten minutes I sat there, musing, brooding, breathing heavily, turning over thoughts more gloomy than I care to remember. I had been forced to retreat in the face of the first Alp I had come to. Unless I could find some way of working round the back of the *Dent*, there seemed nothing for it but to walk back towards the lake and start again.

I looked at my rucksack. A rivet had broken. I patched it up with a shoe lace. I looked round at the little flowers, the rock cinquefoils as fragile as snowflakes, the mauve-coloured milk-worts, the minute pinks and campions, the tufts of saxifrage, but decided that of all sights nothing looked near so attractive as a spire of smoke from a hamlet down in the valley, and there I trudged to a place called Trossy.

If the proprietress of the famous restaurant there remembers the occasion it will not be, I think, to my advantage, for I came within an inch of setting fire to the place. From a menu hand-written on parchment I chose *Bœuf à la Bourguignonne*, imagining it to be that rich casserole of meat, vegetables and mushrooms reputed to be the favourite dish of Henry the Fowler. To my surprise she carried in a huge plate of various sauces, some diced and toasted bread and a silver bowl of uncooked beef cubes topped by a long-handled trident. And out she went.

I looked at her offering with some perplexity. Not my idea of a casserole. Could it be a variation of *Bœuf Tartare*? Dipped in mustard with capers, the raw meat still tasted like extremely raw meat. After chewing on one gobbet with uncommon vigour, I pretended to be smacking my lips when Madame returned, this time with a salver of boiling butter mounted on a spirit stove. With contrived nonchalance I enquired about *la technique*.

'*C'est facile*,' she replied. She harpooned a cube and dipped it first in the sauces and then in the boiling fat, lightly. The liquid bubbled furiously, but at a mere touch, as if from a fairy's wand, the meat came out nicely seared. '*Comme ça*,' she said, and left me to it.

Had there been any other diners in that room, I might have tackled that *fondue* with the delicacy it deserved, handling it a piece at a time. But gluttony got the better of me. By skewering two or three cubes, I built up a little stockpile. No hanging about for the stuff to cool. Carried away by the simplicity of mass production, I built up alternate layers of toasted bread and meat, eventually adding a couple of anchovies as an experiment in *poisson fondu*. That did it.

The fish disintegrated. In a vain effort to scoop out the bits, I lost two cubes of meat. The liquid began to bubble and smoke. As I jabbed into the vat, the over-heated metal portion of the fork fell off, and that too dropped into the boiling butter. When Madame rushed in the situation had already got out of hand. The liquid spilled over. The tablecloth started to burn. She was angry, and she had every right to be, for in my efforts to turn the spirit stove down I had turned it up.

The meal over and apologies fortified by something well over the customary fifteen per cent, I walked out into bright sunshine unsure quite what to do next. From Trossy a road curls round by Chevenoz into the valley of the Drance, completely outflanking the range I had failed to climb. A temptation but a poor-spirited way out. Encouraged by beef, Margaux, cheese and a stiff cognac, I turned my back on Trossy. In the few hours of light that remained I climbed up a logging track behind the restaurant, determined on another tussle with the outliers of the *Dent d'Oche*.

The time may come when the trans-Alpine *sentier* will become as well known as the Pennine Way or the Appalachian Trail. I don't know what records of alternative routes are filed away by M. Alain Chevalier, the *secrétaire technique* of that elusive *comité* in Paris, but for a back-stairs approach, perhaps a small comfort for those who tripped over the first hurdle, as I did, I commend a path between Le Chennay and Les Esserts down to Le Villard and beyond. Above the chalets are neither signposts nor markers, but a rough onward-going track has been trodden out by Savoyards clearly intent on getting somewhere. It winds up through the trees with a great view to the north and the east, rising steadily for mile after mile. When I stopped to regain my breath, as I did pretty often, there occurred a simple truth so obvious I wondered why I had never thought of it before. It's simply that fatigue is directly related to the angle of slope. In a forced march on the flat, especially at night, I can hustle along for three or four hours without a halt. In hilly country, such as the Vosges, I usually manage two hours, but there I puffed and palpitated, looking at my watch after a spell of hard going. Despite the bright light, the mist rose and fell like an inconstant tide. Against one long ridge, it rose so high that, for a time, I might have been walking along a pier, alone above a white and wholly silent sea.

Tucked away among the rocks of those high places, are plants that cling together as Alpines do, for protection. The saxifrages grow in rosettes or else in cushions in the manner of that hardy little pink, the moss campion, for without interlocked roots they would be washed away. Among them bloomed delicate relics of the Ice Age, the mountain avens or, as they call it in Latin, *Dryas* since the leaves resembled miniature oak leaves, and it was among oaks that the dryads dwelt. The white flowers are golden-centred and about them is the exhilaration of sunlight on unbroken snow.

As I strode along, anxious and more tired than I think I knew, I saw, as it were, the Britain of thousands of years ago when all but the uppermost ridges were deep under ice. I might have been some hunter coming back over Helvellyn or Goredale with a slain beast around his shoulders. Such a man would see much that I saw that evening. From plant remains dug out of interglacial deposits near my home I knew that *Dryas*, now so rare in trampled places, had once bloomed there in company with Arctic campions, saxifrage and mountain cinquefoil. And as I walked on the vision of the past enlarged and became audible, for downwind came the rippling call of the Alpine accentor, the nearest relative known to what in Britain folk who love birds call the dunnock or hedge sparrow.

A quiet night. With the tent down behind a great block of dolerite for protection, I turned in early. The mist turned to light rain but I listened to it complacently, feeling that with a few ribs of the range crossed I had made some amends for all that had gone wrong during the day.

At dawn it began to pour down. The hills I hoped to scale were invisible and all plans to rejoin the *sentier* at Bassachaux had to be put aside. Squelching along beside the bubbling beer-coloured waters of the Dranse, I sheltered at intervals, hoping it would clear up but it rained for thirty hours. At each footfall my boots made flatulent noises. The umbrella kept my head and shoulders dry but little rivulets ran off the ribs and seeped down into my underpants. A day best forgotten.

A police car pulled ahead and two gendarmes got out armed with long sticks. Here it comes, I thought. Another search. Rehearsing a little speech about how I walked *pour le sport*, even in the rain, I sidled up, nervously. They never even looked up. They were collecting snails. Wishing them both a good day and good hunting, I asked whether they knew of a path to St Jean d'Aulps.

No, they said.

Did they know of a hotel nearby?

No, they said.

Annoyed at their total indifference to a stranger's plight, I trudged on. Nothing original in that. For a hundred and fifty years or more Savoy has supplied Paris with housemaids, Italy with kings, and tourists with solid ground for complaint.

That evening I sat under the porch of a wayside shrine, munching biscuits, wondering whether to spend the night there or trudge on for another mile or two. Among the pines the rain made a noise like escaping steam. From somewhere downstream came the faint notes of a horn. Did they hunt foxes or wild boar in Chablais? The notion seemed improbable and I wrote up some notes about the disconsolation of wet underwear.

Weeks earlier, on a similar night in the Lower Meuse, I had whiled away the time in a nice dry barn by scribbling down a list of platitudes under the general title of Rafferty's Rules for Long-Distance Walkers and Such. Rule One read: 'If you don't do anything about it, a bad situation can only be relied on to get worse.' Underneath I had scrawled: 'Sweat it out long enough and you'll find something always turns up. But don't get carried away by half-baked aphorisms.' Underlining those words, I added an asterisk and a cryptic footnote: 'Remember Chablais in the rain!' What on earth could I do there except stay put in discomfort or walk on and get even wetter than I was? To hell with Rafferty!

During a lull I heard that horn again. An omen perhaps. Before it died away, I packed up and walked up the road to where it seemed to be coming from. There were no buildings in sight. It sounded again. No doubt about it this time. A high-pitched wail. Harsh but melodic. A horn played by some good old-fashioned blaster of the river-boat school. Around the bend a badly-written sign pointed to *La Discothèque Go-Go – Boissons et Dansant*. A large wooden shack half-hidden among the trees. A weird-looking place.

A muscular young black man, a West Indian, opened the door. He gave me a big grin. He might have been waiting for me. Was I English? I nodded, sadly. 'Man,' he said, 'you sure look wet. My name's Jim. Sit *right* down here and I'll fix a drink.' He switched off something by Louis Armstrong.

Enormous cordiality. I asked if he could put on a meal. Pretty soon he reckoned. When the folks got back. They were out somewhere, but there'd be a real crowd in that night. They'd be all over the place. I drank Jim's health in a rum and ginger. He drank mine and I thought of Rafferty and had another.

Time slipped by. Jim talked about the neighbourhood, the difficulty of attracting customers. He was elusive about who actually ran the place. He said Madame kept them on the run, but she'd gone out with a friend. Jim preferred to stay around.

Night came. He lit a few candles and the oil stove. It continued to rain hard. In between thunderous bursts of jazz from the record player, water plopped into saucepans laid out under some substantial cracks in the roof. In an effort to fill the social vacuum, Jim jumped around, chatting incessantly, putting on one disc after another. He tap-danced. He helped out Duke Ellington with a fine imitation of an alto sax, but he obviously had something on his mind. He kept listening and looking out of the window. 'Thought it was the car,' he said. But nobody turned up. Nobody at all.

Towards ten o'clock, feeling enormously hungry, I asked outright about something to eat. Jim suddenly looked downcast.

A portion of his expansive ego expired in a long sigh. He guessed there wouldn't be anything until the folks got back from the village. They ought to be back soon. Something must have held them up.

What it was I never discovered. Everything about the place seemed a bit odd. The air of desolation. The girl who had gone out. His questions about the police car. Were they in the smuggling business or something even more sinister? As I slip in and out of people's lives on these walks I often have the feeling of seeing part of a play without ever knowing how it started or how it would end.

Jim heard the car at once. I saw him tense. Before the pair walked in, he ran to the record player and slammed on another disc.

The girl looked young and pretty but utterly downcast. Her boy-friend carried two laden baskets. They had been having a row and continued to shout and gesticulate in the open doorway. Jim joined in and apparently got told off, but above the roar of the music I saw all this as if in mime. I could scarcely hear a word. At length the girl switched the machine off and burst into tears, saying they did nothing except make her unhappy.

The argument continued in the kitchen. Jim seemed to be trying to pacify the girl, but she was inconsolable. It looked as if the boy-friend had slipped up somewhere that night. He should have kept quiet, she said. Why had he spoken at such a time? They had no money to spare. Even *he* knew that.

Embarrassed by the situation, I sat in the empty bar, wondering what it was all about. Until the girl reappeared and asked apologetically what I'd care to eat, I thought they had forgotten I was there.

She brought in soup and a large plate of cold meat and salad. I ate it alone, but they all came in for coffee. They had made it up. There was love in the air. The girl sat next to Jim, smiling and addressing them both affectionately. The relationship seemed somewhat complicated. Both men got on extremely well, defending each other at any ill-turn in the conversation. I gathered that business was bad. They hadn't had a customer for two or three days. They were too far off the main road to attract many cars, but if they could put up more signs they reckoned they could make a success of the place.

The girl showed me up to a little room that hadn't been used for months. It smelt of mice and mould and old newspapers. 'A little primitive,' she said, 'but it's all we have. I hope you will be comfortable. My husband will get breakfast for you, early. *Bonne nuit et bon voyage.*'

In the morning Jim handed me a very modest bill. 'Sorry about the row last night,' he said. 'That girl o' mine sure gets mad at times. I think she's gonna have a baby.'

I contend that a man with a good pair of feet can walk in almost anything: boots, shoes, sandals, even carpet slippers, and go barefoot on soft ground. My preference is for medium-weight shoes with heavy Commando-type soles made of stuff called Vibram. I had been talked into buying boots for this trip. With hindsight I think I might have done as well in shoes, but, if boots it had to be, I wanted the best on the market. After trying several makes, I chose an Italian-made pair which were very supple and light (they weigh twenty-six ounces apiece) and expensive. Each day they had been carefully washed and waxed. In Vevey they were re-soled by a saintly-looking cripple. You felt that no man who had overcome that much could be anything but a first-rate craftsman. And I liked the look of his hands as he stroked the leather. They were fine boots, he said. They ought to be taken care of. He knew just what to do. The soles would have to be stuck on under an infra-red lamp. They would be ready the following night. The thirty francs he asked seemed a bit steep, but with the Alps in sight I would have paid more.

On the stiff climb up to Montriond that day the sole of one boot began to gape like a panting dog. It flapped as I walked, and the other looked in bad shape. It had buckled around the welt. I sat down and took them off, and as I turned those boots over in my hands, I tell you I could have wept. There seemed nothing for it but to buy another unbroken-in pair somewhere, and down I flapped, towards Morzine, cursing all new-fangled ways of foot protection. Had I found the international headquarters of the Guild of Cobblers I would have set fire to it.

Nine had struck before I flapped into that drab little town, but, being France, the well-shod citizenry were still about their well-stocked shops. Without much hope I turned into a flashy-looking place that sold gear *pour tous les sports*. The young salesman sounded too glib by far. A man out to sell anything, I thought. But not a bit of it. He picked up the worst of the two boots and bent it, professionally. 'What do you want another pair for?' he asked. 'These can be repaired.' I asked where. He gave me an address, but not of a cobbler's shop. At that hour, he said, M. So-and-so would be with his girl-friend.

And there he was, a surly fellow who all but told me to go away. He was still at work in a corner of the kitchen beside a robust woman ironing a patched shirt. For some people, he said, it was necessary to work. Others could amuse themselves all day and when they were in trouble to whom did they come? They came to him, late at night.

I explained the situation, laboriously. I had many miles to go, I said. For me it was necessary to have a good pair of boots.

He stopped hammering and looked at me. 'Tell me something,' he said. 'Do you really like to walk *all* day?'

A powerful question. I had thought about it a lot. Turning it round, evasively, I said I was a professional just as he was. Did he like to sit there, hammering away all day?

At this he laughed and held out his hands for the boots.

With exaggerated scorn, he pulled off one of the soles as if it were the skin of a banana. 'So it has come to this,' he said. 'A man who can use a dab of glue now calls himself a *savetier*. I have wasted a lot of my life learning how to use a hammer and a needle.'

For ten francs that surly man stitched and hammered on a pair of soles which have left prints from Morzine to the Mediterranean. I shook his hand. I hope his girl-friend looks after him and his business flowers, and I'm sorry for what I said about modern cobblers.

From Morzine an easy path ambles up behind the cliffs of Nyon to the chalets of Charny and beyond, a continuation of that *sentier* at the foot of the *Dent d'Oche* from which I had strayed two days earlier. The path skirts the Golèse to the south-west of the *Dents du Midi* and curls down behind the farmsteads of *La Rosière* and the *Chantemerle*, the Rose Queen and the Singing Blackbird. That morning the wind sprang up, shaking showers of sleet from leaden clouds, but I strode on, eating up the miles. confident both in the route and my well-found boots. The

Riquewihr

Maquisard 'tué par les balles Hitleriennes'

The widow of Vaud

Edge of the Vanoise

Col de Bonhomme

Val d'Isère

Crest of the Iseran

Curraz

Hannibal's gorge

High Alps

Last obstacle

Over the Bonette

mountains thereabouts are part of a strange, lost world rampart know to geologists as the Pre-Alps. They are foreign to their surroundings and the bedrock on which they stand. Among them are fire-baked deposits unknown anywhere else.

Long before the Alps emerged from the Tethys Sea the whole region was dominated by a mountain range in places about twice as high as Mont Blanc, but it must have been a very unstable range. The topmost layers began to slide westwards on a cushion of gases and water vapour injected by volcanoes. The rocks came to rest along a line extending from Savoy to Lake Thun in Switzerland. Escher van der Linth, the first man to investigate that gigantic landslip, gave a short lecture on the subject regretting that if he published his sections no one would believe him. 'They would put me in an asylum,' he said. That was over a hundred years ago, but time and much patient research has shown he had discovered the remains of the Pre-Alps.

The mountains are carpeted with pale barberries and azalea and that colourful rhododendron, the rusty *alpenrose*, a botanical token of a limefree soil. Rhododendrons are closely related to the heathers. They have populated the roof of the world from North America to China, and they flourish best in wind-swept country that resembles their Tibetan home. Among the fissures of the Golèse they resembled rose-coloured cascades, the colour nicely offset by bright green beds of sphagnum which, as I recall, are known to practical young lads in the West Riding as wet arse.

In Samoëns it began to snow. Concerned about what it would be like on the *col d'Anterne* the next day, I went round to the *Syndicat d'Initiative* for a brief chat with M. Pourquoi, an aggressive little man with a square jowl, like a tomcat.

'Good day, M'sieur. Are you the Director?'

'*Pourquoi?*'

'Because I wish to speak to him.'

'*Pourquoi?*'

'I have much need of advice.'

'About what?'

'The weather. You have a telephone here. Is there much snow around Chamonix? To that place I intend to walk tomorrow.'

He said it again.

'*Pourquoi non?*' I said, and made for the door.

'Wait!' he said. 'It is not necessary to use the telephone. You can see for yourself. The weather is bad everywhere.'

'How do you know?'

'Because this morning I talked to a hunter. He has seen the bear again.'

The most that can be said for the old brown bear of Samoëns is that, unlike the great wolf of Gévaudon, the animal managed to survive. Several unimaginative people, including the local baker, said they had seen it up on the slopes of Mont Buet. In bad weather it padded down towards the village and rooted among their vegetables. Other stories about how it regularly knocked off a chamois hunter and once chased the postman on his bicycle for miles and miles, are, I suspect, being worked up by M. Pourquoi for tourist consumption. But I may be prejudiced.

I spent the night in a cosy little hotel where the *patron* said that at one time or another all the world had some trouble with that fellow. '*Pourquoi?*' I asked, reflectively.

He shrugged his shoulders. 'Perhaps it starts in the bedroom,' he said.

On the question of getting over the Anterne opinion seemed divided between optimists who, I suspect, had never been there, and pessimists who told terrible stories of ten-foot drifts on the *col*. All they could say about the weather was that the bear knew a thing or two. It must be pretty bleak up there. And I went to bed uncomforted.

Small triumphs are easier and more pleasant to describe than protracted defeats. I tried and failed to cross the *col d'Anterne* direct, but as I managed to reach the back of the barrier the next day, the defeat can be dismissed briefly.

From the last thread of road at Salvagny, the trail winds up through a gorge to the Falls of the Mourners and out towards a knife-edged escarpment to the west of Mont Buet. A hard slog under good conditions. Alone there that morning, in worsening weather, it looked grim. One by one the chalets slipped from sight and I fell back on the old comfort I derived from being able to recognize plants and animals or put them into some pattern of association.

This is marmot country. The little squirrel-like animals scamper about on boulder-strewn slopes in colonies of a dozen or more where they are far more often heard than seen. The alarm is a high-pitched whistle. It usually comes from a solitary animal on sentinel duty. The warning is quickly repeated by the others. The sentry sits bolt upright for a few moments as if assessing the situation, and then he too dives for shelter, uttering another call in quite a different key. If left undisturbed for a few minutes, their heads reappear like toast from a pop-up toaster. The youngsters are extremely playful, rolling over and nipping each other in the manner of kittens. One animal appeared to be dragging another one along by its tail which may account for an old belief that they stock their burrows with grass for hibernation purposes by using each other as living haywains.

During the afternoon it began to snow, heavily. There seemed no chance of making much progress that day. Feeling like an ant on a large sheet of white paper, I put my tent down on the edge of the *col* and spent an unpleasant night there.

Dinner went down rather badly. I couldn't work up much enthusiasm for some very cold boiled eggs and pressed beef. To fill in time I patched a shirt, sewed on a few buttons and read a hair-raising account of the ascent of the Matterhorn. An appropriate moment. Outside, the wind gave a pretty fair imitation of a wind machine. After what seemed a lifetime sentenced to my little igloo, I crawled out to find the wind fitful and the sky still heavy. It cast a deathly pallor on the snowfield. All the trails were buried and this stormer of great mountains walked back to Salvagny as timidly as any old maid in a marsh.

By keeping to the black waters of the little river Giffre, I managed to outflank Samoëns without encountering anyone who saw me off there the previous day.

At Morillon, to the west of that village, the pylons of a ski-lift climb steeply to one of the crests of the Esserts. The sun came out. Encouraged by that God-sent warmth and light, I clambered up through the trees, through Christmas-card scenery, following the pylons to a high place where all seemed mountain-tops and sky. In marked contrast to the long waves of the Jura, the peaks of the Pre-Alps resemble a choppy sea. They are disorderly. Their tops rear up one behind another, some gleaming white, some piebald and some untouched by the storm.

After much uneasy pacing about on that windy platform, I chose what looked like a fairly gradual descent and zigzagged down towards the valley of the Arve.

Fear is something most people prefer to say little or nothing about and on this I'm with the majority, but it would be glossing over a chronic factor in those early days in the Alps if I didn't admit plainly that I was often afraid about what I'd let myself in for. When I see climbers inching their way up cracks in a vertical rock-face I know very well that what I tackled would be regarded as ridiculously easy, even by beginners on a mountaineering course. All I managed to learn was how to scramble down from one platform to another by utilizing scraps of hard-won experience and information picked up from books. At this distance from events it now seems rather like taking your first girl out with a five-pound note and a manual of sexual instruction. I kept thinking, 'Look where you're going. Keep to the visible ridges. Don't be tempted by the gullies of streams that take short cuts and usually end in a sheer drop. Don't clutch at clumps of scrub. Safety lies in good footholds, not in hanging on by your hands.' On the whole I didn't do too badly, but I was in much too much of a hurry. I hadn't served a sufficiently long apprenticeship in that little private war with death, the serious business of grappling with gravity.

Take that ridge beyond Vercland. It looked easy enough. The mule track wandered into a snow drift. No joy there. I outflanked it, holding to gently rising contours under a jut-jawed overhang of grey granite rock. Fairly easy going. To the east of that promontory, almost hidden in the soft green haze of birch, a fissure gaped invitingly. A short cut as I saw it. It turned out to be a trap. The fissure skewed from side to side, hiding what lay beyond until, from a glimpse of open sky, I began to climb steeply, hopeful that once over a short face I had got the better of the uppermost ridge. Foot- and handholds fell easily for some twenty feet up a moderately angled profile, but they came to an end abruptly and, worse, the old story, I couldn't easily clamber down what I had clambered up. I tried to edge out of the crack sideways in a poor effort at a traverse. O God, where had I got to? Lead thou me on.

What would a mountaineer do? A fool question. No mountaineer in his right mind would have got into a crack that led nowhere. Above fragments of prayer and self-recrimination I seemed to hear the theme of Gershwin's *Rhapsody in Blue*: tumultuous chords imperfectly remembered, but enough to take the mind off the paralysing effect of fear.

God didn't lead me on. He led me down, down a dry gully. Whenever I hear scraps of that Gershwin composition today I go back in memory to grey rock and what it feels like to be scared and enormously alone. That afternoon I conveniently forgot the incident as soon as I regained the mule track and jogged down fairly comfortable paths towards the national highway between Cluses and Sallanches. The discords lasted only about ten minutes. Mountaineers play it cool the whole time.

In *The Alps from End to End*, a splendid book written towards the end of the last century, Sir William Conway says that the sound of hysterical shrieks coming from a party they had left behind 'informed us that a man had fallen into a hole and was in the process of being hauled out'. In his opinion:

> There was no reason to shriek and, indeed, every reason not to do so for help was not required and we might easily have been betrayed into going back. . . . Excitable novices are a nuisance on a mountain. . . . Good and careful guides seldom fall into a crevasse. They discover and avoid them. The process takes a little time, but the discomfort of being hauled out is worth avoiding.

With guides and porters including two of their own Gurkhas who had never been to Europe before, Sir William and his friend, Colonel Fitzgerald, climbed twenty-one peaks and nearly forty passes in just under three months. They tackled everything they saw. If mist hid the mountain they were heading for they marched on and tackled another one. Fitzgerald didn't approve of rucksacks. He filled the pockets of his jacket with whatever he needed. Sir William says it took him some time to gather momentum, but when he fell into his stride all he had to do was to keep pace with his pockets. The Gurkhas had the time of their lives and the village girls couldn't take their eyes off them. Karbir put orchids in his hat. Amar Singh sported a Kashmir turban so big he used it as a rug at night. They couldn't speak anything except Nepalese which made things difficult when they got lost in their search for provisions. But once he knew they were safe and could be picked up somewhere, Sir William pressed on. Towards the end of the trip he became a bit testy, but only about minor discomforts, about the mouse in his sleeping bag and the shepherd who scorched one of his boots in an effort to dry them out. For the rest he was the very model of the English gentleman abroad. A little austere perhaps, but always courteous. To the cobbler who repaired his boots he dispatched a litre of wine 'to take the place of conversation'.

Some of the climbers of that heroic age rather overdid the gentlemanly stuff. When one or two of his companions fell to what he calls their destruction, John Tyndall, one of the most famous geologists of his day, reports that Tairraz, the guide, screamed, 'but like the Englishmen the others met their doom without a word of exclamation'.

Tyndall reckoned he could climb wherever a chamois could climb. His accounts of prodigious assaults are studded with notes about the structure and properties of ice crystals and glaciers. He listened to the music of streams or, as he calls it, 'the sound of agitated water' and concludes it comes from exploding bubbles of air of different sizes. Had he slipped in mid-climb you would expect some footnotes on his own momentum. The attitude is one of studied detachment. There is that dreadful morning on the Matterhorn. He says:

> We chose the back fin of the mountain for our track, and from this the falling stones were speedily deflected right or left. . . . We had gathered up our traps, and bent to the work before us when suddenly an explosion occurred overhead. We looked aloft and saw in mid-air a solid shot . . . describing its proper parabola, and finally splitting into fragments as it smote on one of the rocky towers in front of us. Down the shattered fragments came like a kind of spray, slightly wide of us, but still near enough to compel a sharp look out.

Thanks to a friend of mine, a newspaperman who is also a skilful climber, I skimmed the cream of mountaineering literature before I set off, devouring a dozen or more books, old and new. I read much of that stern stuff in the Alps and have since returned to Conway, Tyndall and, in my estimation, to the best of them all, A. F. Mummery and Edward Whymper. 'The true mountaineer,' says Mummery, 'is undoubtedly the noblest work of God.' As for mere footsloggers, those of us 'who cannot be trusted to sit on a crag unroped', they are 'as contemptible an object as may be easily imagined'.

He catches the spirit of those high places. 'The strange inter-folding of the snows, the gaunt weird crags of the ridges, the vast blue icicle-fringed crevasse or the great smooth slabs sloping downwards through apparently bottomless space ... each and all no less lovely than the boundless horizons of the summit view.' But it's not the view he goes for. He says he would still climb, 'even were there no scenery to look at, even if the only climbing available were the dark and gruesome pot-holes of the Yorkshire dales'. All mountains, in his opinion, are predestined to pass through three stages: first an inaccessible peak, then the most difficult ascent in the Alps and lastly 'an easy day for a lady'.

Edward Whymper could climb like a cat. His famous ascent of the Matterhorn and I've forgotten how many other peaks, including mountains in Greenland, the Rockies and Central America, have no place here. What fascinates me is his abounding self-confidence and whimsical asides. On his first trip to the Alps he describes how he put in a bit of practice in Paris by climbing up to the apartment of a friend on the seventh floor of a house in the Latin Quarter. The friend was engaged in fighting someone at the time. 'He recommended me to go up to the towers of Notre Dame. Half an hour later I stood on the parapet of the west front, by the side of the leering fiend which for centuries has looked down upon the great city, and then took rail to Switzerland. . . .'

Thereafter he conquers one mountain after another. In the Dauphiné he slows down slightly to scale Mont Pelvoux, 'a peak of rather a monotonous character'. Defeated by Mont Viso, he returns crestfallen to Abries. On the way there, his guide, a shepherd whose boots were much out of repair, slipped down a steep slope,

... and performed some wonderful and alarming gyrations which took him to the bottom of the valley much quicker than he could otherwise have descended. He was not much hurt, and made happy by a few needles and a little thread to repair his abraded garments. The other man, however, considered it wilful waste to give him brandy to rub in his cuts when it could be disposed of in a more ordinary manner.

Whymper's delicate pen-and-ink sketches are no less remarkable than his blow-by-blow accounts of his own misadventures. In one informal self-portrait he depicts himself not only in mid-air, but almost upside down as he fell nearly two hundred feet in seven or eight bounds from the top of the Great Staircase on the Matterhorn which he had ventured up alone. Of that brisk descent he says:

> As it seldom happens that one survives such a fall, it may be interesting to record what my sensations were during its occurrence. I was perfectly conscious of what was happening, and felt each blow; but like a patient under chloroform, experienced no pain. Each blow was, naturally, more severe than that which preceded it, and I distinctly remember thinking, 'Well, if the next is harder still, that will be the end.' ... This bounding through space did not feel disagreeable. But I think that in no very great distance more, consciousness as well as sensation would have been lost, and upon that I base my belief, improbable as it seems, that death by a fall from a great height is as painless an end as can be experienced.

Almost miraculously no bones were broken, but in addition to losing the tips of his ears he sustained two very severe gashes and blood spurted out of several other cuts.

> The most serious ones were in the head, and I vainly tried to close them with one hand, whilst holding on with the other. It was useless; the blood jerked out in blinding jets at each pulsation. At last, in a moment of inspiration, I kicked out a big lump of snow, and stuck it as a plaster on my head. The idea was a happy one, and the flow of blood diminished. Then, scrambling up, I got, not a moment too soon, to a place of safety, and fainted away.

On the large-scale *Michelin* map the roads around the mountains of High Savoy resemble the curves of a laced-up Victorian beauty. There is a bosomy bulge on both sides of Saint-Gervais and Chamonix and another one, broader and more hip-like, converging on Bourg St Maurice. The international *sentier* runs down the middle of that figure, almost in a straight line, passing between the breasts of the Anterne and swerving only slightly on the skirts of Mont Blanc. My own course had been somewhat erratic, but entirely peaceful until that encounter with the great surge of traffic on the national highway between Cluses and Sallanches. There under the echoing walls of the Varan a flood-tide of wheeldom came at me hard.

There is a story about how, nearly a century ago, John Ruskin walked down into Chamonix, intent on a few quiet days in the mountains. At that time it was the custom to celebrate successful climbs in the Alps by firing off cannons and rockets. Somebody had reached the top of Mont Blanc that day. It may have been Albert Smith, who bought a hundred bottles of wine and thirty-five fowls for his assault on the summit. The old man heard the noise. He stared at the crowds on the slopes. Some climbers hired forty or fifty porters 'who usually served only to frighten each other'. Ruskin stamped back to Chamonix and sat up that night writing a rolling piece of rhetoric that began: 'You have made race courses of the cathedrals of the earth . . .'

To get off that fearful highway, I struck up the Roman road at Oex, near the foot of a spectacular cascade, the Arpenaz and made Saint-Gervais by nightfall.

A town firmly for the *touristique* and competently organized for just that. Short walks, long walks, *excursions téléfériques*, climbing (*compagnie de guides*), ski-ing, skating, riding (*centre hippique*), swimming (*piscine chauffée*), gambling, *les bars et cinémas* and the town baths that offered a cure for almost everything *de santé*, *de détente, de rééquilibre psychosomatique de quiétude et euphorie*. In a dissertation of those baths when men and women used to gambol in the water together naked Fynes Moryson remarked that 'many having no disease but that of love, howsoever they faine sickness of body, come thither for remedy, and many times find it'.

In the *gendarmerie* the man at the desk gave me firm directions about how to attain my next major obstacle, the *col de Bonhomme*, adding that if the fat one would let him off the hook he would come along himself. As to weather prospects, he thought I might do better at the *Syndicat*.

There I tapped a deep well of goodwill. They telephoned a research station and were given encouraging news about that high pass to the south. Snow on the high points certainly, but likely to melt. General outlook: fair. They offered to find a hotel and gave me free tickets for a trip on the mountain railway to see Mont Blanc.

* * *

At intervals along the track the train stopped; the passengers got out, but never far and never alone. They followed each other, cautiously. When someone discovered a patch of gentians to pluck he was soon joined by others. It became a communal grazing ground. The more venturesome peered over a railed-off ledge at Chamonix far down in the valley, but they were soon back in the train.

The great moment came above Bionnassay. The train suddenly stopped. The passengers shouted and pointed. High up, so high we had to shove each other to get at the windows, the topmost peak of Mont Blanc broke through a veil of clouds. They slipped off her shoulders, slowly as if in a strip-tease act. The highest mountain in Europe put in an appearance as finely timed as a commercial. The peak remained coldly poised for perhaps three minutes and then slowly faded from view. A curious experience. I had never seen the top of the mountain before and I never saw it again. But we rattled back towards Saint-Gervais satisfied that we had got what we came for, a glimpse of one of the world's most famous vistas.

The Range of Light

The mountaineers looked up with no surprise. I didn't expect an uproarious welcome, but felt that the sudden appearance of a snow-sprinkled fellow-traveller at the door of La Balme, the mountain hut below the *col de Bonhomme*, merited something more than a muttered '*Ca va?*' from the more eloquent of the two. His companion nodded and went on reading the tablecloth, an old copy of the *Journal de Genève*.

As for myself, I had had more than ample time to rehearse introductions since I had looked down on that little hut for more than three hours.

It lies on the GR5, some three or four miles above Les Contamines, a refuge on the first platform of a bleak pass. With the sky bright and the air crisp, all seemed set for a solo assault. But though I tried and tried hard to get over that *col* by three different routes, it literally beat me flat. I fell on my face twice. I couldn't make any headway. A repetition of the Anterne venture. The track lay buried beneath a *cirque* of snow, quite soft on the floor of the cleft, but in places deep. I tackled the rocks on the rim; I floundered about on the slopes. After an unnerving and wholly unpremeditated *glissade* head-first into a drift, I slunk back to the hut convinced that nobody could get through without snow-shoes or skis.

All this I intended to relate in studied understatement to whoever inhabited the hut. I had seen a tent near the door. But something about the two young men recommended caution. Their ice-axes looked very professional. They were out for a walk, they said. Not to be outdone by this show of Gallic non-chalance, I said I had been doing a bit myself, trying to give the impression I had merely been up to the *col* to see what it looked like.

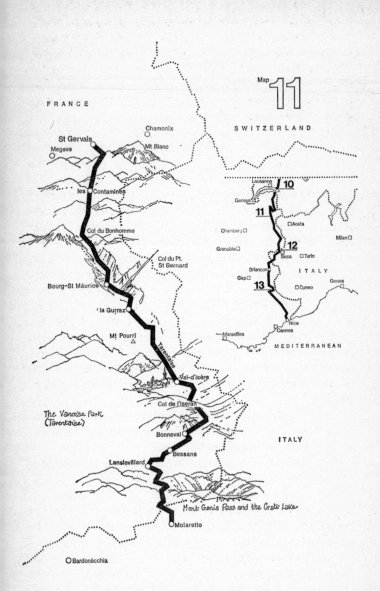

Map 11

FRANCE

Chamonix

SWITZERLAND

St Gervais

Megève

Mt Blanc

les Contamines

Col du Bonhomme

Col du Pt.
St Bernard

Bourg-St Maurice

la Gurraz

Mt Pourri

Tarentaise

The Vanoise Park
(Tarentaise)

Val-d'Isère

Col de l'Iseran

Bonneval

Bessans

Lanslevillard

Mont Cenis Pass and the Crater Lake

Molaretto

Bardonècchia

ITALY

Lausanne

Geneva

10

11

Chambery

Aosta

Milan

12

Grenoble

Susa

Turin

Briançon

ITALY

Gap

13

Cuneo

Genoa

Nice

Cannes

Marseilles

MEDITERRANEAN

Henri and Alain were making the *Tour de Mont Blanc*, keeping to the trail that winds round the whole *massif* by way of Entrèves, La Fouly, the Forclaz, Montroc and the *col du Brevent*, a brisk nine days' walk around as many glaciers in a range of light. They knew the *Bonhomme* pretty well, they said. They usually went over it once or twice a year. Sometimes they scrambled over Mont Tondu, but that week they intended to take it easy, starting with the *col* the next morning.

'At what time?'

'Half past four.'

'Why so early?'

'To see the sun rise,' said Henri.

A cool pair. Friendly but not given to small-talk. The tradition is that, more than any other race, the British are particularly reticent among strangers, but less so, I think, than young Frenchmen with the disconcerting habit of answering questions in two or three words. The two came from Lyons. No, they said, they didn't work there. They designed reactors at Pierrelatte, the atomic centre. A good place to escape from. As for Savoy, they reckoned it the finest place in the world. With M. Pourquoi in mind, I asked weren't the people *un peu* – I struggled for the word – *cassant, insociable*? Henri looked surprised. The local people, he said, were mostly hotel-keepers and like hotel-keepers everywhere, their manners changed at the sight of money. As for themselves they came to Savoy to get away from people.

We British are a sensitive race. For the better part of an hour I sat in a corner deciphering a dull article on the Common Market in the *Journal de Genève*.

Dark came down, coldly. It began to snow. Henri and Alain yawned and made for the door. They slept outside, saying it felt warmer and more comfortable in a tent. I pitched mine alongside, and they were both snoring exuberantly before I managed to work out that remark about getting away from people.

Henri woke me with a mug of hot coffee and a thimbleful of *marc*. By the time I had packed and crawled out into the pale blue light, they were waiting. Although they carried a tent and cooking gear, my pack seemed twice the size of their own.

'*Formidable*,' said Alain, lifting it up gingerly. 'Where is your *piolet*?' I didn't know what he meant. He tapped his ice-axe. I had no *piolet*, I said.

We walked together, rapidly, over a thin powdering of snow. When it became deep, the uncommunicative Alain took the lead. He mounted a steep slope at right angles to the floor of the *col*, and struck out along a barely discernible ridge.

At first they affected to ignore my performance as a person might charitably look aside when his partner fluffs a golf shot or miscues at billiards. For a time they may have thought they were in the company of somebody who had evolved a new technique of tackling snow slopes by digging his heels in. If so, they were quickly disillusioned. Whilst they trudged forward resolutely, step by step, scarcely altering their pace however steep the traverse, I floundered and slipped. At one point I tried to scramble back to the ridge on all fours. It soon became clear I didn't know a thing about how to walk on snow.

Henri showed me how to dig my toes in so that I trod deep, impelled by my own momentum. He advised me to keep close so that when he began to chop steps, usually with a single stroke of his axe, I had something firm to put my feet on. I kept my eyes on those steps, scarcely daring to look down the appalling sweep of the slope below, but when, to give me confidence, Alain handed me his own *piolet*, the feeling of acute nausea passed and I merely felt chronically giddy. My instructors were patient and highly professional.

Dawn broke. Clouds as delicate as the tails of egrets glowed and caught fire in the first great shafts of light from the east. Peak after peak appeared around Mont Pourri in the Vanoise. With its white walls and rose-coloured roof that great dome looked like the pavilion of a chief among the tents of his men. The light also disclosed shameful evidence of what I had done wrong the previous day.

Far below my footprints stood out as if some distracted creature had scampered about, trying to avoid some threat from above which, I suppose, is more or less what it amounted to. The tracks wavered about uncertainly, and at the point where I lost my balance and rolled over they ended in a long blue-grey smudge. Observing merely that it must have been an experience,

Henri threw back his head and began to yodel, invoking a series of echoes from the crags around.

About high mountain air in the morning there is a super-tonic quality. It confounds that pompous stuff called human gravity, which, as somebody put it, serves only to conceal the defects of the mind. Any reticence there might have been between us blew away. We joked and fell about each other, throwing snowballs. Alain sang barrack-room songs and Henri whirled down a slope in the manner of a *ramasseur*.

To perform that feat you sit on your heels and push off, using your *piolet* as a handbrake. He carried out some remarkable acrobatics culminating in a series of broad loops, controlled at speed by digging his axe in at full arm's length. When I tried to do the same I succeeded only in rolling over again, breaking another rivet in the frame of my rucksack. After much of this we struck out for the second ridge, the *Croix de Bonhomme*.

I have often thought about setting off for a long walk in the company of one or two friends, but, with cautionary memories of a few sailing trips, I have never actually tried it. Toleration for the close and prolonged company of all but a few intimates tends to diminish progressively until you can't bear the way somebody drums his fingers or repeats an irritating little phrase. But at the beginning, before the hard corners of mannerisms and personality begin to stick out, all is conviviality. We go out of our way to show what companionable fellows we are, and so it was with us that morning. We swopped addresses and bits of chocolate. I gladly sacrificed a quarter of brandy bought only for the most dire of emergencies. We told tales of what we recalled most vividly and since the two were for climbing rather than walking, my stock of adventure in lonely places seemed meagre beside their own, especially on the subject of storms, for on one occasion they had actually been struck by lightning.

As Henri described the incident, they had climbed up to a high ledge in winter, determined on reaching a *réfuge* in the *col de Chavannes*. It became overcast. Fearing snow, they climbed rapidly, cutting deep steps, hauling themselves up steep places by using their axes as *grappins*, that is as anchors or grapnels to which they tied their ropes. On one ledge they put an extra heavy strain on an axe that began to emit a high-pitched whine, 'like a bee'. As if in sympathy, the other axe started to whine in the same way. This is the song of the ice-axe, *la chanson du piolet*, an electrostatic effect that occurs when the atmosphere is heavily charged.

Suddenly, all at a blow, they were deafened as a discharge struck at the lightning conductor dangling from the ledge. The two men were thrown into the snow. They weren't hurt, but they felt completely numb, *engourdi* as they put it, and they lost about thirty metres of rope. It didn't burn up. The fibres opened and they were left with a few handfuls of fluff and the charred shaft of one of their axes. 'Down from that place we came like rabbits,' said Henri.

When I look back I consider that brief stage as the high point in what little I have learned about walking through snow-covered places. Without it, I doubt if I could have got through what came later, but it seemed nothing but pleasurable at the time. If Henri and Alain remember those four or five hours between La Balme and the Cross of the Good Fellow, it will be, I hope, with amusement. We parted on the cliffs of Les Chapieux. They were making for the Miage glacier. I had a less appealing appointment in Bourg St Maurice with some television people from London.

They turned up with two car-loads of equipment. They were considerate, and as most of their shots were taken through powerful telescopic lenses, it wasn't necessary to modify my cross-country route. I walked on for two or three days acutely conscious of the cameras and the loss of privacy. For all that, I have an uneasy feeling that the technique of filming exposed a bit of what I was missing by walking fast. The camera is a relentless instrument. I can look at objects from a distance, yet it can poke and probe about in the intimacy of a close-up. The film crew invaded village wash-houses and churches, clambering up into belfries and bedrooms to look down on courtyards and little back streets I might never have seen on my own. Christopher Brasher, the producer, chose the Val d'Isère and the Vanoise for its spectacular beauty, and also because it shows plainly what's happening to most of the Alpine parks.

The Vanoise is a very large park, the refuge of the golden eagle, the chamois and the ibex with its huge backward-pointing horns.

If the French authorities manage to hold on to their absolute authority over the place, conserving it for those who want peace and quiet, it's possible that the townships on the edge of the park will absorb most of the squalor of uncontrolled tourism, but it doesn't look as if things are turning out that way. Big investors have got their eyes on the interior. Entrepreneurs are offering local communities hard cash for concessions to build hotels. There is a plan for a massive ski station up in the mountains and some of the park commissioners are in favour of the project. The irony is that, but for the creation of the reserve with its little tracks leading up into the hills, the traffic that now thunders down the highway might have thundered on, ignoring the place that used to be difficult to get into. But the little tracks are becoming roads and as the townships expand, the tourists are looking for new places to go.

The valley of the Isère is a remarkable example of what economists mean by shifting economies and the decay of rural self-sufficiency. Ski-villes are springing up like mushrooms; the old villages have all but dropped to bits. The old folk who stayed on when their children left are living in poverty. The investors' answer to what can be done for them is simply 'develop the place'. They argue that the park is vast and the exploitation of one small corner unlikely to make much difference to the peace-and-quiet seekers. But open space is like virginity: once lost it can never be regained.

I know very well that a high moral tone usually creeps into most things written about the decay of the countryside. Conservationists are usually right, but too often they sound only righteous. They use the words 'us' and the 'others', the spoliators, the people guilty of myopia, venality or, what is almost as bad, indifference. As we're all in this appalling mess together, I wish we could always use the word 'us' to mean us all.

It had been agreed that for film purposes we should give some impression of both sides of the valley, rustic and modern. Waylaid at intervals by the cameraman, I kept to a track on the very edge of the park. The gorge thereabouts is dissected by scores of streams. Fascinated by the noise they made, the sound engineer tried to capture the difference between a brooklet and a thin cascade. During rare intervals of quiet near a road, he carried what he called 'actuality' to a high pitch by recording the rustle of my boots as I walked through grass and scrub and fields of knee-high flowers. He also tried to record birdsong. Nightingales bubbled and, occasionally, a kite screamed, the sound echoing eerily among the cliffs, but never when that diligent man happened to be around. Hearing those cries when it seemed as if all my powers of observation were being overlooked by cameras and microphones, it cheered me up a lot to think that some of the greatest pleasures we encounter are often those unlooked for.

The trail winds through the timbered shacks of La Gurraz, a hamlet full of woodworm and history. An old woman who might have been the wife of Time himself waddled past with an immense scythe over her shoulders. The wealth of her neighbours used to consist of about a dozen cows, large flocks of sheep and snuff-coloured goats and a communal patch of vegetables; nowadays they are selling their dilapidated homes for high prices. They are being done up as *chalets modernes pour vacances*.

The cameramen drove off to find a new location, leaving me on a path with very little in its favour. It looped through a wood on an acute slope and came to an extremely dead end some five hundred feet above the turbulent river. A landslip. The old story. The trees had been cut down. After a vain search for a path up to the summit of the cliff, I zigzagged down to some hovels on the main road, resigned to a three hours' march in the company of heavy traffic.

Of all kinds of vehicle drivers, I normally fear truckers the least and mountain hogs the most. There is a sub-species, *alpestris*, of whom I may have something to say later. The majority, I suspect, are ski-bums, frustrated young men, the self-appointed presidents of suicide clubs who take blind corners at speed and regard pedestrians as a curious kind of mirage that dissolves when approached. By contrast, the man behind the wheel of a forty-tonner is like the captain of an ocean-going liner in the presence of busy little speed-boats. He has a sense of responsibility; but for the enormous draught he creates, I feel safe in his presence, or at least I did until I met shoals of the monsters on the road to Val d'Isère. The dangers are not so much the sharp bends in the road as the long tunnels into which the juggernauts thunder with their lights full on. And there are no sidewalks inside.

'*Allumez vos lanternes*' it says at the entrance. During a lull, I ventured into the first, nervously, carrying a torch that gave scarce more light than a candle on a Christmas tree. Black as hell. The tunnels are sinuous and the little eye of light at the other end offered no encouragement. Several trucks roared past with no noticeable diminution in speed. At their approach, I scampered for the nearest cranny and flattened against the wet and dripping rock, hoping to make a few more yards before the next monster bore down.

I emerged feeling distinctly shaky, but there was no going back except through the same tunnel. Overhead the crags of the Sassière and far below the fast-flowing river.

Streams of water poured down through the roof of the second tunnel and a loose rope on the tarpaulin of an articulated truck thrashed my shoulder. I emerged again and walked on. At the sight of yet another fearful hole ahead, my nerve went and I turned back towards a small roadside café.

The man of the house spoke English slowly, but fluently. He had been an interpreter during the war. Perhaps he sensed my mood for after questions about how far I had walked he said: 'Are you not sometimes afraid to travel alone?'

'Yes, sometimes,' I said. 'But not in good country. What I'm frightened of are *those* things,' and I nodded towards the cars that raced past.

He looked through the window dispassionately. 'Those things are my business,' he said. 'Everyone has a car these days.'

'Not everyone. I haven't got one.'

He poured out another drink, professionally, twisting the bottle so that the very last drop fell into my glass. 'Accept this, please. Perhaps I am being a little impertinent, but I have another question. It is perhaps more tranquil to travel your way, but I should not like to be alone all the time. What do you think about?'

I gave him the stock answer, about how it depended on where I was and what I saw, and it sounded as thin as it always does when you try and put something close to your heart into a few words. He nodded, but there was clearly something else on his mind. I can't remember exactly how he put it, but he wanted to know how one kept *bad* thoughts at bay. Was it not a fact that when people were alone they lived through their lives backwards and forwards? There emerged those thoughts they kept from their friends. Was that a good thing? But with company he felt

227

it was different. Then you were obliged to live in the present. And that was much easier.

'Another drink?' he said.

'No thanks. You've given me a lot to think about. Don't you spend much of your own time alone?'

'Not at all,' he said. 'I have my little ones. Come and see them.'

In a garden at the back of the hut a little girl sat on a swing, staring moodily at her brother who was reading a fairy story to a very old and very uninterested sheepdog.

'My grandchildren,' he said. 'They are very fond of each other and I am glad to have their company.'

The old man went back to attend to a customer. I sat down. The boy continued to read and the girl tried vainly to attract his attention. He never looked up. Perhaps there is something about a dog and a fairy story that you can't get from an importunate sister.

At length the girl tiptoed up and struck him lightly on the shoulder. A mere love-tap, but he turned on her, angrily. The dog ran off and the boy ran after it, almost crying. 'Come back, Pépé,' he shouted. 'Oh come back. I have something *very* important to tell you.'

I'm pretty sure I could have got through that last tunnel on my own, but fortunately I didn't have to try. A car pulled up and Brasher leaned out. 'Thought you'd got lost,' he said. 'I tell you, that tunnel ahead's an absolute stinker. Black as the inside of a cow. You'd better pop in,' and he opened the door.

I went through the ritual patter. Sometimes it's difficult to remain a full-time pedestrian. We argued. We reached a compromise. I walked on. Brasher drove close behind with his headlights full on. I waved happily at the oncoming drivers. I don't know what they thought of us, but most of them looked very surprised.

What I have to say about Val d'Isère is tinged with knowledge of the disaster that happened there months later. The hillside collapsed. A landslide rolled down on to a school and eighty children were buried alive. You could argue it was predictable. Trees were being uprooted with steel hawsers that afternoon. They were dredging the river for sand and gravel. The water flows fast and muddy and in flood it bites deep into the loose clays. But all this, I say, is being written with hindsight. My first impression was of violence. Pollution is violence and environmental pollution is environmental violence. From the gaping holes in the bare ground, it looked as if a stick of bombs had fallen across the floor of the valley. Tower cranes whined among dozens of chalets and half-completed hotels. A little army of workmen were building the Super Ski-ville of the Tarentaise.

Ski-villes reproduce themselves much like waterweed. Bits break off; they float away and take root elsewhere. Holiday-makers want ski-runs. The local people desperately want business. There is every reason in the world for developing miles of slopes on both sides of the highway, but few if any valid ones why a park should be ripped open in the process.

Val d'Isère was ripe with rumour. The concessionaires were out hunting. Their clients are the big construction companies and finance corporations; their go-betweens, a host of small entrepreneurs, including those well-dressed young vagrants of the snow-line collectively known as ski-bums. Many are just nice young kids who have developed a passion for snow in the way young girls get hooked on the smell of a stable. Several I talked to were well-mannered bilinguists, competent to handle all kinds of sports gear, especially fast cars and those diabolically noisy little power-driven sleighs called skidoos.

They are not averse to washing dishes during hard times. A few act as ski-instructors for the cheaper hotels. They all get a rake-off for introducing visitors to almost anything and most of them eventually drift back home. But for the hard core who hang on for season after season the going is usually pretty perilous. With jobs ranging from concession-finding to pimping, they are the uninhibited fixers.

Cars poured into the town that weekend. Heavy snow had fallen on the *col de l'Iseran*, that high ridge between the Isère and the valley of the Arc. The *Syndicat* had fixed up an international ski-ing contest. I mooched about moodily, impatient at the delay. When I'm in top gear the scenery seems to flow towards me, easily. But when I'm held back the process is reversed and accelerated. Everything seems to be rushing ahead, leaving me stranded. Through field-glasses I looked up at the *col*, the highest I had seen. I wanted to get to grips with it. But when? Brasher kept asking for just another day. I growled like a chained dog and left on the morning of the ski-ing contest.

A glorious morning. At eight o'clock I looked down on Val d'Isère from a height of six thousand feet. The way is by the Ouillette, a stream that leaps down through a larch wood strangely dressed for spring in early July. A difficulty arose above the tree-line where the pools looked too deep to ford and the rocky falls too rocky to be jumped over with any confidence. Remembering how Hilaire Belloc managed to ford a flooded Italian river, I collected some hefty lumps of rock and lobbed them in to gauge the depth of the water. Through some acoustic effect beyond my comprehension, a stone thrown into a deep pool produces a hollow *ploonk* easily distinguishable from the high-pitched *plonk* you get from the shallows. After several *ploonks* I got an encouraging *plonk* and waded through two feet of bitterly cold water. Pausing only to empty my boots and wring out socks, I reached the snow before seven thousand feet, climbing rapidly, remembering to dig my toes in.

That joy of escape, that feeling of getting away, of being unshackled. If I could write of it as easily as I swung along that morning there would be pages here of the wind that blew a pencil of snow spume from the breast of the Solaise, of a sharp-winged peregrine soaring on an uplift, of mountain flowers and the thin cry of marmots. Much of that pleasure came from confidence, for on the way up to the Isèran, after walking close on a thousand miles, I knew I could make a fair showing on rocks and snow. I write this down firmly, knowing it for a fact though I had cause for concern that morning.

In working my way up a gully under the Pyramide, the snow gave way and I sank in up to my waist. From below came the sound of running water. I had strayed over the edge of a buried stream. In leaning backwards to get out, I wrenched my knee and for a moment thought it done for. But some brisk massage and a swig of brandy put me in good shape for a clamber round a cliff. From there on a long easy slope led up to the crest at nine thousand feet.

On the far side of the *col*, the skiers flocked in their hundreds, but in that enormous bowl of mountains they were no more than a pinch of dust on a soup plate.

I trudged down. They were being hauled up to a high point on a cable and released. I trudged on. They swooped on me as swallows might swoop on a tortoise. I trudged round that ski-yard and down towards Bonneval, sad at losing height laboriously gained. Of all those skiers only one showed any marked determination to get away from the rest. He appeared, briefly, in silhouette against the shoulders of the Lessières and down he skimmed, into the recesses of the park. Was he, I wondered, a professional who had done badly in the contest? More likely a passionate amateur. The élite ski on their own, or at most in parties of two or three.

Years ago, a friend of mine, a newspaper correspondent in Sweden, told me how his brother Erik, a passionate skier, joined a border patrol in Finland, largely for the sport. They had never seen a Russian in that sector. The war seemed a long way away. But out they went for three or four days on their own, ski-ing in the silver grey light of the pine forests.

Just before dusk one evening the young Swede saw a lone figure in the distance. Thinking his officer had come out to meet him, he waved. The man waved back. From opposite sides of a slope they swooped down towards each other. When they were only a few yards apart Erik realized the man wore an unusual uniform. He was a Russian. They both swung their sub-machine guns off their shoulders, but Erik managed to fire first. He fired and kept on firing until he had emptied the magazine.

My friend said: 'I don't know what he did after that. He must have stood beside the body for a long time. At the farm they told me he tried to carry it away. He came in spattered in blood and could scarcely speak. They sent him off to a mental home and he's been in and out ever since. They say he's getting a bit better, but I don't see much change myself. It's all so sad.'

The snow thinned at seven thousand feet and gradually disappeared. There was no orderliness in its going. Long white tongues could be seen far down in the valley of the Lenta. At the foot of the first escarpment it became patchy, and there, as marvellously displayed as jewels on green baize, were myriads of little alpine flowers, all fresh sprung from the melt. I looked at them with love and a little regret, since on the way down from the *Bonhomme*, I had lost my illustrated copy of Egli's *Alpen-*

flora. I remember using it to identify a superb lily at Chapieux and never saw it again.

Without its aid, I could recognize a few of the saxifrages, the gentians and some of the soldanellas and campanulas. The beds of bright yellow whitlow grass I knew from the ruined walls of a castle in South Wales. In company with the glacial buttercup, it manages to pierce the last puttering of snow. But what were those little rosettes like drops of blood on a curious sort of mottled rock? I know little about the alpines. Shameful this, since hosts of new species were collected abroad and grown in gardens for the first time by one of my illustrious neighbours, Reginald Farrer.

Farrer lived at Ingleton in Yorkshire. In case you imagine we were over-neighbourly, he travelled the world and died in Burma before I was born. But mention his name to serious rock gardeners anywhere and their eyes gleam. There is Farrer's gentian, Farrer's primula, Farrer's saxifrage, geranium, globe flower, and I forget how many more, including an entirely new genus, *Farreria*, represented by a little ground Daphne with clusters of citron-yellow flowers.

A photograph shows a plump man with a large upturned moustache of the kind favoured by Victorian lion-tamers, which, in a way, he was. He wrote some furious polemics. The moustache hid a hare lip, but the impediment in his speech subdued neither his tongue nor his pen. He turned out a string of novels, much poetry and several plays, all now forgotten, except for what he had to say about his abiding passion for alpines and gardens.

Farrer never married but, under the name of Lady Little Willow Tree, he refers tenderly to his friend, a geisha girl in Tokyo. On the subject of permanent attachments, he reckoned nothing 'less stable, no guide more delusive and treacherous than that which the young call love and the old, more wisely, instinct'. It is appropriate that the great plant-collector became a vegetarian, although his biographer, Geoffrey Taylor, thinks it may have stemmed from his discovery in Japan that his pet kitten had been served up the previous night as *fricassée* of chicken. A many-sided man.

There is the whimsical Farrer. He possessed a very famous bunch of *Daphne rupestris* which never failed to blossom exactly in time for the Royal Horticultural Society's summer show, no matter how the date varied. This became the subject of a scurrilous pamphlet. Farrer happened to be in Tibet at the time, but, as he explained later, his beloved plant always appeared at her best in public. As he put it: 'The flowers open the day before the show and the nervous tension is such that they all drop off the day after it is over.'

There is the pre-eminently practical Farrer. He infused new life into rock gardening, insisting constantly on 'a faint adulteration only of soil and perfect drainage'. He poured scorn on the rich 'out to purchase the glories of the Alps at so much a yard'. He castigated rock gardens he disapproved of as so many plum buns, dogs' graves or drunkard's dreams.

But above all there is Farrer on the subject of the plants he loves best. Here his prose is profound and often purple. Of an iris (*Oncocylus*) that usually only blossoms once in a garden, he says they 'are a doomed and lonely race of irreconcilable Troads in weeds of silken crêpe, sullenly and grandly unresigned to exile . . . ' A certain campanula (*Miranda*) that took away his breath when it bloomed, he described as 'diaphanous and pale china-blue, like a fine cloud at night with the moon behind it'. As for primulas he said, 'a cold awe sweeps across the gardener as he comes at last into the shadow of that grim and glorious name'.

Farrer died of some chest infection during an expedition to Burma. Unable to take any sustenance except whisky and soda, he died, his servants said, 'without giving any pain or trouble to us'. Perhaps he had achieved his dream. This dream, he wrote, was 'to have some illustrious plant to bear his name immortal through the gardens of future generations, long after he himself shall have become the dust of their paths'.

From the crest of the Isèran, the trail drops more than seven thousand feet through a series of hanging valleys. The impression is that each is the floor of that range. They look so vast, you cannot imagine yet another steep descent, but they are no more than steps in a huge staircase. On those slopes, some little way past the Bridge of Snows, the peaty loam became unstable and puffed up from frequent freezing and thawing. This is solifluction or soil creep. The feeling is of walking on slippery mattresses.

To my consternation, a portion about the size of a tennis court began to slide as I trod on it. It didn't slide very far, perhaps fifty feet in all and the slope wasn't particularly acute, but I had the notion, momentarily, that a portion of the mountainside had come unstuck. There is no arguing with earth in motion. If you move at all, you move together. My arms flailed wildly. I lost my balance and when the unnerving motion stopped, suddenly, I rolled over, tearing my pants on the branches of a recumbent spruce that rolled down with us. I rose and walked down to Bonneval plastered with chocolate brown mud and draughty at the rear.

This Bonneval is a ski-ville in embryo, a township on the way up. Enormous notices proclaim the good intentions of the *Syndicat*. You are repeatedly assured of a welcome. *All* sports, it says, are catered for. I promised myself the best food at easy prices. But at half past two that afternoon the woman in charge of a brassy-looking restaurant used a phrase I hadn't heard in close on sixty days. She said the kitchen had closed and she said it firmly. A singularly uninformed local said there were no other restaurants in town and I hastened out of the place, scowling horribly at a young lad, who, in defiance of all the park regulations, tried to sell me a bunch of edelweiss. But good luck in the shape of that selfsame lad ran after me. Do you want a room? he asked. No! I said. He persisted. Then what about something to eat. I stared at him. A meal? Where could I get one? Come with me, he said.

He led me back to a tumbledown shack where an old woman, who was, I discovered, his grandmother, greeted me warmly. I gave him a franc and had I known what I was in for I would have given him more.

Granny produced a small home-made quince liqueur unbidden, murmuring that it was on the house. Pausing only for reassurance as to its palatability, she banged open the wooden shutters and began to bawl like a street vendor. Up rushed four cheerful scruffy-looking children, three boys and a girl, all grandchildren. One she sent for wine, another for ham and cheese and a third for something else. The girl followed her down to the kitchen whence came the puff and roar of a bellows-blown fire. An offer of another liqueur and up they all trooped within half an hour. They stood round the table respectfully as Granny with a flourish uncovered a large *Croûte Savoyarde* as daintily done up and garnished as ever you could have wished for in a three-star restaurant. With it went a litre of Gamay, several cheeses and a bowl of fresh peaches. Price: eight francs.

Feeling wonderfully looked after, I took coffee with Granny, who stitched up my pants, holding the material an inch from her nose. They had a future now in Bonneval, she thought. They had built the ski-lift. With a subsidy she might be able to repair the house and give it a lick of paint. When the visitors pour in, as I sincerely hope they do, there won't be time to devote half an hour to a *croûte*. Refrigerated trucks, full of what the trade calls convenience foods, are already making weekly trips into the remote valleys. But I feel better for having written something about the other side of ski-villedom.

On the bridge out of town I turned my back on that *sentier* I had followed indifferently well from St Gingolph. It looped away west, into the park. Through field-glasses I scanned the ranges to the south where I had nowhere to go but everywhere.

To the south-east, at the far side of a series of towering defiles, lay Italy, but the only passes for which I had maps were clearly deep under snow. The Ribon under Charbonnel looked possible, but a venture there meant coming down into the Stura, too far to the east for a walker intent on Briançon and the High Alps. With a kneecap that throbbed uncomfortably when I put too much weight on my right leg, I decided to try to find an easy way up to the *col* of Mont Cenis, avoiding the roads by working round the flanks of the Arcelle Neuve. But where to spend that night? For weeks I had been telling myself I ought to find a site fit for contemplation and cool off for a day or two, but somehow there always seemed better reasons for bustling on.

It is sad to discover that even among enormous mountains these sites we dream of are as elusive as any other kinds of prolonged content. Perhaps it's just a matter of time, of having the leisure to weigh up the relative merits of slope and vista, of wind protection and a soft underlay. After looking keenly at several potential boudoirs I came at length to a stream from the green glaciers of the Lombarde and though not much liking to wander off course, I followed her into the Averole which is a *vallée* by Bessans. That stream ran too straight for comfort, so I took up with one of her daughters and blessed that switch in affection when, above a cascade, she led me to a pool hemmed in on the one hand by trees and on the other by crags that went straight up into the sky. To the north I gazed on the Vanoise and to the south on the outer walls of Italy, and there in my own name I took possession of an untouched corner of the world.

With tent up and bedding down, I lit a crackling fire of old larch and thought about supper. With half a bottle of wine, the rolls packed up by an innkeeper in far-away Val d'Isère were ample enough. They bulged with creamed egg and veal and a lettuce heart for garnish, but for such a night as I hoped for, they were not inspiring. The upshot was that I spent the better part of an hour lying on the bank of the stream that fed the pool, tickling trout. I caught three scarcely six inches in length. Now trout grilled on a stick are uneatable, as I had discovered in the Ardennes, but wrapped in tin foil they can be nicely steamed. One fish exploded in a fit of posthumous pique, raising a shower of ashes, but the others came out done to a turn.

As I lolled in front of that fire, weaving fantasies from the flames, I thought how much urban man has lost by substituting hot-water pipes for an open hearth. Coal is valuable stuff. Smoke is foul. There is no going back to yesterday, but a room with central heating is like a church without an altar; it lacks orientation.

As the flames sank, I had an uneasy feeling that my own store of energy was sinking too. It wasn't so much physical tiredness as a diminution of drive. I had lost much of that feeling of conquest that puts miles to flight. I pulled out maps of various sizes and tried to work out the distance to Monaco or Nice, or indeed anywhere on that coast. Without making allowances for detours and counter-marching, it came out at something well over two hundred miles, say ten or eleven days of hard going. The problem was whether to stay there and nurse that knee or press on. I decided to press on, knowing that if my drive petered out it would take much more than a few days' rest to charge it up again. I went to bed in the dark, the fire a discouraging heap of grey ash and charcoal.

O blessed sleep. I awoke to find the world new-made and shining. A touch of red in the eastern sky might betoken rain for the goatherds of the *Val di Ala*, but not, I felt, for me. It smelt dry. It looked good. To the west, where a great hog's back of ridge hid Mont Cenis, the peaks were gold-plated and only lightly veiled in mist. In the mountains there are as many dawns as there are different kinds of days and the man who sets off in the morning worrying about a red sky ought first to check the wind.

Mont Cenis is less of a peak than a sprawling *massif* with a cloven crown between the Cottian and the Graian Alps. The route that looked best lay by Chantelouve and St Sebastian of the Blessed Arrows and then straight up on what from the map looked like a mule track. I looked again, closely, for there is little to distinguish between the dotted line of a *route forestière* and a *limite de commune* which usually lies along ridges fit only for chamois.

I went up cheerfully as a bird, breasting outliers, picking my way through screes and expecting always to encounter something formidable. Ridge followed ridge. The going steeper now, I seemed to be in the heart of the forest. Not quite what I expected, but no hardship. You could have taken a cart up that zigzag track. High above I saw a long rim of rock and braced myself for a smart climb.

Nothing of the kind. A mere step in the forest. I looked down on the crown of trees cut by the loops of National Highway Six, the road up from Lanslebourg. Around a horseshoe bend chugged a red truck.

The dramatic moments of life are apt to fall singularly flat. I reached the *col* by a series of forest rides. I scarcely climbed at all and the consolation, if any, came from beating that red truck to the transport café by twenty minutes, although, of course, it may have stopped on the way. I took a drink with the driver with a feeling of mild disappointment. E. M. Forster has pointed out that actual life is full of false clues and signposts that lead nowhere. He says that 'often with infinite effort we nerve ourselves for a crisis that never comes. The most successful career must show a waste of strength that might have moved mountains, and the most unsuccessful is not that of a man who is taken unprepared, but of him who has prepared and is never taken.'

What the crater of Mont Cenis looked like before *Electricité France* turned it into an immense lake is difficult to imagine. The scene now is one of industrial frenzy. In recent years the water-level has been raised at least twice, submerging the trail, the main road and now the trail above the road. There can be no quarrel about turning that high-altitude depression into a source of power; the vista in all directions is markedly unappealing. The question is why development of this kind produces a tide line of permanent squalor. The tin shacks and barrack-like bungalows of ferro-concrete built to house an army of workmen are still there. Entrepreneurs have put in bars and amusement centres. A shanty town has sprung up beyond the barrage. A driver for *Transports Internationaux* confided that if I wanted a girl or a blue film there was a place at the back. Through a dirty window I saw the girl. She looked like an old doll in a bankrupt toy shop.

Feeling desperately tired, I marched on. To save a few miles, to escape the interminable loops of that road, I disregarded the notice about guard dogs and slunk across the lower end of the construction. Down I went, past bulldozers and forests of cranes, right down to the floor of the unfinished reservoir.

There may be no fool quite like a fool in search of a party on the top of Mont Cenis, but that night I felt I deserved one. When I came to write up my notes I found I had walked just over a thousand miles. In the little bar at the Grand Croix, where they speak mostly Italian, they said there was no *ristorante* nearer than Cenisio about five miles away. I set off at once.

The road thrashes about like a wounded snake, shaking off five thousand feet in a few miles. On all sides great mountains. To the east the summit of Rocciamelone turned from bronze to purple and slowly faded from view. I pounded on through in the transparent dark. At the frontier posts the French saluted and asked no questions. The Italians were volubly co-operative. They might have guessed they were dealing with a man on his way to a feast. A glance at my passport and they waved me on, ahead of a line of waiting trucks.

When the restaurant appeared with its lights blazing, I had already worked out the ground plan of a menu starting with half a bottle of champagne. Perhaps a little *vitello* followed by a chicken or a pheasant cooked in wine. How it came about that I walked out without so much as a biscuit had to do largely with Madame's curious aversion to Swiss francs. In addition to a little

French money and a book of travellers' cheques, I carried about twenty pounds' worth of that hard currency. She had lost on the exchange rates before, she said. But the cheques, I argued, surely they were worth their face value anywhere. She wasn't having any. Maybe she didn't altogether like my appearance.

After I had changed some money back at the frontier post she gave me a table within fifteen feet of a hypertensive television set. Could it be turned down or turned off? No! Could I eat elsewhere? No! Not even at a side table in the bar? The same answer.

Given a few minutes to think up something guileful, I might have remembered Gaston's ploy at Liège and made some reference to my old friend in Rome, no less than the director of the All-Italian Tourist Board or some such similar fiction, but my salivary glands had begun to secrete bile. '*Tutto impossibile*', I said, and stamped out.

To walk alone among mountains in the moonlight, to hear no sound except your own footsteps, the chirrup of crickets, the passionate complaint of nightingales; all this is what, in retrospect, I had walked a thousand miles to enjoy. But it found no receptive fellow in me that night. I felt tired and ravenously hungry. With nothing more sustaining than a tin of warm sardines and a roll of yesterday's bread, I would have swopped that vast and warm-scented emptiness for the meanest tavern in the Finchley Road. A cottager said the *albergo* in Molaretto, miles away, might still be open. Without much hope I trudged on, wondering what on earth you say to a Piedmontese innkeeper awakened long after midnight by a handful of gravel on his bedroom window. Had a car come along I might have broken a still unbroken rule and taken up this narrative from some room in distant Susa. But no car came, and what happened in Molaretto still has about it something of the air of a miracle.

The inn appeared, an unpretentious-looking place from the outside, but wonderfully full of light and bustle. Far from looking surprised at a customer at that hour, the innkeeper, a tubby little man, waved me towards the dining room with a splendid sweep of his arm. There around a candlelit table sat about a dozen men. They were mountaineers. One seemed vaguely familiar. He rose to greet me. 'The Englishman from Val d'Isère,' he said.

'So you have come to join us. Welcome!' Signor Scribante Oreste shook my hand and introduced me to his president and fellow members of that élite of the climbing fraternity, the *Club Alpino Italiano*. They invited me to join their table.

Sandwiched between a man who spoke French and another who knew a bit of English, I answered questions; I talked of the pleasures of a wandering way of life and, with Madame at Cenisio in mind, I said something about its rubs and indignities. They were intrigued and puzzled. They were passionate climbers. Each day, they said, they tried to achieve *una grand' altitudine*. Height meant everything. They had not even heard of the *Sentier de Grande Randonnée*, but at my immodest mention of a thousand miles, the president ordered half a dozen bottles of sparkling Soave as something to remember them by. *Per ricordarti di noi.*

Outside on the balcony, until long after midnight, they sang *canzone piemontese*, those soft airs of the mountains. They pointed out peaks ghost-pale in the moonlight. They told of stern adventure on the Cross of Ferro, Charbonnel, Uia di Ciamarella, and Monte Pietramorta. Yet, as I look back on that evening, Molaretto stands higher than any of the Italian Alps.

High Alps

We parted at dawn. Laughing and talking, laden with coils of rope, the mountaineers set off for some crack in the roof of the Rocciamelone. I ambled down into the valley of the Dora alone, intent on avoiding anything arduous that day. Parked by the roadside in the glow of a shrine to St Martin were three transcontinental trucks, enormous affairs, their drivers sleeping, stretched out full length on the front seats. They slept amid the noise of nightingales. It seemed strange to hear that full-throated song in July. In Britain the early birds tune up in late April; they give their best concerts during the first three weeks in May. By June they are mostly silent, brooding, starting to moult and store up fuel for their flight back to tropical Africa in August, but in the Cenisio that morning they were bubbling as if newly arrived.

The light spilled over the peaks. It saddened me a little to think I had grown accustomed to vistas on the grand scale. No range, however spectacular, could have taken me entirely by surprise. But suddenly, as if in reproof, I looked down on the heart-touching beauty of a little Italian town tucked away in an armpit of the hills. All seemed so intimate, so exquisitely Lilliputian that some benign giant might have arranged those little houses with hats on, those plumes of cypresses as playthings for a child. I walked down into Giaglione among the huckling of hens, the bleat of goats and warm staccato voices. Here are the Piedmontese, the people who live at the foot of the mountains, and from near Susa to the source of the Dora they treated me well.

The air came up from the vine-terraced valley, aromatic and full of the warm south. There, if anywhere, I might have stayed and built up some of that drive lost beyond the Isèran, but prolonged rest alone would have sufficed. With no time for such

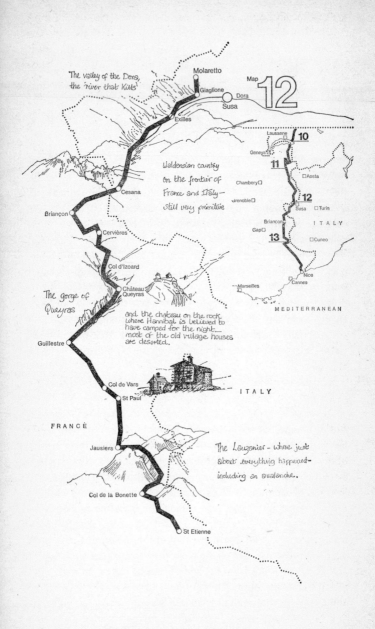

The valley of the Dora, the 'river that kills'

Molaretto

Giaglione

Dora

Susa

Map 12

Exilles

Lausanne

Geneva

10

11

Chambery

Grenoble

Aosta

Cesana

12

Susa Turin

Briançon

Cervières

Gap

Briançon

ITALY

13

Cuneo

Col d'Izoard

Château Queyras

Waldensian country on the frontier of France and Italy — still very primitive

The gorge of Queyras

and the chateau on the rock where Hannibal is believed to have camped for the night — most of the old village houses are deserted.

Marseilles

Nice

Cannes

MEDITERRANEAN

Guillestre

Col de Vars

St Paul

ITALY

FRANCE

Jausiers

The Lauzanier — where just about everything happened — including an avalanche.

Col de la Bonette

St Etienne

respite, I began to pencil in lines on maps scarcely opened. About a dozen heights had still to be gained: the Montgenèvre and the Rochebrune, the Bûcher beyond Château Queyras, the *col de Vars* and the Bonette. A more adventurous walker might have struck due south, into the country of the Waldensians, those heralds of the Reformation burned in batches for their faith, but I settled for the Dora, and, except for one misguided descent, I clung to the heights of that wild river until near sundown.

Under a church bell kicking wildly in its tower, I walked out through narrow slots of streets, past houses all pink and yellow and peeling, past women in black shawls around the pump. On, out – far out – to a mule-track, scarcely two feet in width, but made for walking on, purposive. It drove through hillside holdings so steep that bare-chested men clung to knotted ropes as they hoed and pruned. I kept to that track for ten miles, and but for an obsessive notion to cross the river ahead of a bridge far upstream, would have kept to it for more. The descent entailed losing hundreds of feet in altitude and an hour or two in time, for there were no crossing at the narrows I came to. The Dora thundered white through a gorge. Nor was there any going on there for the river undercut a cliff too steep to be scaled, and I scrambled back to the ridge, among grass and rocks that danced in the heat.

There are two Doras. The one they call the Dora Baltea rises at the foot of Mont Blanc and gushes down in the Po by way of Aosta. The other, the *torrente assassino*, 'the river that kills' whets its knife on the boulders above Cesana-Torinese and runs off to Turin. It flows fast and, in places, deep. Valdoranians seem proud of the number of people the stream has swept away. They are at one with those Tillmen of Flodden Field, just over the Scottish border, who will tell you that

> Said Till tae Tweed
> Though ye rin wi' speed
> And I rin slaw,
> Where ye droon one man
> I droon twa.

The sun struck down hard, with malice, burnishing the walls of rock. Seeking shade, I made for a group of old chestnut trees in a cleft, their wrinkled trunks propped up with crutches like a party of pilgrims bound for Lourdes. Among the trees appeared the shell of a wooden house, the boards rotten, the steps all but collapsed. One shutter hung down from a rusted hinge. An old woman beckoned from the blind eye of a window. In that silence she had about her the air of an apparition. In what appeared to be the only habitable room in the place, a flock of little yellow finches fluttered in and out through the open window or remained twittering on the sill. One or two flew up into the rafters. They were mostly serins, the wild canaries of Europe.

The old lady shook with silent laughter. *Miei piccoli compagni.* They were her little friends, she said. She made clicking noises and scattered a handful of seed. A few birds flew down on to the white-spattered floor, seemingly unmindful of a large grey cat. With part of her flock reassembled, she sat down and motioned me to a chair.

From what I could make of her Italian, she lived there alone but *mio figlio viene qui.* Her son visited her occasionally. *Anche il prete.* A priest, too. He lived down in the valley, at Chiomonte. It was clear she didn't want to leave that dilapidated house. *Non me ne andrò mai.* 'I will never go,' she said.

Throughout most of Italy and France, the serin, the nightingale, the *gentille alouette* and hosts of other small birds are reckoned valuable only when shot and roasted. The old lady with her finches may have established the last sanctuary in Piedmont.

Before I got far that day I thought the heat of the Upper Dora had done me in. It came at me from above and below, like a tangible thing. The track snaked to the top of the ridge and went on and on and on, winding about among jaw-broken hills, white rocks and sand. Nothing to look at except cistus scrub. No soil worth the name, no trees, no shade, no sound except the papery rasp of red-winged grasshoppers. Everything else appeared burnt out, dead. I walked on because there was nothing else to do. I took off my shirt. I made a cushion out of a vest and put it under the bite of my shoulder straps, but it gave scant relief.

Years ago, on a walk through the deserts of Kenya, I imagined I had been acclimatized to the sun for the rest of my life, but there I walked unburdened by a rucksack. That morning it hung down, heavy and inert, a bag of misery.

Towards midday I began to sway like a drunk and recognized, nearly too late, the onset of heat exhaustion. The symptoms were unmistakable: giddiness, nausea, acute thirst and impaired vision. A peak on the opposite side of the valley seemed to wobble and a portion became detached, hanging as if suspended in the sky. This surely is what the psalmist meant by the destruction that wasteth at noonday.

I left the track and scrambled down the slope towards the hamlet of Molière. A desperate and unprofessional scramble, but effective since it took me where I wanted to go. A young girl handed me a mug of cold water. She looked surprised when I stirred in two handfuls of salt and swigged it off in a couple of gulps. The taste is remarkable, the effects galvanic. A rocket seemed to explode in the top of my skull. The background snapped into focus. I felt marvellously reinvigorated. They served me a large dish of onion-laden veal and wine and cheese, and I ate and ate and slept in a chair for close on three hours.

There are gaps in this journey which I find it difficult to account for accurately, largely, I suspect, because things went badly, or maybe because, like any tourist, I hurried on, eager to see somewhere else. There is a mostly unremembered length of sheer slogging between the little *ristorante* at Molière and that great rock in the gorge of the river Guil, the Château Queyras where Hannibal is believed to have camped for the night during his march from Spain into central Italy. From diaries and maps, I know it took me three days to get there. I tramped through Ulzio in the rain and over the pass in the Montgenèvre to Briançon, working due south by way of the Col d'Izoard, but they were restless, zestless stages, chiefly remarkable for getting that seventy miles over and done with, quickly.

Exilles is a crumbly old town guarded by an immense fortress. All the spy-holes and gun-ports look out to where Napoleon's dragoons galloped down the valley, but it began to pour and I trudged on, conscious more of nature than of man and his works. Within half an hour the Dora began to rise, angrily, intent on mischief, and on I went, throughout a day of torrential rain. The place-names did nothing to relieve the gloom. Up in those hills you pass, successively, through the Ruins, the Deserted

Place, the Point of Darkness, the Crest of Suffering and thence down into the Infernal Forest. On the crest I sat and watched the lights of Clavière go out one by one. I thought morbidly of the *Tenebrae*, that service during Holy Week in which candles are extinguished, slowly, to commemorate the darkness that fell over the earth. I thought, too, of my wet tent and wished to God I'd bought half a bottle of Scotch in Cesana-Torinese.

The next day I crossed the frontier and walked down into Briançon. No gloom there. They were celebrating something, maybe a patronal festival or the mayor's birthday. A dozen brass bandsmen played Chabrier's *Joyeuse* as if they really felt that way, and the coaches poured in, hissing and honking through the crowds: huge *Dieselomnibüsse* from Zürich and Dortmund, Italian *torpedoni* with flag-decked television aerials, coaches from Marseilles to Malmö, including the Bluebird (Super-Coaches Ltd) from Stockport, Cheshire with a tourist aboard who sold dehydrated shepherd's pie.

'Processed,' he corrected me, firmly. 'The word dehydrated went out years ago. Sounds like all that crap they sold at the end of the war. In the trade, we call them "controlled convenience foods", for that's just what they are.'

Alfie had come out with the tour to look the field over. As he saw the situation over a drink, decent English people coming out to a decent hotel expected decent English food. 'I mean, we don't all go in for fancy French stuff, do we?'

'Fresh or French?'

'French,' he said. 'If you ask me, some of it's not all that hot anyway.' He looked over his shoulder, conspiratorially, towards the kitchen door. You could sense the bugs on the fresh-sliced beans, salmonella in the *bisque aux légumes*, and worse, far worse, some Gallic variant of acute gastritis in dishes lightly disguised as *pot-au-feu* or *consommé*.

I shuddered theatrically. 'What's the alternative?' I asked. 'Processed Lancashire hot-pot, Yorkshire pud or bangers and mash?'

Mild ironies bounced off Alfie like dehydrated peas. He never even noticed them.

'My firm,' he said, 'puts out a very, *very* nice processed farm-house stew and a savoury mince. Two new lines we're proud of. And, of course, we've got a whole range of soups. About a dozen kinds in gallon packs. All the same price. You don't want to confuse the customer, do you? He wants to know where he stands with his budgeting. And he can have curries, sauces, gravies, green beans, peas, carrots, diced apple, lemon meringue pie, and crème caramel.'

My mouth didn't water. It became dehydrated. I may be a bit prejudiced about Alfie. It all came out so pat. He might have come straight from some salesman's course on anything from encyclopedias and insurance to pep pills or pesticides. He looked the part: precociously worldly, like a page boy, and wholly sold on what he had to sell which, I suppose, is what salesmanship is all about. For all that, I learned a great deal about what processed foods are and, equally important, something of the language in which they're sold. The customer, for instance, is not the consumer. The consumer is some poor drip at the bottom of the production line who either wants a quick mouthful between lunchtime drinks or, as Alfie put it, 'something leisurely at night to impress his bird'.

'*The* customer' is the publican or hotel-keeper who, in the gilded double talk of contemporary salesmanship, 'understands his obligations to save "the industry" hundreds of thousands of vitally needed man-hours'.

'Needed by whom?'

'By all of us,' said Alfie. 'I mean we're not in the game for peanuts are we? As we see it, all the customer has to do is to follow our instructions, properly printed on the label of the job he's buying, and then he's happy and we're happy, too. Makes sense, doesn't it?'

He warmed up to the subject. 'Now take instant potatoes. The customer doesn't want to go fiddling about with something dry in a tin, adding salt and a bit of butter. It takes time. *We* do all that for him, supplying the condiments, the milk and fat ready-built into the mix. All *he* has to do is to take one gallon of nearly boiling water and whirl it round for two minutes. And there it is. The stuff never varies. We guarantee that.'

'How about crème caramel?'

'Same thing,' he said. 'You need a tube of caramel and a packet of mix, but only half a gallon of water. It makes enough for twenty moulds.'

'Still all the same consistency?'

'Funny you should mention that. As a matter of fact, it's not,' said Alfie. 'We've found that some caterers drop a few eggs in when it comes off the boil, and we're rather proud of that. Makes us feel we're advancing the whole art of cookery. I mean, you don't want everything to taste the same, do you?'

'Then why don't you supply a bigger range of products?'

Alfie looked pained. 'Listen!' he said. 'You've missed the whole ruddy point. We're out for *instant* efficiency. We supply a *controlled* product. It's not what the customer wants. It's what he *needs*.'

They tell a tale in Briançon of how, shortly after the war, a party of elderly scholars arrived from Berlin, not realizing how unpopular Germans were in that town. On the face of it their mission seemed innocent enough. They were investigating that old problem: where did Hannibal cross the Alps with his elephants? They came armed with trunk-loads of documentation. They had read every word you can find on the subject by Polybius, Coelius, Varro, Strabo, Livy, and I forget who else. With Germanic thoroughness, they narrowed the number of accessible passes down to five, the first being the *col de la Traversette* from which you can stare down into Italy. Other passes may have been equally accessible in the year 218 BC, but as a precaution against invasion, some have since been blown up by both the Italians and the French. Knowing this, the Germans came to Briançon to ask a distinguished military historian which pass he would have chosen had he been given the task of invading Italy.

After looking at their maps and listening to their theories, the Frenchman advised them to tackle the problem the hard way, that is to climb the *Traversette* and see for themselves. He advised them to get a move on as he had recently given the same advice to a party of Americans. He didn't say who they were.

The Germans set off at once. They scrambled up to Monte Viso by way of Château Queyras and the Belvédère du Cirque. The *col* lies some ten thousand feet above sea-level. Once within sight of their goal, their leader, an authority on Polybius, made a fine speech and staggered up the last fifty feet alone. Hannibal, he believed, had stood there, Polybius had followed him. To weigh up all the possibilities, historic, strategic and geographic, he proposed to stand there himself and look down.

Coming up the other side, he saw eight circus elephants and a calvacade of cinematographers. The Americans were making a film with all the realism that could be put into it.

For over two thousand years Hannibal has ranked among the few indestructible heroes of history. Had he left behind a personal account of his great march, as Xenophon did, scholars might have been saved a great deal of trouble. As it is they agree, if on nothing else, that he carried out one of the boldest strategic strokes of all time. The struggle was for the mastery of the then known world. Carthage, for long the dominant power in the western Mediterranean, had been hemmed in by Rome. She had lost her command of the sea. Nothing could stop her from being invaded. Hannibal foresaw this. He attacked Rome from where she least expected attack, that is he crashed down into Lombardy from the Cottian Alps. But how did he manage to get up there? Mark Twain said the researches of antiquarians have already thrown much darkness on the subject and if they continue it is probable we shall soon know nothing at all.

Now it's the turn of the scientists. One of the big difficulties about deciding where Hannibal marched is that the descriptions of the country he passed through are fragmentary. There is mention of an island in a river here, a bare rock at the end of a gorge there and oblique references to trees and snow seen at certain times of the year. The problem is complicated by the way the place-names have changed since Gaulish times.

Sir Gavin de Beer, a former director of the Natural History Museum in London, re-examined the classical texts, looking for clues about the vegetation, the weather and such things as the speed and depths of rivers on the much disputed line of march. It was necessary, for example, to work out the probable height of the alpine tree-line and the exact date of the setting of the Pleiades in 218 BC. But with the help of his colleagues and other distinguished botanists, climatologists and astronomers, he discovered a host of little facts that give weight to certain texts and showed others to be inaccurate commentaries.

All this is laid out in his book *Hannibal's March* which served as guide to my own amble down through the Queyras. Sir

Gavin says plainly that he can't say precisely which pass Hannibal used, but he reckons he can narrow the choice down to two, fairly close to each other, to the north and the south of Monte Viso.

Hannibal, he believes, marched from south Spain to the Rhône which he crossed between Fourques and Arles. He followed that river to its tributary, the Drôme, striking out towards Gap and the upper waters of the Durance. Thence he went either up the valley of the Guil to the *col de la Traversette*, or to the *col de Mary* and down the Maira to Turin. If you consider these conclusions a modest return for much time and labour expended by many people it can be argued that problems, like mountains, are there to be tackled. But what happened to the man called the Joy of Baal?

For fifteen years he rampaged up and down Italy, smashing one army after another. What might have been the final blow to the Roman state was delivered at Cannae, that village of Apulia, the scene of the death of sixty thousand men. Sir Gavin says:

> On that field the great general, the terrain, the sky and all nature conspired to bring about the annihilation of the unlucky Roman army. For Hannibal not only sent out bogus deserters who subsequently fell on the rear of the combatants, but he took advantage of the nature of the terrain where the sun burned fiercely; there were clouds of dust, and the wind blew steadily from the east. He drew up his army in such a position that the Romans suffered from all these disadvantages while his men fought with the aid of the wind, the dust and the sun. Hannibal's tactics at Cannae have never been surpassed nor even equalled. . . .

Despite that defeat the Roman federation stood firm. Had it cracked, European civilization might have been based on what de Beer calls the commercial culture of Carthage. There would have been no Roman invasion of Britain and outer Gaul, no Renaissance. Christianity itself might have flickered out or remained an eastern religion. But Carthage was eventually destroyed by Rome and Hannibal fled to Syria. To avoid capture some years later he took poison, saying 'Let us now put an end to the great anxiety of the Romans who have thought it too lengthy and too heavy a task to wait for the death of a hated old man.'

A typical remark. From glimpses of his character that came down from classical sources he was clearly a sagacious man with a dry sense of humour. And he knew when he had met his match. Livy tells how, years after his defeat at Zama by Scipio Africanus, the two army commanders met in Crete. Scipio asked Hannibal who he regarded as the greatest general in the world.

'Alexander the Great,' replied Hannibal.

'Who do you put next?' asked Scipio.

'Pyrrhus.'

'Who do you put third?'

'Myself.'

Scipio laughed and continued: 'What would you have said if you had defeated me?'

'I should have regarded myself as the greatest general of all,' said Hannibal.

During his almost ceaseless campaigns, he was parted from his wife, Imilce, for about sixteen years. Silius Italicus relates how she pleaded with Hannibal to let her accompany him on his march across the Alps: 'Does our union and nuptial joys make you think that I, your wife, would fail to climb the mountains with you? Have faith in a woman's hardihood.' But Hannibal would have none of it. He bade her stay at home and bring up their son in the image of his father: the hope of Carthage and the dread of Rome.

To see that great gorge, the Queyras, where the Gauls rained down rocks on Hannibal's army, I followed a turbulent little stream, the Cerveyrette, from Briançon to the foot of the Izoard Pass, striding out with confidence on an old track under the Rochebrune. On the heights of the *Casse Deserte* are landscapes from old Western films, utterly bare with gaunt spires of rock implanted, you might think, by some devil to spite heaven. Skirting the summit I took a chance on the *col Tronchet* and heartily regretted venturing on that incoherent slope. The loose earth slips and had done so, I suspect, the previous day, but I came out unscathed above the great rock of Queyras and spent the night there.

The gorge looks as if the Alps have been gashed deep by one tremendous blow from an axe. Walls of rock overhang the shadowy floor of the defile. They are of a curious purplish colour, due, perhaps, to manganese. They resemble amethysts in the sunlight and dark red wine in the shade. Here grow those flannel-leafed emblems of the alps, the edelweiss, together with the sun-rose, wild rhododendron and an exquisitely symmetrical green-flowered lily of the woods, herb paris or leopard's bane, for centuries reckoned sure protection against the maledictions of witches, epilepsy, pox and the plague. Perhaps old Culpeper had his tongue in his cheek when he pronounced it 'fit to be cultivated in every good woman's garden', for it is, in fact, a powerful purgative and, in relatively small doses, poisonous.

I can't understand why Hannibal should have been attacked by the Gauls here, for, of all local tribes, they had most reason to hate and fear their common enemy, Rome. Yet from the heights of the gorge they rolled rocks down on his forces and he suffered heavy casualties. Of his thirty-seven elephants, all but one had perished before he flung his troops against the legions at Trebbia, and on that battle-scarred beast Polybius says he rode. The Romans called the elephants Lucanian cows and affected to despise the beasts, but to the Gauls they must have been more terrifying than the first appearance of tanks in the First World War.

A bird detached itself from the steep rock face of Escoyères and dived down, skimming so low that I felt the flutter of its sickle-shaped wings on my close-cropped hair. Several others followed in quick succession, intent, apparently, on seeing me off. They were pallid swifts, the southern relatives of those roof-top screamers that enliven my summer evenings in a London apartment. It may be that, in foreshortened perspective, my head and red-ringed beard is somewhat fox-like in appearance. But what fox ever threatened the existence of that most aerial of high-nesting birds? A more likely explanation is that, in trudging along half-naked and perspiring, I attracted a cloud of flies.

The walls of the gorge are pierced by road tunnels – not the dark and serpentine affairs of the Val d'Isère, but airy places, scarcely a hundred yards in length. In one such tunnel I walked beside a pathetic drift of butterflies, mostly Black-veined Whites. They were piled inches high in the gutter, like the aftermath of a wedding, some still fluttering feebly, but the majority dead, their life spark extinguished. They were the casualties of nature's prodigious out-scattering of genes and, like the wind-borne seeds of the dandelion, many are doomed to fall on stony ground.

Many kinds of butterflies and moths are notorious migrants. At certain times of the year they flutter through the alpine passes like chains of flowers, flying north, striving to establish new colonies as an insurance against the destruction of the parent stock. On the coasts of Sussex I have seen Painted Ladies and Clouded Yellows coming in from the sea in countless thousands. A lighthouse captain told me that the butterflies had passed through his beam of light for half an hour, resembling a snowstorm.

Of all migrant insects I look on that beautiful tawny-orange creature, the Painted Lady, with most affection. We have wandered together in the highlands of Scotland. On this trip I met her in Belgium and Switzerland, in Savoy and the valley of the Dora. From the arctic to the tropics, she is found in every continent except South America. I saw several that morning and walked on with the thought that two of the world's most widely distributed creatures are Man and the Painted Lady.

At the foot of the gorge lies the little township of Guillestre, walled and guarded by crumbling towers built, they will tell you, to resist the Saracens. Most of the inhabitants that morning were jam-packed in the *place Sainte Catherine*, awaiting the arrival of the cyclists in that most celebrated of French sporting events, the *Tour de France*. But that I didn't know as I tried to cross the square. A gendarme hauled me back; several spectators shouted angrily. I might have walked on to the pitch at Lord's at a critical point in a Test match.

Down swept the cyclists, the leader only a few yards ahead of his rivals. With noses on their handlebars and bottoms high in the air, they cycled at a furious speed, but in concert, like a swarm of bees on the tail of a queen. The crowd cheered wildly. They cheered the leader; they cheered the man who pedalled past last of all with his back wheel wobbling in the manner of an eccentric hoop. Cars drove past advertising Pneus Michelin, Cinzano, Peugeot, Gauloises, scattering leaflets, and Guillestre took the day off.

* * *

Behind a paper-littered desk in what I took to be a particularly dilapidated *Syndicat*, sat an upright, grey-haired man.

'You are the Director, M'sieur?'

'No,' he said. 'I am the mayor, Général Guillaume. At your service.'

A most distinguished mayor. He fought his way through Italy. He commanded the French Occupation forces in Germany. They made him the governor of turbulent Morocco. A French Academician has spoken of his *bravoure au combat, son audace, sang-froid, sentiment de l'honneur* and on top of all they will tell you locally he is *un homme de lettres connu et estimé*. Augustin Guillaume describes himself simply as *un enfant de Guillestre*.

He motioned me to a chair. I didn't question him. He questioned me, with tact. Where had I been? How far had I walked that day? What did I do for a living? Quite unexpectedly he asked. 'Do you know Montgomery?'

'The Field Marshal?'

He nodded.

'I don't really know him,' I said, 'but he once spoke to me.'

'What did he say?'

Now I remembered very well what that sharp-faced little man in the black beret said. He asked me how long I had been in the gunners, and when I told him three years he said, 'Good show! And when we catch up with the Hun we're going to knock him for six, eh? Give him a dam' good hiding. That's what he needs. Stand at ease, Gunner.'

'He was encouraging,' I said.

The General invited me to lunch, to an old villa with a great garden and an even greater view. All around were terraced holdings, trimly cultivated. The soil of Guillestre is poor but well cared for. Somebody once said that greed shows up more clearly on a landscape than on a man's face, and so does kindness.

In his study he talked of his life abroad as a soldier and of his passion for local history. Today he is the co-ordinator of a series of international highways that will eventually stretch from Spain to the Balkans. He still travels extensively, but Guillestre has become the centre of his life. He looked up at the ceiling reflectively. 'There is a room above here,' he said. 'It's my bedroom. I was born there and there I hope to die . . .'

Friends came in after lunch, joining us for coffee. Madame brought me into their affairs, gracefully, asking about different places and whether my wife *wholly* approved of my excursions. For my part, I sat there in boots and torn jacket, answering as best I could, feeling rather oafish and, suddenly, very, very tired.

I yearned to relax, to talk without effort among my own people. With the General I could just about hold my own, but not in the company of five strangers. I seemed to be playing a part and playing it badly. In the diary he kept during his walk through the Alps, William Conway observes:

> A man's apparent character varies with the society in which he is cast. . . . It has sometimes seemed to me that whenever two men meet and enter into communication with each other a third creature may be conceived as arising, wherein their two personalities are merged. What is true of two is true likewise of many, where mutual communion is established; they generate by their assemblage a sort of social individual whose image would be their composite photograph, allowance being made for the preponderance of the stronger characters. This composite individual has a character of his own. One never meets the same twice. He lives as long as the assemblage lasts; the dissolution of the bond that unites his component parts involves his death.

Between Guillestre and Jausiers lies the *col de Vars*, an easy pass outflanked by a pathway under the brow of Paneyron. I ambled over it like an old bear, padding down to St Paul on the Ubaye, a little anxious about what I should find there. Jausiers, I had decided, should be the springboard for my last leap into the void, the Lauzanier, that semi-circle of peaks between the *Hautes Alpes* and the *Alpes Maritimes*. Once across the Raspaillon or the Bonette, one of the highest passes in western Europe, I had done with path-finding. In my mind's eye I saw a little rivulet, the Tinée, rising beyond that great barrier, a rivulet that would lead me down to the sea.

There is a curious kind of mental tiredness more insidious by far than any amount of bodily fatigue. It comes from constantly poring over maps, from chronic worries about the route and the weather. My legs and shoulder muscles were in fine shape. My feet felt indestructible but I seemed to be pounding along in a mental vacuum. Perhaps there is a simpler way of putting it:

to the civilized man there comes sooner or later a desire for civilization.

They had bad news at Jausiers. The road over the Bonette had been blocked by snow for several days. But I didn't want the road, I said. What of the Val d'Abries, the Parassac and the Lauzanier? Was there snow on the *col de Larche*? At that word Larche, the only place he knew anything about, the postman shook his head. There would be only a little snow there, he thought. It was lower by nearly a thousand metres. But how did I propose to get there without going back to St Paul and up the valley of the Ubayette?

Across country, I said. '*Je marcherai là, direct.*' At this he looked at me, blankly. '*Ce n'est pas pratique,*' he said, and he said it twice.

They are courteous, helpful folk in Jausiers. The police confirmed what the postman had said. They were divided only on the best route to take, for nobody appeared to know the way from personal experience. With ample supplies I set off early, imagining, romantically, I heard the sound of fife and drums.

I trudged due east, up towards the source of a stream, the Abries, keeping to a narrow valley under Siguret and the Beak of the Eagle. In contrast to the lush pastures of the valley floor, the slopes are bald and cut by cascades. Overhead the high clouds sailed against the wind which, in mountainous country, is a bad sign, auguring change. But I reckoned hopefully that if I could breach that regiment of peaks by high sun I should come out on the Ubayette, above the *col de Larche* and encounter the elusive *sentier* I had shadowed for some hundreds of miles.

On the few occasions when it became necessary to climb, I climbed, steadily, remembering all I had learned, not trusting anything but tried toe-holds, using my hands solely for balance. This is an intriguing exercise. If your toes are dug into something reliable, the mere feel of a plant stem between your fingers instils confidence. At nose level I looked at sticky catchflies, tough-stemmed hawkweeds, small and hairy willows and those wild chrysanthemums, the alpine moon daisies, all marvellous comfort in wild places, and an excuse for not looking down.

Vowing not to scramble up anything that couldn't be easily scrambled down, I gained the first crest in a little over two hours and didn't much like what I saw. No sign of the Larche or L'Ubayette, but a field of snow ahead and another crest beyond with its profile roofed in cloud.

More detours. Towards noon a warm breath of air came up from the south. Looking for a gap in the wilderness of rock I tried one gully after another, sweating profusely. Three chamois appeared on a ridge. A scrabble of hoofs on loose shale and they plunged over what appeared to be a sheer cliff, seeming to float down from ledge to ledge. I turned back, inching down a scree, laboriously, to find the valley below wholly immersed in cloud. A depressing sight. I had imagined, vainly, that by tackling the face of the Abries in one outburst of energy I could break through that last remaining barrier to the sea, but there I seemed marooned, between cloud and sky. There was nothing for it but to spend the night there.

A long night. Stretched out under the fly sheet I tried to read, but though I scanned the lines and chewed over an occasional idea, I listened and heard only the occasional cry of a bird and the moaning of the wind. There were also ticks to be contended with. One company of adventurers managed to climb up the nylon sheet and drop off at intervals. These, I suspect, were diversionary tactics since most of the little beasts staged a ground attack, emerging from some dried-up droppings around my pack. After much brisk brushing and beating they fell back, but not for long. Ticks can hang around for years, waiting for a meal. As a science writer, I recall the publicity given to a tick identified as a Syrian species found, of all places, on the altar cloth of Canterbury cathedral. Its ancestors, the dean thought, might have come originally from Jerusalem, perhaps under the chain mail of a Crusader home on leave. But a specialist at the British Museum thought otherwise. He said it probably got in under the wings of a dove or maybe on the belly of the cathedral cat. The Parassac brood gave me a lively time until long past midnight and by then I had other things to think about.

From somewhere above came a rumble and a series of subdued thumps. The ground shook as you feel it shake under a distant bombardment and then all became quiet again. Mountaineers may be used to this sort of thing. I stiffened, nervously, the more since I had been reading Gosset's famous account of how his party was swept away by an avalanche.

At dawn, the clouds, the mist, were denser than ever, and through them, until they dispersed towards ten o'clock, the sun appeared as an immense pearl. To the east at least two crests remained to be scaled and both were covered in snow. The snow-line bore no apparent relationship to the altitude since some distant peaks seemed almost bare, but the blanket sufficed to show up the gullies and angles of the slope, covering places where the ground fell away gradually. A wide ledge roughly parallel to the valley floor sufficed for a path. Remembering what happened on the *Dent d'Oche*, it would have been more prudent to have clambered down to the lake and made what I could of the southern wall, behind the Bonette, but I felt miserly about height so hardly gained and I had no mind to tackle snow if it could be avoided.

Above an outlier of the Parassac soared a white-headed vulture, that huge carrion-seeker they call the griffon or *vauture fauve*. I scarcely gave it a glance. Marmots piped, bees bumbled upside down, seeking nectar among the pendulous bells of the heather, but I had eyes and ears only for the rise and fall of the wind and swirls of cloud that betoken storm. Far ahead, perhaps half a mile away, appeared the strange, ant-like figure of a man, the first I had seen in thirty hours. With one claw-like forearm rigidly doubled up under his chin and a goitrous bulge of flesh around his neck, he shambled up. To my dismay he could scarcely speak a word. Unintelligible noises crackled out of his throat.

I tried French and splinters of Italian. Pointing to a gap in the hills I asked him whether *that* was the route, *il sentiero per Santo Dalma ou Saint Etienne*. He stared at me with the warm eyes, the gentle expression of a cripple, but shook his head and I wondered whether he meant he didn't know or that he didn't understand. Or that the answer was no. Impossible to say. I murmured some thanks. We touched hands. He grasped mine tightly, and we went our different ways.

Towards noon a feathery wisp of snow curled off the face of the peak immediately above and floated down to a *couloir*. It seemed so light, so ethereal in substance, that I took it for wind-blown spume. But when the wisp enlarged perceptibly, obscuring the peak as if enveloped in mist I stopped, at first curious and then alarmed. The snow no longer floated down the gully. It began to spew down with the noise of escaping steam. The foremost wave flapped violently, like washing hung out on a windy day. The noise changed to a hollow roar. Gusts of air shoved me backwards. I tried to run, looking over my shoulder. I remember stumbling. I felt trapped. There was nothing I could do, but to my inexpressible relief the avalanche folded in on itself and veered off, pouring down into some unseen depression from which emerged a slender tongue of snow that rippled gently as it came to rest.

Most journeys end more abruptly than they begin. This one came pretty close to a full stop in the Lauzanier that afternoon. After the onrush of snow I couldn't relax. I became apprehensive and unutterably tired of staring at the map, of looking at the sky, at distant horizons and wondering what on earth to do next. I might have thrown my hand in then and there and called it a day, but as it looked safer to plod on than plod back, I made for the crest of the Pelousette in the hope of finding something manageable on the other side.

Crests are deceptive things to head for. Walls of rock crouch behind what you take to be the very last obstacle on the way up. After scrambling over several tantalizing little ridges, I reached a steep *cirque* of snow, brittle at the surface, mushy below, on which I tiptoed as delicately as a cat. It cracked under my boots. No comfort there. I clung to the rim of that rotten stuff, edging along, nervously, until it became apparent that either I had to tackle the snow or else climb an ugly little cliff of reddish rock.

I climbed, desperately badly, cursing and praying. How in God's name had I managed to get *there* of all places? For answer came that jangly bit of Gershwin played flat, a parody of a parody. I turned it off mentally, saying primly: 'Take a slow deep breath and watch your step, me boy. Don't fumble about with your fingers.' What fools climbers were. What on earth did they *do* it for? *Les conquérants de l'inutile*. In Saint-Gervais they said forty people had already died on Mont Blanc that year, nearly all of 'em amateurs. If I don't do better I'd be the first of the season in the Lauzanier. Fine place to be found dead. About as heroic as falling off the roof of a truck. A bit of rock crumbled under my right toe. Shaley stuff. I grabbed a ledge and did what nobody should have done, that is haul myself up on to what I couldn't see. The crest or a hidden overhang?

To my surprise, to my immense relief, I had topped the crest and looked down on a ribbon of snow-lined road scarcely fifty yards below the rim. By working almost imperceptibly west, I had come out on a loop of the Bonette, that great pass on the fringe of the Maritime Alps. To compound the feeling of anti-climax, a car-load of boisterous Americans chugged up and offered me a lift. They had been stuck for hours in a drift. We had a party on the spot and the last but one of the maps I used is still stained with wine I knocked over, trying to explain how I got there.

That evening I scampered down several thousands of feet to the source of that torrent, the Tinée, and slept there and woke up in what seemed a different world.

The Warm South

How fresh and sweet that morning was. A solitary warbler, a busy little creature like a goldcrest, piped cheerfully above the chatter of the stream. The sun poured down on hard-won patches of corn and pasture flecked with flowers. Here is the north-west frontier of the Mediterranean, an austere country ringed by ramparts of red slate and schist, but in the deep clefts of the Tineée deliciously warm. The contrast between the *ubacs*, the north-facing slopes and those in Provence they call *adrets*, the ones that look south are as cold March to the very bosom of June. From a makeshift encampment beside a fallen pine I stirred indolently. Each day on a journey such as this I am reborn. Each day, I know, I must begin again, but on that day I foresaw yet another journey all but done. Slowly, carefully, a little reluctantly, I packed up and ambled down into St Etienne for breakfast. Then south, at first as if with all the time in the world.

Pace is what you are accustomed to. I ambled for maybe an hour, pausing only to look at a praying mantis, that emblem of predacious piety, but it's difficult to squander a small fortune in acquired momentum. I strode on, faster, through the coarse aromatic leaves of strange evergreens. Wild figs sprang from cracked rocks in gorges clad in small prickly oaks and huge heathers. They clutched at thin soil. They will soon be washed away. Forests came before man. Deserts follow him. Here in the making is another desert. A butterfly, the *Apollon* or sun-seeker, a gorgeous creature with black and blood-red spots on its wings, hovered over a solitary clump of saxifrage and made off, dancing madly in the fierce light.

Below the ravine of Auron, that last easy length of the *Grande Randonnée*, the river roars between walls of naked rock, and down I went with the stream. Faster still. All seemed downhill. The

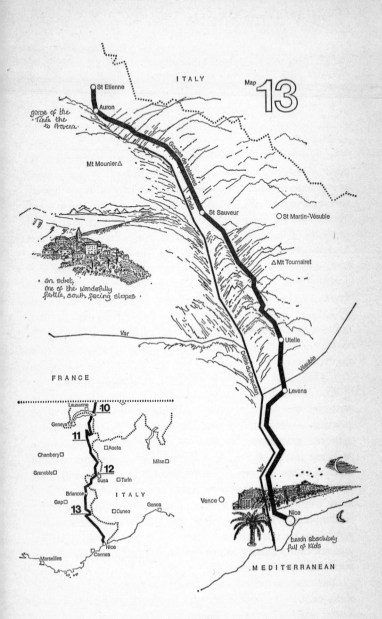

ITALY

Map **13**

St Etienne

Auron

gorge of the
Tinée the
to Provence.

Gorges de Valabres

Mt Mounier△

Tinée

St Sauveur

○ St Martin-Vésuble

△ Mt Tournairet

an adret,
one of the
wonderfully
fertile, south facing slopes.

Var

Utelle

Défile du Chaudan

Vésuble

Levens

FRANCE

Lausanne
10
Geneva

11

Chambery□
□ Aosta

Grenoble□
Milan□

12
Susa □Turin

Briancon
ITALY

Gap□
□Cuneo Genoa□

13

Vence ○

Var

Nice

Nice○
Cannes

Marseilles

beach absolutely
full of kids

MEDITERRANEAN

geometry is flowing and it flows south, into *la grande chaleur* of Provence in the season of cicadas. From dawn to dusk the chorus is incessant, interrupted only when a cloud lightly masks the sun and the temperature wanes, an infrequent event in July. To the ancient Greeks the creatures were the earthly embodiments of a race of demi-gods who so loved singing that they gave up all eating and drinking. When they died, the story is they returned to the Muses in heaven to tell of those who still love song on earth. At close quarters, the staccato *zay-zay-zay-zay* of the soloists is harsh and unmelodic, but strange rhythms emerge as they sing in unison, and at a distance the sound is of a waterfall. The singing is confined to the males.

> O happy the cicadas' lives
> Since they all have silent wives.

In the watershed of the Tinée the hamlets cling to the hillsides. Even under the great cedar in the *place*, the air is hot at midday. You can push it with your hand. A barefoot toddler stands in the moist dust under the fountain, staring wide-eyed at the swallowtail butterfly quivering on his outstretched finger. Grandad nods over what he protests is only his second *pastis*. Mother breast-feeds her last-born from a cane chair in the shade, interrupting neighbourly chatter only to greet you in the slow, curiously articulated speech of Provence. The menfolk are out in the terraced holdings, raking meagre crops between what may be the last generation of olive trees inherited from their forbears. From rise to fall of cicada song, this is woman's world.

Provence lies across the ancient kingdom of the Ligurians, a people who, together with the Etruscans, the Basques, the Picts and other elements in the west of Europe, spoke a neolithic or pre-Indo-European language. They occupied the southern Alps before the Celts fought their way to the Mediterranean to be beaten back, in turn, by the Romans. Writing from his embassy in Carthage, Cato said they were ignorant liars about whose origins nobody could remember anything, but from recent discoveries in such things as linguistics and blood groupings we are beginning to learn more about these people. The existence of the Ligurians is perpetuated in hundreds of place-names, especially those ending in *-inco* and *-asca* on the Franco-Italian border. They were almost certainly a matriarchal, a mother-venerating society. Hanging from cottage doorways in the gorges of the Tinée and the Var, you may still find little plaited figurines called corn-dollies, an essentially feminine symbol used at harvest-time to propitiate the Corn Goddess for the damage done by the sickle and to ensure the fertility of the next crop. It has to be hung there, reverently, by a newly-married woman.

Neolithic societies were matrilinear, that is the chieftain or king was not succeeded by his son, even if he had one, but by his mother's nearest male relative who might be the brother or the nephew of the previous king. There was some certainty in that system. A big belly is more positive evidence of parenthood than talk about who the father was. The daughter of the Ligurian chief who received a delegation of Phocean Greeks at Marseilles took one look at their handsome leader, Euxenos, and unpinned her girdle. She scented an amiable and profitable alliance. For women, exogamy, the practice of marrying outside the tribe or family group, must have been infinitely preferable to expansion by warfare.

The matriarchal system is a very old one. The moon, one imagines, became a female deity because her phases were directly associated with menstruation. The queen reigned as the incarnation of the mother-goddess. The oldest clay figurines known to prehistorians are Venuses with big breasts and bellies, the symbols of generation and fertility. But the matriarchal cults were swept aside at the coming of the warlike Indo-Europeans; their patriarchal warrior-pastoralists worshipped the gods of thunder, the sky and the sun. The womb-like tomb-chambers of the megalithic farmers were replaced by masculine phantasies in the shape of enormous phallic stones. Their legends described how even the gods waged war against each other. Man's monopoly of wisdom became symbolized in the story of the birth of Athene from the brow of Zeus, an event which apparently took place without any maternal participation. Civilization, I'm inclined to think, took a wrong turn when man forsook the female principle of survival and stability. In Mexico today the word for the ultimate, the best in anything from a straight flush to the sight of beautiful country, is *a todo madre*, something which is 'wholly mother'. It may be that Ligurian elements in Provence brought about that veneration of women, that far-reaching upsurge of love poetry which reached its peak in the days of the troubadors.

If I moved fast on that last two-day stage of sixty miles, the journey moved even faster. Far from coming to an end, abruptly, as I thought it would, it scampered on ahead from somewhere just south of St Etienne and I never really wanted to catch it up. The physical details are of small account. The track trickles down through the herb-scented hills by way of St Sauveur and the Mountain of the Madonna above Utelle. I left it at Levens some twelve miles from the coast and took to the valley of the Var. There on the autoway, beside the river, the rich herdsmen of Europe hooted their way down to what the regulars call the Old Blue Strip, the Côte d'Azur, a modern fringe to an ancient garment.

In that noisy company I walked for three or four hours, mentally turning over the dividends of not just this trip, but also what it meant in relation to others I had made.

> I am part of all that I have met;
> Yet all experience is an arch wherethrough
> Gleams that untravelled world whose margin fades
> For ever and for ever when I move. . . .

I have described some of the highlights and shadows of this journey, but they are for the most part the view from the hill or the rural bypath. On the few occasions when, through pressure of time, I took short cuts across industrial areas, I was appalled by what I saw. I am thinking particularly of the abject condition of the Lower Rhine, the Meuse, the Moselle, and the layer of rotting fish on the surface of Lake Geneva. Many of the Swiss lakes are all but done for. They are communal cesspools, almost entirely devoid of any form of wholesome life, and as for the Mediterranean, that mother sea of civilizations, the belt of frothy scum, composed in part of oil and undecomposed human excrement, around many of the holiday centres is frightful to look at. It makes even the thought of bathing abhorrent. Pollution is not merely confined to sea coast and heavily industrialized regions. It is creeping into Alpine villages where those who have stubbornly stuck it out, such as the oldsters of Gurraz and Ceillac in the High Alps, are bluntly advised to sell out and die somewhere else.

They are squatting on an unexploited goldmine of tourism. If they remain they will be obliged to act as servants of that industry, as dishonest mimics of themselves got up in costume their grandparents wore. They will become the lay figures of the guided tour, of travel adventure advertised and sold in packages, guaranteed like processed farmhouse stew, hamburgers, and scampi and chips to be consumed without risk. The price is degradation.

As I see it, we are not much moved by waste, by pollution, by exploitation unless it offends our sight or hurts our pockets. The precepts of land-management, of living in harmony with the environment, are as clear as the ten commandments, but until they are written round the walls of junior schools they can't be repeated too often. The first is that the wholly commercial, the industrial way of life, with its ethos of expansion, is simply not sustainable. It cannot last. The rapidly closing circle of enjoyable space must constrict to the point of intolerability within the lifetime of someone born today.

I recall the start of this journey vividly: the cold grey sea, the young people on the beach, the feeling that anything might happen from that moment on. After months of planning I knew I wasn't getting away from it all; I was trying to get *with* something. Essentially, it was the rediscovery and enlargement of a portion of the world of which I have the joy of being a part. That world is what's left of unspoiled land, of land brimful of self-sustaining energy, a community of plants and animals, the ground floor of people and cultures, of changing landscapes which, I believe, can be seen and enjoyed best by striding across its subtle graduations on foot.

In the process of rediscovery many of my preconceptions have been modified or completely changed. Much of western Europe is undergoing social and cultural convulsions so profound and at such a pace that I could only wonder at what point I had stepped in and where it would all end.

The changes are evident in the tide-like drift of people from remote rural areas to the towns and cities, a process which has been going on since Roman times at least, but now at an unprecedented rate. Cultural diffusion is being accelerated by wandering gangs of labourers from Spain, Italy, Algiers, Greece, and other places. The peaks of local individuality are being smoothed out by droves of tourists with money to spend on what the city agencies have largely made up for their diversion. 'It's not what the customer wants; it's what he needs.' Everywhere I went I tried to meet people with most claim to be called natives. Through the barriers of language I knew I should miss a great deal, but I guessed that a lone traveller on foot has a better chance of breaking down those barriers than most.

As for the route itself, rather more than half the distance between the North Sea and the Mediterranean has already been surveyed and signposted indifferently well by national committees of *sentiers* in France and Belgium. Unfortunately, they confine their activities strictly to trails within their own frontiers. There is no co-ordination that I could discover between the French, the Swiss, the Dutch and the Italian authorities, who between them might, if they were interested or encouraged, work out a wonderful international trail with alternative routes. The first major gap lies between the coast of the North Sea and the start of the serpentine *Sentier Ardennais* near Liège; the second is from south Luxembourg to the Vosges by way of Lorraine, and the third from Masevaux at the foot of the Vosges to Lake Geneva where the trans-Alpine trail begins. Hopefully, these gaps will be bridged within the next few years.

The argument that only a few walkers would use a long-distance trail is usually put forward by those who don't want to get involved in the self-centred politics of the organizations concerned. As matters stand at the moment, the map of western Europe is fly-specked with isolated reserves and sanctuaries with here and there a big park like the Vanoise, a wilderness area in danger of human erosion. Trails are vitally necessary to keep the way for tomorrow open. They are the least we can hope for within contemporary patterns of development. With a little ingenuity they could be used to link up some splendid country in the Netherlands with the Ardennes, the Vosges, and the southern Alps. They can be picked up from most of the nearby roads and cities are relinquished just as easily.

One well-found trail from coast to coast might well become the trunk of an ever-growing tree with outward-spreading branches. It offers an opportunity for striding out for hundreds of miles. It affords an escape from the grey disease of conformity. Certainly whatever remains on those trails of the essential differences between varying kinds of country, of people and their cultures will resist the smoothing-out processes longest.

Long after dusk I reached the lights, the indolent palms, the rowdy manic traffic of Nice, the fifth city of France but for *divertissements en tous genres* second only to Paris. Empty *Gauloise* packets in the gutter. Bougainvillaea and baskets of pink geraniums. Clip joints. Lines of hotels like wedding cakes. Cafés that sell coffee and brandy, eight different kinds of *pastis* and Smith's Potato Crisps. Two Algerian winos, dead drunk, their mouths open, lay near a traffic sign that advocated *Prudence*. High over the Bay of Angels, streaks of rockets burst in scarlet chrysanthemums, briefly illuminating what is claimed to be the biggest supermarket in the world. Crowds flocked round an open-air cinema. They cheered wildly at the news-flashes. 'They have got there,' they said. Who'd got where? 'The Americans,' they said. 'They are actually walking on the moon.' Near midnight I scratched myself trying to cut a corner off the approach to the *Promenade des Anglais* by pushing through the prickly pears around the perimeter of the airport. Then down to the beach, walking among the youngsters sleeping there, not stopping until I had waded into the warm sea.

The Quest for Arthur's Britain

Edited by

Geoffrey Ashe

The story of Arthur and the Knights of the Round Table is the chief myth of Britain. But is it something more than myth? Most scholars now regard his reality as probable and accept 'Arthurian Britain' as a meaningful historical term.

Solid facts have emerged through the recent work of archaeologists. *The Quest for Arthur's Britain* examines the historical foundations of the Arthurian tradition, and then, in five archaeological chapters, presents the results of excavations to date at Cadbury (reputed site of Camelot), Tintagel, Glastonbury and less-known places. An outline of Arthurian Britain takes shape, and several fascinating questions emerge. For example, were the Dark Ages in Britain a transitory, unimportant period? Or did the Celtic resistance against the Anglo-Saxons – a resistance identified with Arthur – have a profound effect on the development of the British Isles?

'The best sort of historical detective story.'

ECONOMIST

'A useful compendium of information about the Arthurian problem, the Arthurian legend, and about what archaeology says of western Britain between A.D. 400 and 600 . . . this work is of great importance and interest: long may it continue and prosper.'

Glyn Daniel, GUARDIAN

'Ideal for romantic patriots and for those with a serious interest in our national origins.'

Cyril Dunn, OBSERVER

Journey Through Britain

John Hillaby

An account of an eleven hundred mile walk from Land's End to John O'Groats by 'one of the world's greatest walkers'.

'A social and natural history of Britain for the happy wanderer . . . he has done supremely well.'
Donald Gould, NEW SCIENTIST

'An enviably good writer as well as a pedestrian extraordinary . . . Every word of his splendid book enriches us.'
Alan Wykes, EVENING STANDARD

'His knowledge is prodigious; stories slip off his tongue like gossip . . . the book is immediately attractive, entertaining, informative, simply and well written.'
Angus Wolfe Murray, THE TIMES

'Delightful and engrossing . . . He emerges from his book as a gentler and less gamey Norman Douglas, equipped with that marvellous old monster's scepticism, wit, curiosity and scholarship.'
Philip Toynbee, OBSERVER

'. . . as exciting as any trip through the Amazon jungle.'
David Holloway, DAILY TELEGRAPH

Journey to the Jade Sea
John Hillaby

An account of an eleven-hundred-mile walk through Africa by 'one of the world's greatest walkers'.

Tired of city life and ashamed at his toleration of boredom, John Hillaby decided to go on a three-month safari in the Northern Frontier District of Kenya. With five natives, six camels, 1400 pounds of baggage, twelve pairs of gym shoes, a shot-gun, a Swahili phrase book and a floppy hat, he travelled from Wamba to Lake Rudolf and back.

'Hillaby's book, beautifully written and illustrated, is a "must" for armchair explorers.'
DAILY MIRROR

'Very entertaining, deftly instructive, and in places beautiful.'
Gavin Maxwell, OBSERVER

'Mr Hillaby has written about his tremendous adventure with great skill, with considerable humour at his own expense, and with an enthusiasm for his ordeal which is absolutely incomprehensible.'
NEW YORK TIMES

'Something different . . . strips exploring of its inessentials. That is why I enjoyed this book so much.'
Cyril Connolly, SUNDAY TIMES

'Full of humanity, and leavened with wry humour. Few would make the journey and fewer still would describe it half so well.'
FINANCIAL TIMES

'One of the best pieces of writing about Africa I have encountered.'
GLASGOW HERALD

'An urbane, intelligent and wryly amusing book that will stir many a dream of paradisal innocence.'
TIMES LITERARY SUPPLEMENT